Practical Process Automation
Orchestration and Integration in Microservices
and Cloud Native Architectures

Bernd Ruecker

Beijing · Boston · Farnham · Sebastopol · Tokyo

Practical Process Automation

by Bernd Ruecker

Copyright © 2021 Bernd Ruecker. All rights reserved.

Published by O'Reilly Media, Inc., 1005 Gravenstein Highway North, Sebastopol, CA 95472.

O'Reilly books may be purchased for educational, business, or sales promotional use. Online editions are also available for most titles (*http://oreilly.com*). For more information, contact our corporate/institutional sales department: 800-998-9938 or *corporate@oreilly.com*.

Acquisitions Editor: Melissa Duffield
Development Editor: Michele Cronin
Production Editor: Deborah Baker
Copyeditor: Rachel Head
Proofreader: Kim Wimpsett

Indexer: Potomac Indexing, LLC
Interior Designer: David Futato
Cover Designer: Karen Montgomery
Illustrator: Kate Dullea

March 2021:   First Edition

Revision History for the First Edition
2021-03-16:   First Release

See *http://oreilly.com/catalog/errata.csp?isbn=9781492061458* for release details.

978-1-098-10648-5

[LSI]

Table of Contents

Part II. Process Automation in the Enterprise

Part III.   Get Going!

Preface

I remember very clearly when I first decided to use a small open source workflow engine, implemented in Java, to write a piece of business software for a friend 20 years ago. This decision changed my life. I got very enthusiastic about process automation and engaged in the community of that open source project. Ultimately this experience pushed me toward cofounding my own company, which went on to become the leading vendor of source-available process automation tooling (I could never, ever have dreamed of the big names now using our software!). My aim with this book is not only to share my excitement about process automation, but also to explain how to apply process automation technology in real life, in a pragmatic and developer-friendly way.

But first, an anecdote. During high school a good friend of mine started their own business; a specialized retail store for graphics cards. You may remember these cards if you've assembled a computer—they could be "modded" to get more power out of the chip, which allowed gamers to buy cheaper cards and achieve better performance. The business model required handling each physical graphic card as an individual item and establishing very specific procedures around sales and distribution.

My friend was successful with this business model. Actually, very successful. So successful that the process, which was based on manual handling and emails, broke down. Orders were delayed, and piles of graphics cards, as well as unprocessed returned parcels, started filling the rooms.

We discussed remedies to this situation and finally ended up developing a piece of custom software that automated some of their processes while supporting the specifics of their business model. It had a pretty narrow focus, but helped them to remove all the piles of stuff. They reduced the cycle time so that orders were shipped within a day. Manual work in the redesigned process was reduced to steps that involved the physical goods (e.g., packing the parcel), while other tasks were automated (generating and printing the invoice and the shipping label, sending customer confirmations, etc.). Customers got transparency into the status of their orders, and we even provided a very simple self-service tracking portal. The software escalated issues if some process got stuck for too long, so it was no longer necessary to wait for customers to complain to take corrective action. Overall, as hands-on as the software was, it was a huge success.

Back then I would never have phrased it like this, but I experienced the advantages of process automation firsthand: improved process quality, reduced cycle times, automation of boring tasks, ability to scale, and reducing operational spend.

Over the next 20 years, I saw core processes and support processes being automated in all industries. I saw NASA processing data from the Mars robot using an automated process on Earth in order to send back control signals to space. I saw insurance companies automating onboarding and claim handling processes, including the reporting of accidents via apps and fully automated handling of these reports. I saw process automation technology being applied to trading and money transfer use cases, and to many different processes in telecommunication. I even saw actual lab robots being controlled by a workflow engine.

Process automation is everywhere, and it is super exciting. The need for automation is growing almost on a daily basis. Digital transformation is happening, allowing completely new business models and requiring companies to change business processes at a fundamental level. Recently, the COVID-19 pandemic brought this into focus: businesses needed to switch from paperwork being signed on-site to electronic processes basically overnight; companies needed to scale complete processes that had been relatively uncommon before, like airlines canceling tickets and compensating for flights; and organizations rapidly pivoted to completely new business models, like the distribution of face masks.

These are only a few examples of the bigger trend Gartner calls "hyperautomation."

Companies embark upon this journey for many reasons: existing processes might be too inefficient, too slow, too expensive to operate, impossible to scale, or simply not flexible enough to support new business models (or all of those things at the same time!). And manually executed or poorly automated processes don't provide enough data to gain actionable insight into what is going on, making it hard to learn and adapt. This makes the business vulnerable to competitors that have already embraced digital transformation and process automation.

Process automation typically addresses processes that need to be tailor-made to an organization's needs. Therefore, they cannot be bought as off-the-shelf application software. Even if these processes are often the same across different organizations (e.g., customer onboarding, order management, claim settlement), the way each organization designs and implements them is unique and can be a differentiator for them in their market. Process automation enables organizations to be more competitive, conduct their business more efficiently, save cost, increase revenue, and progress in their digital transformation.

Chances are high that you work in such a company, maybe as a software architect, enterprise architect, business analyst, or developer. Process automation will be one of the key tools in your toolbox.

My mission with this book is to help you on your journey by sharing what I've learned through 20 years of firsthand experience with process automation.

Process Automation Tools and Techniques

There are many ways to automate processes, from plain software development to batch processing, event-driven microservices, and any other development practice you can think of.

But automating processes has specific characteristics and requirements, and there is dedicated software built for addressing these. Analysts define different software market categories that are related to process automation: for example, digital process automation (DPA), intelligent business process management suites (iBPMSs), low-code platforms, robotic process automation (RPA), microservice orchestration, process orchestration, process monitoring, process mining, decision support, and automation.

All the different software categories provide tools and technologies that allow organizations to coordinate, automate, and improve business processes. These processes can include people, software, decisions, bots, and things.

That's a broad scope. So what will we focus on in this book?

The Scope of This Book

This book looks at how process automation can be applied in modern system architectures and software development practices. It examines how tool support needs to look like to become a vital part of every developer's toolbox. It demonstrates that the core component to make this happen is a lightweight and developer-friendly workflow engine, which will be explored in great detail throughout the book.

Along the way, we'll discuss some typical misconceptions. Workflow engines are not alien in software development, like some people may expect. And even if neither analyst reports nor tools from big vendors are particularly developer-focused or developer-friendly, there are alternative tools available today, as you will see throughout this book. Some of these might not fit into the categories mentioned earlier, but others do.

That said, I will not dedicate a lot of time to what analysts say about process automation software, but focus on giving practical advice about workflow engines in the context of software development in modern architectures. In this context, I will weave together ideas from microservices, event-driven systems, and domain-driven design.

This might give you a new perspective on process automation.

Who This Book Is For

This book targets software developers and software or system architects who want to learn about process automation.

 You might prefer to be called a software engineer instead of a developer, and that is perfectly OK. In this book I use the term *software developer*, simply because I had to decide on one.

If you are a software developer, you might want to use a workflow engine in your application, service, or microservice to solve hands-on problems. This book will help you understand which problems a workflow engine can solve for you, and how to get started.

If you are a system architect, this book will help you understand opportunities and pitfalls around process automation. It will guide you through some tough architectural decisions and trade-offs, including how using a workflow engine compares to alternative approaches or whether a workflow engine should be operated centrally.

But you can also benefit if you work in other roles. For example:

- If you are an IT manager, this book can help you make better-informed decisions and ask the right questions internally.
- If you are a business analyst, this book can help you if you are motivated to think outside the box and understand the technical side of things.

Overall, you will need some general experience in the field of software engineering, but no other specific knowledge.

The Architect Always Implements

Discussing concepts is only half the fun if you cannot point to concrete code examples. Runnable code forces you to be precise, to think about details you can leave out on the conceptual level—and, most importantly, it often explains things best. I am personally a big fan of the motto "the architect always implements." The downside is that I have to decide on a concrete technology (which might not be the technology of your choice) and on concrete products (which might be outdated by the time the book is printed). I've attempted to be as vendor-neutral as possible, but as cofounder of a process automation vendor, Camunda, I am of course opinionated and tend to use the tooling I know best, which is that my company provides.

My opinions of course also influence our product, which means some alignment is unavoidable. But as a process automation addict with 20 years of real-world experience, this book is rooted in the frontline customer engagements that have formed those opinions.

In some places I do use executable source code, as anything else would make it harder to understand certain concepts. In these cases I use the process automation platform from Camunda.

Accompanying Website and Code Examples

In addition to this book, you can find supplemental material (code examples, etc.) for download at *https://ProcessAutomationBook.com*. This website also links to source code available on GitHub.

These examples will not only help you better understand the concepts described in the book, but also give you a great opportunity to play with technology whenever you are bored with reading.

If you have a technical question or a problem using the code examples, please send an email to *bookquestions@oreilly.com*.

This book is here to help you get your job done. In general, if example code is offered with this book, you may use it in your programs and documentation. You do not need to contact us for permission unless you're reproducing a significant portion of the code. For example, writing a program that uses several chunks of code from this book does not require permission. Selling or distributing examples from O'Reilly books does require permission. Answering a question by citing this book and quoting example code does not require permission. Incorporating a significant amount of example code from this book into your product's documentation does require permission.

We appreciate, but generally do not require, attribution. An attribution usually includes the title, author, publisher, and ISBN. For example: "*Practical Process Automation* by Bernd Ruecker (O'Reilly). Copyright 2021 Bernd Ruecker, 978-1-492-06145-8."

If you feel your use of code examples falls outside fair use or the permission given above, feel free to contact us at *permissions@oreilly.com*.

Feedback

I am always happy to take any feedback via *feedback@ProcessAutomationBook.com*.

How to Read This Book

In general, I recommend that you read Chapter 1 and Chapter 2 first and sequentially. This gives you the basic knowledge to understand what the book covers and how it applies to your scenario.

From there on, you might simply continue reading or fast-forward to the chapters that look most interesting to you. While there is of course some logical plot throughout the book, I tried to cross-reference in case you jump over certain parts.

However, there are a few deviations I can recommend:

- If you've had bad experiences with business process management (BPM) in the past, you might want to read "Not Your Parents' Process Automation Tools" on page 14 first, as this should assure you that you have the right book in your hands.

- If you have experience with event-driven systems and believe you don't need orchestration, you might want to sneak a peek at Chapter 8 to get a better feeling for why this book is relevant to you. Also look at Chapter 2 to get a better understanding of what I mean by process automation.

- If you are a fan of microservices or domain-driven design (DDD), you might be skeptical about how process automation can fit into this world. I recommend that you read Chapter 7 early on, as this best demonstrates how the thinking about process automation in this book is different from many traditional approaches in the field.

- If you are an IT manager who has been pulled into a business or process automation project in an off-guard moment, you might want to start with Chapter 12, as this will give you some guidance on how to shape your journey.

- If you are happy to follow my recommendation to use a BPMN-based workflow engine, you can skip Chapter 5.

Conventions Used in This Book

The following typographical conventions are used in this book:

Italic
    Indicates new terms, URLs, email addresses, filenames, and file extensions.

`Constant width`
    Used for program listings, as well as within paragraphs to refer to program elements such as variable or function names, databases, data types, environment variables, statements, and keywords.

This element signifies a tip or suggestion.

This element signifies a general note.

This element indicates a warning or caution.

O'Reilly Online Learning

For more than 40 years, *O'Reilly Media* has provided technology and business training, knowledge, and insight to help companies succeed.

Our unique network of experts and innovators share their knowledge and expertise through books, articles, and our online learning platform. O'Reilly's online learning platform gives you on-demand access to live training courses, in-depth learning paths, interactive coding environments, and a vast collection of text and video from O'Reilly and 200+ other publishers. For more information, visit *http://oreilly.com*.

How to Contact Us

Please address comments and questions concerning this book to the publisher:

O'Reilly Media, Inc.
1005 Gravenstein Highway North
Sebastopol, CA 95472
800-998-9938 (in the United States or Canada)
707-829-0515 (international or local)
707-829-0104 (fax)

You can access the web page for this book, where we list errata, examples, and any additional information, at *https://oreil.ly/Practical_Process_Automation*.

Email *bookquestions@oreilly.com* to comment or ask technical questions about this book.

For news and more information about our books and courses, see our website at *http://www.oreilly.com*.

Find us on Facebook: *http://facebook.com/oreilly*

Follow us on Twitter: *http://twitter.com/oreillymedia*

Watch us on YouTube: *http://youtube.com/oreillymedia*

Acknowledgments

I want to thank all the people who helped me to write this book. First and foremost that includes all the people I've met over the last decade, for example in the Camunda community, within customer projects, or at conferences. Countless discussions helped me understand the world of process automation, and constant feedback shaped not only the Camunda platform, but also my teaching material around it.

I want to thank each and every person at Camunda. Camunda is not only a great place to work, especially because of all the great colleagues, but it is also changing the world of process automation. What we've achieved with the company is far more than I could have ever dreamed of when I cofounded it. And every day is still a lot of fun, so let's keep rolling. :-)

Furthermore, I want to thank my good friend Martin Schimak, who helped me shape the initial thoughts captured in this book. Martin was also a great sparring partner for structuring the book. I am also very grateful to all the great tech reviewers who provided super-helpful feedback. These folks invested a bunch of free time helping to improve this book, so thank you to (listed alphabetically) Tiese Barrell, Adam

Bellamare, Rutger van Bergen, Colin Breck, Joe Bowbeer, Norbert Kuchenmeister, Kamil Litman, Chris McKinty, Surush Samani, Volker Stiehl, and all the others.

Of course, I also thank my family for having endured not only a pandemic, but also me working on this book. And last but not least, I want to thank the whole team at O'Reilly for making the book-writing process not only painless, but pretty enjoyable.

CHAPTER 1

Introduction

Let's get started! This chapter discusses:

- What I mean by process automation
- Specific technical challenges when automating processes
- What a workflow engine can do and why this provides a ton of value
- How business and IT can collaborate when automating processes
- How modern tools differ very much from BPM and SOA tooling from the past

Process Automation

In essence, a *process* (or *workflow*) simply refers to a series of tasks that need to be performed to achieve a desired result.

Processes are everywhere. As a developer, I think of my personal development process as being able to manage certain tasks that go from an issue to a code change that is then rolled out to production. As an employee, I think of optimizing my process around handling emails, which involves techniques for prioritizing them quickly and keeping my inbox empty. As a business owner, I think of end-to-end business processes like fulfilling customer orders, known as "order to cash." And as a backend developer, I might also think of remote calls in my code, as these involve a series of tasks—especially if you consider retry or cleanup tasks, because a distributed system can fail at any time.

Processes can be automated on different levels. The main distinction is if a human controls the process, if a computer controls the process, or if the process is fully automated. Here are some examples that highlight these different levels of automation.

After high school, I helped organize meals-on-wheels deliveries to elderly people in their homes. There was a daily process going on to handle the meal orders, aggregate a list of orders that went to the kitchen, package the meals, and finally ensure that all the orders were labeled correctly so they would be delivered to the correct recipients. In addition to that, there was the delivery service itself. When I started, the process was completely paper-driven, and it took an entire morning to accomplish. I changed that, leveraging Microsoft Excel to automate some tasks. This brought the processing time down to about 30 minutes—so it was a lot more efficient. But there were still physical activities involved, like packing and labeling the food as well as driving to the recipients' homes.

More importantly, the process was still human-controlled, as it was my job to press the right buttons and show up in the kitchen at the appropriate times with the appropriate lists. Only some tasks were supported by software.

During my last hospital visit I chatted to the staff about how the meal preparation worked. The patients were required to fill out a paper card to mark allergies and meal preferences, and this information was typed into a computer. Then the IT system was in charge of transporting that information to the right place at the right time, and it needed to be done in an automatic fashion. People still played a role in the process, but they did not steer it. This was a computer-controlled, but not fully automated process.

If you take this example even further, today there are cooking robots available. If you were to add these robots to the process, it would be possible to task the computer with not only automating the control flow, but also the cooking tasks. This moves the process closer to a fully automated process.

As you can see, there is an important distinction between the automation of the control flow between tasks, and the automation of the tasks themselves:

Automation of the control flow
> The interactions between tasks are automated, but the tasks themselves might not be. If humans do the work, the computer controls the process and involves them whenever necessary, for example using tasklist user interfaces. This is known as *human task management*. In the previous example, this was the humans cooking the food. This is in contrast to a completely manual process that works because people control the task flow, by passing paper or emails around.

Automation of the tasks
> The tasks themselves are automated. In the previous example, this would be the robots cooking the food.

If you combine automation of both the control flow and the tasks you end up with *fully automated* processes, also known as *straight-through processing* (STP). These processes only require manual intervention if something happens beyond the expected normal operations.

While there is of course an overall tendency to automate processes as much as possible, there are specific reasons that motivate automation:

High number of repetitions
> The effort put into automation is worthwhile only if the potential savings exceed the cost of development. Processes with a high volume of executions are excellent candidates for automation.

Standardization
> Processes need to be structured and repeatable to be easily automated. While some degree of variance and flexibility is possible with automated processes, it increases the effort required for automation and weakens some of the advantages.

Compliance conformance
> For some industries or specific processes there are strict rules around auditability, or even rules that mandate following a documented procedure in a repeatable and revisable manner. Automation can deliver this and provide high-quality, relevant data right away.

Need for quality
> Some processes should produce results of consistent quality. For example, you might promise a certain delivery speed for customer orders. This is easier to achieve and retain with an automated process.

Information richness
> Processes that carry a lot of digitized information are better suited to automation.

Automating processes can be achieved by different means, as further examined in "Limitations of Other Implementation Options" on page 93, but there is special software that is dedicated to process automation. As mentioned in the Preface, this book will focus on those tools, and especially look at workflow engines.

Automating processes does not necessarily mean doing software development or using some kind of workflow engine. It can be as simple as leveraging tools like Microsoft Office, Slack, or Zapier to automate tasks triggered by certain events. For example, every time I enter a new conference talk in my personal spreadsheet, it triggers a couple of automated tasks to publish it on my homepage, the company event table, our developer relations Slack channel, and so forth. This kind of automation is relatively easy to implement, even by non-IT folks in a self-service manner, but of course is limited in power.

In the rest of this book I will *not* focus on these office-like workflow automation tools. Instead, we'll explore process automation from a software development and architecture perspective.

To help you understand how to automate processes with a workflow engine, let's quickly jump into a story that illustrates the kinds of real-life developer problems it can solve.

Wild West Integrations

Imagine Ash is a backend developer who gets tasked with building a small backend system for collecting payments via credit card. This doesn't sound too complex, right? Ash starts right away and designs a beautiful architecture. In conversations with the folks doing order fulfillment, they agree that providing a REST API for the order fulfillment service is the easiest option to move forward. So Ash goes ahead and starts coding it.

Halfway through, a colleague walks in and looks at Ash's whiteboard, where the beauty of the architecture is captured. The colleague casually says, "Ah, you're using that external credit card service. I used to work with it, too. We had a lot of issues with leaky connections and outages back then; did that improve?"

This question takes Ash by surprise. This expensive SaaS service is flaky? That means Ash's nice, straightforward code is too naive! But no worries, Ash adds some code to retry the call when the service is not available. After chatting a bit more, the colleague reveals that their service suffered from outages that sometimes lasted hours. Puh—so Ash needs to think of a way of retrying over a longer period of time. But darn it, this involves state handling and using a scheduler! So Ash decides to not tackle this right away but just add an issue to the backlog in the hopes that the order fulfillment team can sort it out. For now, Ash's code simply throws an exception when the credit card service is unavailable, with fingers crossed that all will work out well.

Two weeks into production, a different colleague from order fulfillment walks over, alongside the CEO. What the heck? It turns out Ash's system raises a lot of "credit card service unavailable" errors, and the CEO is not happy about the amount of orders not being fulfilled—this issue has resulted in lost revenue. Ash tries to act immediately and asks the order fulfillment team to attempt retrying the payments, but they have to iron out other urgent problems and are reluctant to take over responsibilities that should be handled by Ash's service (and they are totally right to be reluctant, as you'll read about in Chapter 7).

Ash promises to fix the situation and get something live ASAP. Back at their desk, Ash creates a database table called `payment` with a column called `status`. Every payment request gets inserted there, with a status of `open`. On top of that Ash adds a simple scheduler that checks for open payments every couple of seconds and processes them. Now the service can do stateful retries over longer periods of time. This is great. Ash calls the order fulfillment folks and they discuss the changes needed in the API, as payments are now processed asynchronously. The original REST API will hand back HTTP 202 (Accepted) responses, and Ash's service can either call back the fulfillment service, send them some message, or let them periodically poll for the payment status. The teams agree on the polling approach as a quick fix, so Ash just needs to provide another REST endpoint to allow querying the payment status.

The change gets rolled out to production and Ash is happy to have dealt with the CEO's concerns. But unfortunately, the peace doesn't last too long. A caravan of people arrive in Ash's office, including the director of operations. They tell Ash that no orders can be shipped because no payments are successfully being taken. What? Ash makes a mental note to add some monitoring to avoid being surprised by these situations in the future, and takes a look at the database. Oh no, there are a huge amount of open payments piling up. Digging a bit into the logs Ash discovers that the scheduler was interrupted by an exceptional case and crashed. Dang it.

Ash puts the one poisoned payment that interrupted the whole process aside, restarts the scheduler, and sees that payments are being processed again. Relieved, Ash vows to keep a closer eye on things and hacks together a small script to periodically look at the table and send an email alert whenever something unusual happens. Ash also decides to add some mitigation strategies for the exceptional case to that script. Great!

After all these stressful weeks, Ash plans to go on vacation. But it turns out that the boss isn't too happy about Ash leaving because nobody except Ash actually understands the tool stack that they just built. Even worse, the boss instead pulls out a list of additional requirements for the payment service, as some business folks have heard about the flaky credit card service and want more in-depth reports about availability and response times. They also want to know if the agreed-on service level agreement (SLA) is actually being met and want to monitor that in real time. Gosh—now Ash has to add report generation on top of a database that hadn't seemed necessary in the first place. Figure 1-1 shows the resulting mess in its full beauty.

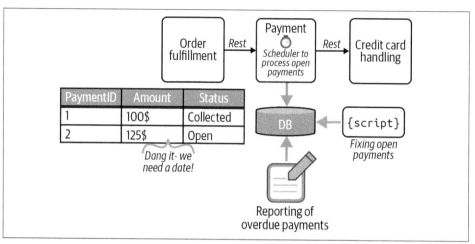

Figure 1-1. Wild West integration at play—the usual chaos you actually find at most enterprises

Unfortunately, Ash just used a far-too-common approach to automate processes that I call *Wild West integration*. It's an ad hoc approach to creating systems without any kind of governance. It is very likely that such a system doesn't serve the business as a whole well.

Here are some more flavors of Wild West integration:

Integration via database
  A service accesses some other service's database directly in order to communicate, often without the other service knowing it.

Naive point-to-point integrations
  Two components communicate directly with each other, often via REST, SOAP, or messaging protocols, without properly clarifying all aspects around remote communication.

Database triggers
  Additional logic is invoked whenever you write something to the database.

Brittle toolchains
  For example, moving comma-separated (CSV) text files via FTP.

Ash needed to write a lot of code for features that are built-in capabilities of a workflow engine: keeping the current state, scheduling retries, reporting on the current state, and operating long-running processes. Instead of writing your own code, you should leverage existing tools. There's really nothing to gain by rolling your own solution. Even if you think that your project doesn't need the additional complexity of a workflow engine, you should always give it a second thought.

Coding processes without a workflow engine typically results in complex code; state handling ends up being coded into the components themselves. This makes it harder to understand the business logic and business process implemented in that code.

Ash's story could also easily lead to the development of a homegrown workflow engine. Such company-specific solutions cause a lot of development and maintanence effort and will still lack behind what existing tools can deliver.

Workflow Engines and Executable Process Models

So what is the alternative to hardcoded workflow logic or a homegrown workflow engine? You can use an existing tool, such as one of the products contained in the curated list on this book's website (*https://ProcessAutomationBook.com*).

A workflow engine automates the control of a process. It allows you to define and deploy a blueprint of your process, the *process definition*, expressed in a certain modeling language. With that process definition deployed you can start *process instances*, and the workflow engine keeps track of their state.

Figure 1-2 shows a process for the payment example introduced earlier. The process starts when a payment is required, as indicated by the first circle in the process model (the so-called *start event*, marking the beginning of a process). It then goes through the one and only task, called a *service task*, indicated by the cog wheels. This service task will implement the REST call to the external credit card service. You will learn how this can be done in Chapter 2. For now, simply imagine that you write some normal programming code to do this, which I call *glue code*. After that task, the process ends in the *end event*, the circle with the thick border.

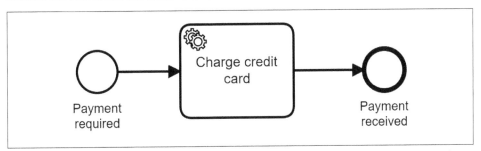

Figure 1-2. A very simple process, which can already handle many requirements in the credit card example

Figure 1-3 visualizes with some pseudocode how you can use this process model to implement payments. First, you will write some code that reacts to something in the outside world—for example, a call to the REST endpoint to collect payments. This code will then use the workflow engine API to start a new process instance. This process instance is persisted by the workflow engine; Figure 1-3 visualizes this via a relational database. You'll read about different engine architectures, persistence options, and deployment scenarios later in this book.

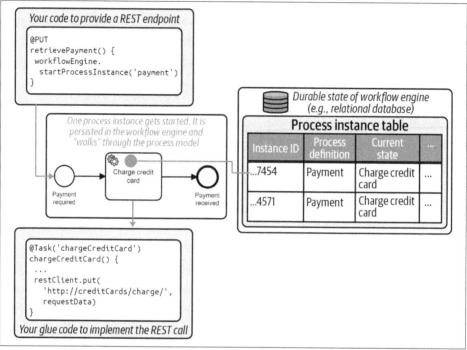

Figure 1-3. Workflow engine

Next, you will write some glue code to charge the credit card. This code acts like a callback and will be executed when the process instance advances to the task to charge the credit card, which will happen automatically after the process instance is started. Ideally, the credit card payment is processed right away and the process instance ends afterward. Your REST endpoint might even be able to return a synchronous response to its client. But in case of an outage of the credit card service, the workflow engine can safely wait in the task to charge the credit card and trigger retries.

We just touched on the two most important capabilities of a workflow engine:

- Persist the state, which allows waiting.
- Schedule things, like the retries.

Depending on the tooling, the glue code might need to be written in a specific programming language. But some products allow arbitrary programming languages, so if you decide to clean up your Wild West implementation you'll probably be able to reuse big parts of your code and just leverage the workflow engine for state handling and scheduling.

Of course, many processes go far beyond that simple example. When retrieving payments, the process model might solve more business problems. For example, the process could react to expired credit cards and wait for the customer to update their payment information, as visualized in Figure 1-4.

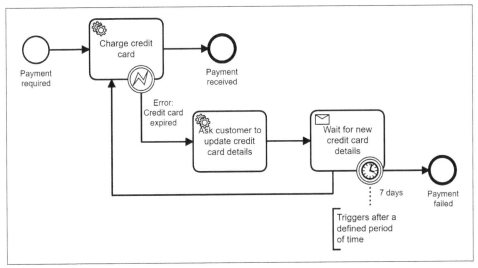

Figure 1-4. The payment process can quickly become more elaborate

So far, the payment process is more of an integration process, which is not the most typical use for process automation. I like starting with it as it helps technical audiences to understand core workflow engine capabilities, but we'll examine a more typical business process in the next section.

A Business Scenario

Let's look at a typical (but imaginary) project. ShipByButton Inc. (SBB) is a tech startup. It provides a small hardware button. Whenever it is pressed, one specific item is ordered. For example, you could put this button next to your washing powder, and when you see that the powder is almost empty, you just press the button, and one box of washing powder will then be ordered and shipped to you (if this reminds you of the Amazon Dash button, this might be simply coincidence ;-)).

SBB wants to automate its core business process, which is order fulfillment. An elaborate discussion of the different roles and their collaboration is provided in "A Typical Project" on page 195. For now, let's just say SBB starts with drawing out the process relating to the physical steps involved, and work their way down to the level of detail that can be automated using a workflow engine. They benefit from the fact that the process modeling language, BPMN, is universal regardless of the level at which you apply it.

The resulting process model is shown in Figure 1-5.

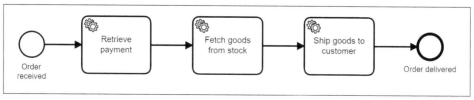

Figure 1-5. End-to-end business process that is subject to automation

This is of course a bit simplified, as in real life you have more exceptional cases; e.g., if payment cannot be retrieved or goods are out of stock.

You can see that this process relies on other services, for example the first task invoking the payment service. This is a typical scenario when applying microservices, as you will learn later in this book.

 Modeling business processes often leads to an interesting by-product: unexpected insights. In a customer scenario close to SBB's, we found that the "business people" did not actually know exactly what the "on the warehouse floor people" were doing. The visual process model not only helped to identify but also to resolve this problem.

Long-Running Processes

Process automation has a broad scope. While it is often about enterprise, end-to-end business processes like order fulfillment, account opening, or claim settlement, it can also help with much more technical use cases around orchestration and integration, as noted in the credit card example.

All these examples share one commonality, though: they involve *long-running processes*. That means processes that take minutes, hours, weeks, or months to complete. Handling long-running processes is what workflow engines excel at.

These processes involve waiting for something to happen; for example, for other components to respond, or simply for humans to do some work. This is why workflow engines need to handle durable state, as mentioned earlier.

Another way to look at it is that long-running behavior is required whenever logic *crosses boundaries*. When I say boundaries, this can mean very different things. If you call a remote service, you cross the boundary of your local program, your local OS, and your local machine. This leaves you responsible for dealing with problems around the availability of the service or added latency. If you invoke another component or resource, you also cross the technical transaction boundary. If you integrate components from other teams you cross organizational boundaries, which means you need to collaborate with these people more. If you involve external services, like from a credit card agency, you cross the boundary of your own company. And if you involve people, this crosses the boundary between automatable and not-automatable tasks.

Managing these boundaries not only requires long-running capabilities, but also requires you to think carefully about the *sequence of tasks*. Failure scenarios and the proper business strategy to handle them need serious discussion. And you might face regulatory requirements around data security, compliance, or auditing. These requirements further motivate graphical process visualizations, which will be covered in depth in Chapter 11; these allow technical folks to consult with the right non-technical people to solve any challenges.

Modern systems have more and more boundaries, as there is a growing tendency to move away from monolithic systems toward fine-grained components, like services, microservices, or functions. And systems are often assembled out of a wild mix of internal applications and services consumed in the cloud.

Business Processes, Integration Processes, and Workflows

To summarize, you can automate business processes as well as integration processes. The boundary between these categories is often not sharp at all, as most integration use cases have a business motivation. This is why you don't find "integration processes" discussed as a separate category in this book. Instead, "Model or Code?" on page 59 will show you that many technical details end up in normal programming code, not in a process model, and "Extracting (Integration) Logic into Subprocesses" on page 211 will explain that you can extract some portions of the process model into child models. This allows you to push technical details into another level of granularity, which helps to keep the business process understandable.

Furthermore, you'll have noticed that I use the terms *process* and *workflow*. Truth be told, there is no common, agreed-on understanding of the difference between process automation and workflow automation. Many people use these terms interchangeably. Others don't, and argue that business processes are more strategic and workflows are more tactical artifacts; thus, only workflows can be modeled and executed on a workflow engine. Similarly, process models can also be called workflow models; some standards use one term, and others the other. Neither is right or wrong.

I often recommend adjusting the terminology to whatever works well in your environment. However, for this book I had to make a choice, and I simply went with what I feel most comfortable with. As a rule of thumb:

- Business process automation is *what* you want to achieve. It is the goal. It is what business people care about. I will use the term *process* (or *business process*) in most cases.

- I use the term *workflow* whenever I talk about the tooling, which is about *how* processes are really automated. So, for example, I will talk about a workflow engine, even if this will automate process models.

In real life, I sometimes adjust these rules. For instance, when talking to technical folks about the implementation, I might prefer the terms *workflow*, *workflow engine*, or sometimes even *orchestration engine* or *Saga*, depending on the context (you will understand the latter terms when you've progressed further in this book).

Business–IT Collaboration

The collaboration of business stakeholders and IT professionals is crucial for the success of modern enterprises. Business stakeholders understand the organization, the market, the product, the strategy, and the business case for each project. They can channel all of that into requirements, features, and priorities. IT, on the other hand, understands the existing IT landscape and organization—constraints and opportunities as well as effort and availability. Only by collaborating can both "sides" win.

Unfortunately, different roles often speak different languages. Not literally—both might communicate in English—but in the way they phrase and understand things.

Putting the business process at the center of this communication helps. It makes it much easier to understand requirements in the context of a bigger picture and avoids the misunderstandings that can happen when you discuss features in isolation.

Visual process models facilitate this conversation, especially if they can be understood by business and IT. All the efficient requirement workshops I've seen were filled with people from business *and* IT.

A common example is that business folks underestimate the complexity of requirements, but at the same time miss easy picks. A typical dialogue goes like this:

> *Business:* "Why is implementing this small button so much effort?"
>
> *IT:* "Because we need to untie a gigantic knot in the legacy software to make it possible! Why can't we just make a change over here and reach the same result?"
>
> *Business:* "What, wait, we can change that over there? We thought that was impossible."

With the right mindset and a good collaboration culture, you will not only progress faster, but also end up with better solutions and happier people. Process automation and especially visual process models will help. Chapter 10 will explain this in much more detail.

Business Drivers and the Value of Process Automation

Organizations apply process automation to:

- Build better customer experiences.
- Get to market faster (with changed or completely new processes, products, or business models).
- Increase business agility.
- Drive operational cost savings.

This can be achieved by the promises that come with the prospect of process automation: increasing visibility, efficiency, cost-effectiveness, quality, confidence, business agility, and scale. Let's look at some of these briefly.

Business processes provide direct visibility to business stakeholders. For example, a business person cares about the sequence of tasks, such as ensuring that payment is collected before shipping, or knowing what the strategy is for handling failed payments. This information is needed to truly understand how the business currently runs and performs. The data that process automation platforms provides leads to actionable insights, which is the basis for process optimizations.

Enterprises care about the efficiency and cost-effectiveness of their automated processes, as well as quality and confidence. An online retailer might want to reduce the cycle time of their order fulfillment process, meaning that a customer will receive a parcel as fast as possible after hitting the order button. And of course, retailers also don't want any orders to fall through the cracks in the system, leaving them not only with a missed sale, but also an unhappy customer.

Some business models even rely on the possibility of fully automating processes; it is crucial for companies to make money, or deliver responses as fast as expected, or scale their business.

Business agility is another important driver. The pace of IT is too fast to really anticipate any trend properly, so it is important for companies to build systems that can react to changes. As the CIO of an insurance company recently said to me, "We don't know what we will need tomorrow. But we do know that we will need something. So we have to be able to move quickly!" Concentrating on building systems and architectures in a way that makes it easy to adopt changes is crucial to the survival of many businesses. Process automation is one important piece, as it makes it easier to understand how processes are currently implemented, to dive into discussions around changes, and to implement them.

Not Your Parents' Process Automation Tools

If process automation and workflow engines are such a great solution for certain problems, why doesn't everybody apply them? Of course, some people simply don't know about them. But more often, people have either had bad experiences with bad tools in the past, or they only have a vague association with terms like *workflow* or *process automation* and think they relate to old-school document flows or proprietary tool suites, which they don't see as helpful. Spoiler alert: this is wrong!

In order to overcome these misconceptions it's good to be aware of history and past failures. This will allow you to free your mind to adopt a modern way of thinking about process automation.

A Brief History of Process Automation

The roots of dedicated process automation technology date back to around 1990, when paper-based processes began to be guided by document management systems. In these systems, a physical or digital document was the "token" (a concept we'll discuss more in Chapter 3), and workflows were defined around that document. So, for example, the application form to open a bank account was scanned and moved automatically to the people who needed to work on it.

You can still spot these document-based systems in real life. I recently saw a tool being used with a lot of phantom PDF documents being created just to be able to kick off workflow instances that are not based on a real physical document.

This category of systems developed further into human workflow management tools that were centered around human task management. They reached their zenith around 2000. With these, you did not need documents to start a workflow. Still, these systems were built to coordinate humans, not to integrate software.

Then, also around the year 2000, *service-oriented architecture* (SOA) emerged as an alternative to large monolithic ecosystems where traditional enterprise application integration (EAI) tools did point-to-point integrations. The idea was to break up functionality into services that are offered in a more or less standardized way to the enterprise, so that others can easily consume them. One fundamental idea of SOA was to reuse these services and thus reduce development efforts. Hybrid tools emerged: tools that were rooted in SOA but added human task capabilities, and human workflow products that added integration capabilities.

Around the same time, *business process management* (BPM) was gaining traction as a discipline, taking not only these technical and tooling aspects into account, but also the lessons around setting up scalable organizations and business process reengineering (BPR).

These developments are summarized in Figure 1-6.

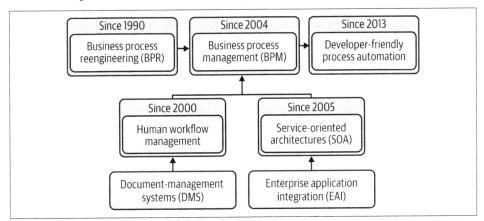

Figure 1-6. Historical development of disciplines

Process automation was a hyped topic in the BPM and SOA era. Unfortunately, there were some major flaws that led to many disappointments, for the following reasons: BPM was too detached from developers, and the tools were too vendor-driven, too centralized, and too focused on low code. Let me explain.

BPM in the ivory tower

BPM as a discipline includes methods to discover, model, analyze, measure, improve, optimize, and automate business processes. In that sense, it is a very broad topic. Unfortunately, many BPM initiatives were too detached from IT. For a long time, the folks doing BPM worked in silos, not considering how processes were really automated within the given IT infrastructure. This led to process models that could not function in real life, and yet these models were given to the IT departments to "simply" implement. Unsurprisingly, this did not work very well.

Centralized SOA and the ESB

In an instance of unfortunate timing, SOA collided with the high times of very complex technologies like the Simple Object Access Protocol (SOAP), which made it difficult for any development team to offer or consume any other service. This opened up the space for tool vendors. Since SOA initiatives were typically very centrally organized and governed, it brought the big vendors into the game, and they sold very expensive middleware that was placed at the heart of many companies in a top-down approach. The tooling was called an *enterprise service bus* (ESB); it was a messaging system at its core, with multiple tools around it to connect services or transform data.

Looking back at SOA from today's perspective, it is easy to highlight some of the shortcomings:

Centralized

SOA and ESB tools were typically installed as centralized systems and were operated by their own teams. This very much led to situations where you not only had to implement and deploy your own service, but also interact with the SOA team to deploy additional configuration into these tools, which caused a lot of friction.

Alien to the development process

Tools broke the development workflow, making automated testing or continuous integration/continuous delivery (CI/CD) pipelines impossible. Many of the tools did not even allow for automated testing or deployment.

Vendor-driven

The vendors overtook the industry and sold products before best practices existed, which forced practices into many companies that simply did not work.

Mixed infrastructure and business logic

Important business logic often ended up in routing procedures that were deployed on the middleware, leaving it without clear ownership or responsibility. Different teams implemented various aspects of logic that better belonged in one place.

But how does this relate to process automation? Great question! SOA typically came in tandem with BPM suites.

Misguided BPM suites

BPM suites were standalone tools that included a workflow engine at their core, with tools around it. Like ESBs, these suites were vendor-driven. They were deployed as centralized tools that were introduced from the top down. In these environments a central team took care of the platform, and this team often was the only group capable of deployment. This dependence on single teams led to a lot of problems.

It's worth mentioning that BPM suites emerged during a time when most companies were still running software on physical hardware—automated deployment pipelines weren't really a thing then.

The limitations of low code

BPM suites came with the promise of *zero code*, which was later rebranded as *low code*. The idea is as simple as it is appealing to business stakeholders: develop processes without IT being involved so a non-technical person can create an executable process model without writing programming code.

Low-code approaches involve heavyweight tools that allow these non-developers to build processes by dragging and dropping prebuilt elements. Sophisticated wizards enable users to configure them, so it's possible to build solutions without writing any source code.

This approach is still sold as desirable by advisory firms and BPM vendors, and the low-code approach indeed has its upsides. There is a shortage of developers at the moment, so many companies simply don't have the resources to do proper software projects as they would like to. Less tech-savvy people (referred to as *citizen developers* by Gartner (*https://oreil.ly/ZNfej*)) begin working on software projects and need these low-code approaches.

But while a low-code approach might work for relatively simple processes, it definitely falls short when dealing with complex business processes or integration scenarios. What I have regularly found is that low-code products do not deliver on their promise, and less-tech-savvy citizen developers cannot implement core processes themselves. As a result, companies have to revert back to their IT departments and ask them to assign professional software developers to finish the job. Those software developers then need to learn a proprietary, vendor-specific way of application development. Developing this skill takes a long time, and it's often a frustrating experience. As a result, there is a lack of sufficiently skilled software developers within the organization, which forces companies to look for outside resources.

Those outside resources are system integrators that partner with the BPM vendor and provide consultants certified by that vendor. Those consultants tend to be either not as skilled as promised, too expensive, or simply not available, often all at the same time.

Furthermore:

- You can't use industry best practices to develop software solutions, like automated testing or frameworks that you might need for integration or user interfaces. You can only do what the vendor has foreseen, as it is hard or even impossible to break out of the preconceived path.
- You are often blocked from open source or community-driven knowledge and tool enhancements. For example, instead of being able to pick up a code example from GitHub, you instead have to watch a video tutorial on how to use the proprietary wizard to guide you through the low-code interface.
- The tools are typically very heavyweight and do not easily run on modern virtualized or cloud native architectures.

These unfortunate dynamics caused a lot of companies to give up on process automation tools, even though not all approaches involve this type of proprietary software or low-code development.

Instead of replacing software development with low-code process automation, the focus should be on bringing software development and process automation together!

It is important to understand that agility does not come from implementing processes without the help of developers, but by using graphical models that different stakeholders can understand and discuss.

As soon as you can combine process automation with "normal" software development practices, you gain development efficiency and quality, you allow normal developers to work on these jobs, and you have a whole universe of existing solutions available to help you out with all kinds of problems. Additionally, workflow vendors might prebuild support for certain integrations, which helps to reduce the effort required to build solutions.

Moving past old-school BPM suites

The good news is that there are now a lot of really useful, lightweight workflow engines available that integrate well with typical development practices and solve common problems.

This new generation of tools are most often open source or provided as cloud services. They target developers and support them in the challenges described earlier in this chapter. They deliver real value and are helping our industry to move forward.

The Story of Camunda

I always like to back this whole development with the story of the company I cofounded: Camunda, a vendor that—as marketing nowadays says—reinvented process automation. As mentioned in the Preface, this book will not be a marketing vehicle for the company, but its story can help you understand the market's development.

I started Camunda together with my cofounder in 2008, as a company providing consultancy services around process automation. We did a lot of workshops and trainings and thus had thousands of customer contacts.

This collided with the peak times of the old BPM and SOA ideas and tools. We were able to observe various tools in use in different companies. The common theme was that it wasn't working out, and it was not too hard to figure out the reasons. I described them earlier in this chapter: these tools were centralized, complex, low-code, vendor-driven.

So we began experimenting with the open source frameworks available at the time. They were much closer to developers, but they couldn't cut it either, mainly because they were too basic, lacked important features, and required too much effort to build your own tooling around them.

At the same time, we collaborated on the development of the Business Process Model and Notation (BPMN) standard, which defines a visual but also directly executable process modeling language.

And we saw a huge opportunity: creating an open source workflow engine that was developer-friendly and fostered business–IT collaboration by using BPMN.

We validated that idea with customers, and soon made a decision to pivot with the company: in 2013 we transformed Camunda from a consulting firm into an open source process automation vendor. Our tool was the complete opposite of the common low-code BPM suites available back then.

Today, Camunda is growing fast and has hundreds of paying customers and countless community users. Many big organizations trust in the vision, and are even replacing tools from big vendors throughout their companies. We accelerate growth globally, as process automation tooling is strongly needed. This is fueled by digitalization and automation programs as well as the trend to move toward more fine-grained components and microservices, which then need to be coordinated. In short: we are doing very well.

Technically, the Camunda workflow engine is engineered the way applications were engineered in 2013. It is basically a library, built in Java, that uses a relational database to store state. The engine can be embedded into your own Java application or run standalone, providing a REST API. And of course, there are a couple of additional tools to model or operate processes.

This architecture has served Camunda very well and can handle most of today's performance and scalability requirements. Nonetheless, a couple of years back we developed a new workflow engine in a completely different architecture, which nowadays is best described as being cloud native. This workflow engine is developed in parallel and backs the managed service offering within Camunda Cloud. As it scales infinitely, this enables the use of a workflow engine in even more scenarios, which is a vision we've had in mind for a long time.

Conclusion

As this chapter has shown, process automation is a centerpiece of digitalization efforts. This makes workflow engines a vital building block in modern architectures. Fortunately, we have great technology available today, which is very different from old-school BPM suites. It is not only developer-friendly, but also highly performant and scalable.

Workflow engines solve problems around state handling and allow you to model and execute graphical process models to automate the control flow of processes. This helps you to avoid Wild West integration and fosters business–IT collaboration when automating processes. You saw a first example of a process model here, directly executed on a workflow engine; this is something that will be explained further in the next chapter.

PART I

Fundamentals

This part of the book will foster a general understanding of process automation with workflow engines:

Chapter 2
>   This chapter introduces workflow engines and the execution of process models on such an engine with a hands-on example.

Chapter 3
>   This chapter answers practical questions on how to implement executable processes and connect them with other parts of your application. This will give you a solid understanding of how process automation can work in real life.

Chapter 4
>   Here, you'll dive into the various use cases process automation can be applied to, which include orchestration of humans, bots, software, and decisions. This should give you a good idea of how process automation is applicable in your context and which projects qualify for leveraging it. Note that Chapter 9 will look at further use cases for workflow engines, namely, how they can be applied to solve certain challenges in distributed systems.

Chapter 5
>   To conclude the fundamentals, this chapter will give you reasons why workflow engines and BPMN are a great choice for automating processes. You'll also read about alternative implementation approaches and process modeling languages.

CHAPTER 2

Workflow Engines and Process Solutions

After the general introduction to process automation, this chapter:

- Introduces workflow engines and process solutions
- Presents a hands-on, executable example to make things concrete
- Explores the developer experience when using process automation platforms

The Workflow Engine

As you saw in the introduction, a workflow engine is the key component for automating the control flow of a long-running process.

If you're wondering why you should use a workflow engine instead of hardcoding processes or using batch processing or data streams, you might want to take a peek at "Limitations of Other Implementation Options" on page 93.

Core Capabilities

The core technical capabilities of a workflow engine are:

Durable state (persistence)
   The engine keeps track of all running process instances, including their current state and historical audit data. While this sounds easy, durable state is still a challenge to handle, especially at scale. It also immediately triggers subsequent requirements around understanding the current state, which means you will need operations tooling. A workflow engine needs to manage transactions, too, for example, handling concurrent access to the same process instance.

Scheduling

A workflow engine needs to keep track of timing and possibly escalate if a process gets stuck for too long. Therefore, there must be a scheduling mechanism that allows the engine to become active whenever something needs to be done. This also allows tasks to be retried in the event of temporary errors.

Versioning

Having long-running processes means that there is no point in time when there is no process instance running. Remember that in this context "running" might actually mean waiting. Whenever you want to make a change to a process, such as adding another task, you need to think about all the currently running instances. Most workflow engines support multiple versions of a process definition in parallel. Good tools allow migrating instances to a new version of the process definition, in an automatable and testable manner.

These core features are visualized in Figure 2-1.

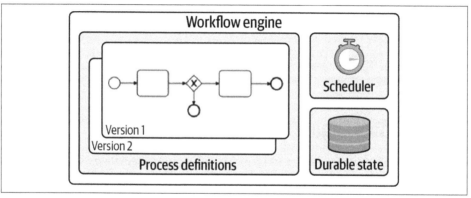

Figure 2-1. A workflow engine is a state machine that is good at waiting and scheduling

Using a workflow engine removes the burden of storing state yourself, leveraging bespoke scheduling mechanisms, and ultimately building your own workflow engine, as described in "Wild West Integrations" on page 4.

Of course, there are trade-offs. The main disadvantage of using a workflow engine is that you introduce another component in your stack. This never comes for free. For example, you need to choose a tool, learn how to use it, and sketch an architecture that makes use of it.

Typically this initially investment pays off quite early, but of course this depends very much on your scenario. At this point in the book it is too early to discuss when it makes sense to use a workflow engine—you first have to understand how these tools work and how they influence your architecture—but we will come back to that question in "When to Use a Workflow Engine" on page 115. To give you a sneak peek, the return on investment also depends on the investment, so lightweight tools with a shallow learning curve can already be helpful for solving "smaller" problems. You can get up and running with such tools relatively quickly.

 Different workflow engines have different architectures and resource requirements. Modern workflow engines tend to be very lightweight and integrate well with your existing architecture, developer experience, and CI/CD pipelines. There are also managed offerings in the cloud. And some workflow engines can scale horizontally and thus be used in high-load scenarios, like trading use cases where latency matters, telecommunications use cases with huge throughput, or retail use cases with high peak loads to be mastered.

Additional Features of Workflow Platforms

Along with these core capabilities, most workflow engines provide additional features. Good tools make these features optional or pluggable, which gives you the ability to choose whether you want a super-lean workflow engine or if you want to leverage some of the additional tooling. You can also adopt more features over time, when you see the need for them.

Typical additional features are:

Visibility
Process models can be expressed graphically, either through relatively simple visualizations or powerful graphical languages (discussed in detail in "Process Modeling Languages" on page 100). Having visibility into how the process is implemented is beneficial for communication and helpful for different roles, from developers ("How did I implement this last year?") to operations ("What tasks happened before that incident?") to business stakeholders ("How is the process currently implemented? Can we improve this?").

Audit data
Workflow engines write a lot of audit data about what is going on, including timestamps (e.g., when a process instance gets started and when it ends), task information (when a certain task is entered, how often it needs to be retried, etc.), and details on any incidents that occur. This data is extremely valuable during operations; for example, for recognizing and understanding a current failure situation, as well as for evaluating the overall performance in order to improve the process itself. Audit data can also be used in business dashboards to provide transparency about the work being done, processing costs, and so on.

Tooling

Most tool stacks deliver not only the core engine, but also tools for graphical modeling, technical operations, or business monitoring. "Typical Workflow Tools in a Project's Life Cycle" on page 38 will go into more detail on this.

Architecture

There are two basic options for running the workflow engine itself, visualized in Figure 2-2:

- The workflow engine is operated as a service, meaning it is a self-contained application that is separate from your business application. This means that your business application talks remotely to the workflow engine.

- The workflow engine is embedded as a library and thus runs as part of your own application.

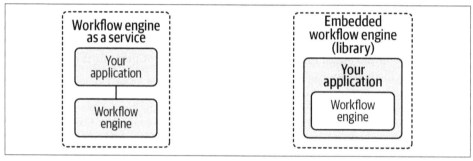

Figure 2-2. Typical architectures of a business application using a workflow engine

Having the workflow engine as a service should be considered the default nowadays. It allows you to isolate your application code from the workflow engine, which can eliminate a lot of problems. When working with support cases around embedded engines, it often takes a lot of effort to figure out how a customer embedded the workflow engine, and how that led to the problems described.

As a bonus, running the workflow engine as a service allows you to use it with different programming languages. Modern environments make it easy to spin up such a workflow engine—via Docker, for example, or by consuming it as cloud service.

Internally, the workflow engine itself implements scheduling, thread handling, and persistence. This is where there are big differences in the products. For example, let's assume that the workflow engine uses a relational database to store state. As Figure 2-3 visualizes, the workflow engine then keeps a record of all process definitions as well as all process instances. Whenever a process instance advances, the state is updated.

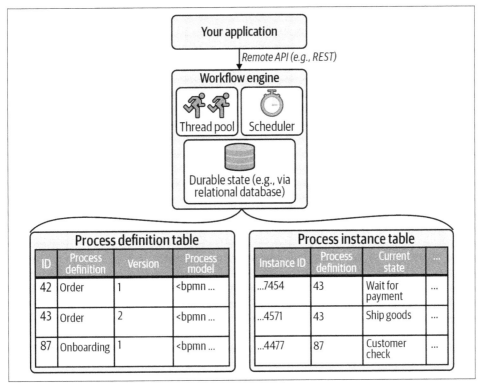

Figure 2-3. *Typical architecture of a workflow engine persisting in a relational database*

Some workflow engines store state using something other than a relational database; for example, they might use a more event-sourced approach. This enables scaling beyond the limitations of a relational database, which allows modern engines to scale horizontally or to support high-throughput, low-latency, or real-time applications. As a user of the workflow engine, the way the state is stored is not your problem, but of course you need to understand the implications that affect you. If a relational database is used, it is important to know which products are supported as you need to operate that database. If other state-handling methods are used, they might impose their own requirements that need to be checked.

One common source of confusion is threading. When I use the terms *waiting* or *long-running* in the context of a workflow engine, I don't mean that the workflow engine thread is blocked, waiting for something to happen. Instead, the workflow engine stores the current state in the persistent database. Then, it's finished; it returns the thread and does nothing.

But because the process instance's state is kept in the database as long as it's running, the process instance logically waits for something to happen; some event that will cause the workflow engine to load the state from the database again and resume processing. This could be a user pressing a button, which yields an API call on the workflow engine that completes the corresponding task. It could also be the engine scheduler that wakes up a process instance because some timer event is due.

A Process Solution

The process model is only one piece of the puzzle to automate a process. You will need to implement additional logic, typical examples being:

- Connectivity, e.g., to call REST endpoints or send AMQP messages
- Data handling and transformation
- Decisions about which path to take in a process model

The core workflow engine is not responsible for handling these aspects, even if most vendors will provide some out-of-the-box help for them. There is a thin line between convenience features you want to use and low-code features that you'd better stay away from, as described in "The limitations of low code" on page 16.

For this book I assume that most of the additional aspects are handled where they can be handled best by developers: in programming code.

So for example, instead of using your workflow engine's proprietary connectors to implement an HTTP call, it might be easier to code this in Java, C#, NodeJS, or whatever language you are fluent in. "Combining Process Models and Programming Code" on page 54 goes into more details of combining process models and code.

This code is logically part of the automated process, so the process model, this glue code and potentially other artefacts form a process solution as visualized in Figure 2-4. Technically, this could mean a single project using Java and Maven, .NET Core, or NodeJS, or it could mean a bunch of serverless functions logically bundled as a process solution.

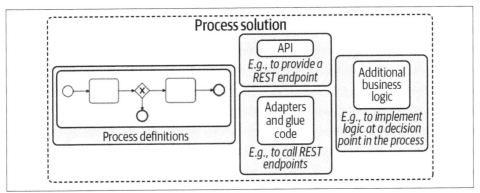

Figure 2-4. A process solution encompasses the various artifacts you need to automate a process, including but not limited to the process model

Note that a workflow engine is not responsible for storing business entities. This data should be stored by your application, and the workflow engine typically just refers to it. So while it can technically store data alongside every process instance, the use of this capability should be limited to keeping references (IDs).

An Executable Example

Let's walk through a concrete example to make things more tangible. The source code is available on this book's website (*https://ProcessAutomationBook.com*).

For this example, I use the following product stack:

- Java and Spring Boot
- Maven, so my Maven project equates to the process solution
- Camunda Cloud, a managed workflow engine in the cloud

Many of the concepts and steps illustrated here can be related to other products, but I need to choose a concrete stack to be able to show real source code.

The example will be extended later in the book and is about the onboarding of new customers in a small telecommunications company. The process model is shown in Figure 2-5.

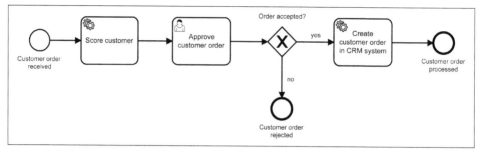

Figure 2-5. Process to onboard new mobile phone customers in a telecommunications company

When customers sign up for a mobile contract, a new instance of the process is started. The process first calculates a score for the customer using some Java code. This is handled by a service task, indicated by the cog wheels. The score is an input for the decision of whether to accept the customer's order. This decision is made by an employee of the telecommunications company, as indicated by the human icon; it is explicitly not automated.

The result of that decision influences the path of the process instance at the upcoming XOR gateway, the diamond with the X. This gateway is a decision point, so either the onboarding process instance continues to automatically process the new customer order, or it ends. Of course, in a real scenario you would add some more tasks, e.g., to inform rejected customers.

Let's briefly explore what you need in order to bring this model to life. This is not about generating code from some business-owned model, but about taking this specific process model and executing it on the workflow engine.

Customer onboarding will be its own microservice with a REST API, implemented by the development project, visualized in Figure 2-6, that contains:

- The onboarding process model. Using BPMN, which will be introduced in "Business Process Model and Notation (BPMN)" on page 45, the process model is simply an XML file stored alongside the project's source code.
- Source code to provide the REST API for clients, which is "normal Java."
- Some Java code to do the customer scoring.
- Glue code to implement the REST call to the CRM system.
- A form for the user to approve customer orders.

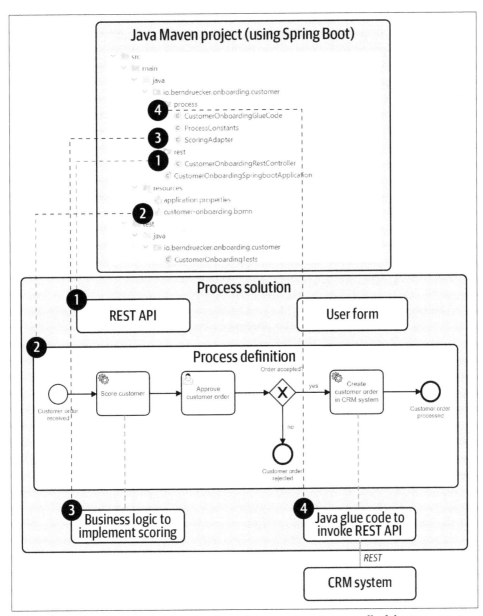

Figure 2-6. A process solution is a development project containing all of the important artifacts, like the process model, glue code, and test cases

Let's see how these pieces look when using Camunda Cloud.

First, the process model needs to be deployed to the workflow engine. While you could do that directly via a graphical modeling tool or via the API of the engine, the easiest option is to hook in the normal deployment mechanism of your microservice. In this case, this is an auto-deployment during startup of the Spring Boot application, as shown in the following code snippet:

```
@SpringBootApplication
@EnableZeebeClient
@ZeebeDeployment(classPathResources="customer-onboarding.bpmn")
public class CustomerOnboardingSpringbootApplication {
}
```

Now you can use the workflow engine API to create new instances of a process, e.g., when a new REST request is received:

```
@RestController
public class CustomerOnboardingRestController {

  @Autowired
  private ZeebeClient workflowEngineClient;

  @PutMapping("/customer")
  public ResponseEntity onboardCustomer() {
    startCustomerOnboardingProcess();
    return ResponseEntity.status(HttpStatus.ACCEPTED).build();
  }

  public void startCustomerOnboardingProcess() {
    HashMap<String, Object> variables = new HashMap<String, Object>();
    variables.put("automaticProcessing", true);
    variables.put("someInput", "yeah");

    client.newCreateInstanceCommand()
        .bpmnProcessId("customer-onboarding")
        .latestVersion()
        .variables(variables)
        .send().join();
  }
}
```

You can find more sophisticated code samples on the website for this book (*https://ProcessAutomationBook.com*), including how to return a synchronous response in case the onboarding process returns in milliseconds.

On the process model, you now need to add an expression to implement the decision of which path to take in the model, as shown in Figure 2-7.

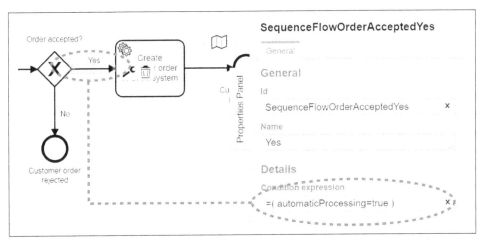

Figure 2-7. Gateways in BPMN (decision points) need expression language on the outgoing sequence flows

Camunda Cloud uses the Friendly Enough Expression Language (FEEL), which is a business-friendly expression language standardized in the context of decision engines. It will be described in "Orchestrate Decisions" on page 76. In the example, the expression simply checks a process variable, automaticProcessing. If it is true, the process continues on the "yes" path.

Then you have to define your glue code, as shown in the following code snippet:

```
@Component
public class CustomerOnboardingGlueCode {

@Autowired
private RestTemplate restTemplate;

@ZeebeWorker(type = "addCustomerToCrm")
public void addCustomerToCrmViaREST(JobClient client, ActivatedJob job) {
  log.info("Add customer to CRM via REST [" + job + "]");

  // TODO some real logic to create the request
  restTemplate.put(ENDPOINT, request);
  // TODO some real logic to process the response

  // let the workflow engine know the task is complete
  client.newCompleteCommand(job.getKey()).send().join();
  }
}
```

This code needs to be connected to the process model. In Camunda Cloud this is done by logical task names, as visualized in Figure 2-8.

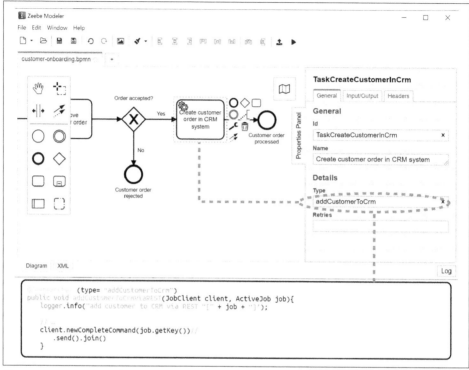

Figure 2-8. Service tasks in a process model can be connected to source code

In order to start the microservice, you need the workflow engine up and running. In the case of Camunda Cloud, this means that you will create a new "Zeebe cluster" via the cloud console, available online (*https://console.cloud.camunda.io*). Zeebe is the name of the workflow engine fueling Camunda Cloud.

You will receive connection details that you need to add to your application configuration, which in our example is a file called *application.properties*. Spring allows you to overwrite these connection details easily, e.g., via environment properties, which will be handy when you want to run the application in a production environment later.

After starting the Java Spring Boot application, you can invoke the REST API with the REST client of your choice, such as cURL:

```
curl -X PUT
    -H "Content-Type: application/json"
    -d '{"someVariable":"someValue"}'
    http://localhost:8080/customer
```

This will execute the REST code shown earlier to start a new process instance in the workflow engine. A good way to understand the nature of a workflow engine is to look at the operations tooling. Figure 2-9 gives an example, showing the just-started process instance and what data is available about that instance.

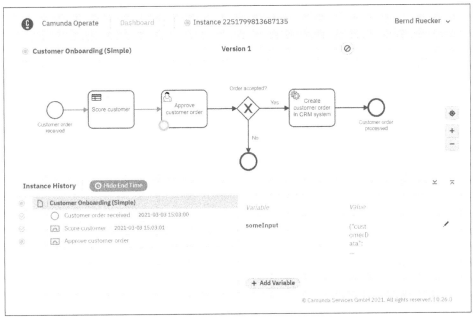

Figure 2-9. Operations tooling allows you to discover, analyze, and solve technical problems related to processes

The process model is source code and implements important parts of the business logic, so you should test it just like you test other parts of your business logic. In Java, this means writing unit tests using JUnit. At the time of writing, the assertion API was still in flux, so please check the book's website for the latest source code. It will look like the following:

```java
@Test
void testHappyPath() throws Exception {
  // simulate an incoming REST call that will kick off a new process instance
  customerOnboardingRest.onboardCustomer();

  // assert that a process was started
  ProcessInstanceEvent pi = assertProcessInstanceStarted();

  // Assert that a job (pub/sub mechanism of the workflow engine) for scoring
  // was created
  RecordedJob job = assertJob(pi, "scoreCustomer");
  assertEquals("TaskScoreCustomer", job.getBpmnElementId());
  assertEquals("customer-scoring", job.getBpmnProcessId());
```

```
// and complete the task, executing some fake logic instead of the real adapter
execute(job, new JobHandler() {
  public handle(JobClient client, ActivatedJob job) {
    // do some fake behavior instead of the real Java code
  }
});

// Verify that human task was created
RecordedHumanTask task = assertHumanTask(pi);
assertEquals("TaskApproveCustomerOrder", task.getBpmnElementId());
// ... maybe do more assertions ...
// and simulate it being completed with approval
Map variables = new HashMap();
variables.put("automaticProcessing", true);
complete(task, variables);

// Assert the next job for the call to the CRM system was created
job = assertJob(pi, "create");
assertEquals("TaskCreateCustomerInCrm", job.getBpmnElementId());
// and trigger its execution with the normal behavior
execute(job);
// A mock rest server was injected into the glue code by Spring,
// so we can verify the right request was sent
mockRestServer
  .expect(requestTo("http://localhost:8080/crm/customer")) //
  .andExpect(method(HttpMethod.PUT))
  .andRespond(withSuccess("{\"transactionId\": \"12345\"}",
                          MediaType.APPLICATION_JSON));

assertEnded(pi);
}
```

The process solution behaves like a normal Java Spring Boot project. You can check it into your normal version control system and build it using your normal CI/CD pipeline, like any other Java project. For instance, the sources of this example live in GitHub and are continuously built by TravisCI.

The full source code is available online, and I recommend that you play around with it, as this will help you to get a better basic understanding of a workflow engine for the upcoming discussions.

Applications, Processes, and Workflow Engines

A typical question is about the relationship between applications, workflow engines, process definitions, and process instances.

If you use the workflow engine as a service, you can deploy many process definitions on that workflow engine. For every process definition, you can run zero to many process instances. You can also use that workflow engine from many different applications or microservices.

All of this is comparable to a database installation, where you can create multiple tables and connect many different applications to them.

However, it might be advisable to use separate workflow engines for separate applications, as this improves isolation. Especially if you embrace microservices, this is the way to go, as described in "Decentralized Engines" on page 117.

For example, the team responsible for order fulfillment might operate a workflow engine. It won't share this with the team doing payments, as it wants to be isolated from anything the payment team does—but it will connect not only the order fulfillment application, but also the order cancellation application to that engine. Both applications deploy their own process definitions. This example is visualized in Figure 2-10.

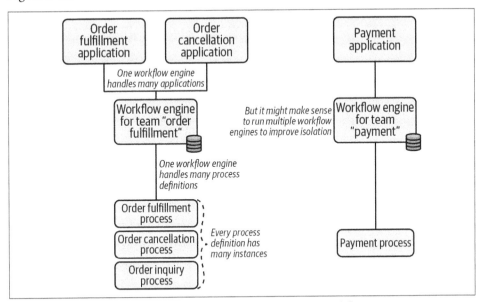

Figure 2-10. A summary of the cardinality of applications, workflow engines, process definitions, and instances

Typical Workflow Tools in a Project's Life Cycle

Most workflow engines are flanked by tools that help you leverage the full potential of process automation. Figure 2-11 shows a typical stack that might be provided as an integrated platform by your vendor. It includes the following tools:

- Graphical process modeler
- Collaboration tool
- Operations tooling
- Tasklist application
- Business monitoring and reporting

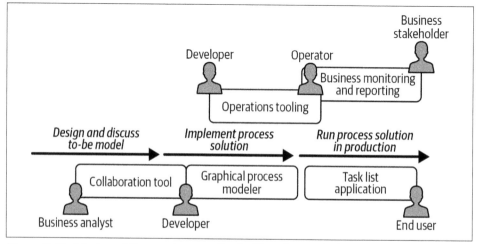

Figure 2-11. Most workflow engines are flanked by other tools that might be valuable at different stages of the project's life cycle, for different stakeholders

Let's briefly go over these tools to see how they are used in process automation projects. Note that good tools allow you to unbundle the platform, so that you aren't forced to use a big pile of tools but can select what really helps you.

Graphical Process Modeler

A graphical process modeler allows you to, well, model your processes graphically. Figure 2-12 shows an example.

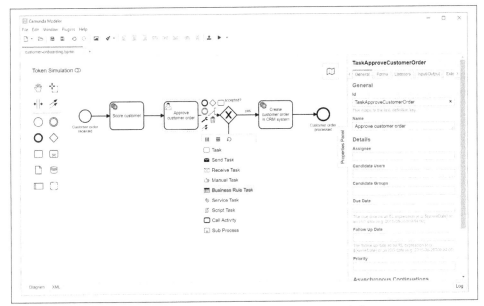

Figure 2-12. Graphical modeling tools allow you to edit process definitions

While a graphical modeler might be a valuable tool for business analysts, the focus in this book is on executable processes, so we'll treat the modeler as a tool for the developer. This is something some tools do a good job with, and some don't.

For example, the modeler should be able to work on files in your local filesystem, allowing you to store the process model along with your version-controlled source code. This makes it easy to keep it in sync with your source code. Some tools force you to use a separate repository, which can make the experience more brittle.

Also, the modeler should provide easy ways to edit all technical details that are important to make a model executable. This includes referencing glue code and other aspects you saw earlier in this chapter.

Graphical modelers are very handy in process automation projects. Just make sure you select a developer-friendly tool stack, as the wrong tool might easily become an obstacle in software development. Look at how the tool fits into your development environment.

Collaboration Tools

During the initial discussion on how to automate a certain process, it is often valuable to have different people collaborate on process models. This includes people from many roles, such as business analysts, developers, and methodology or subject matter experts. So, a good example of a useful feature in a collaboration tool is the ability to share a diagram with others and let them comment on it, as shown in Figure 2-13.

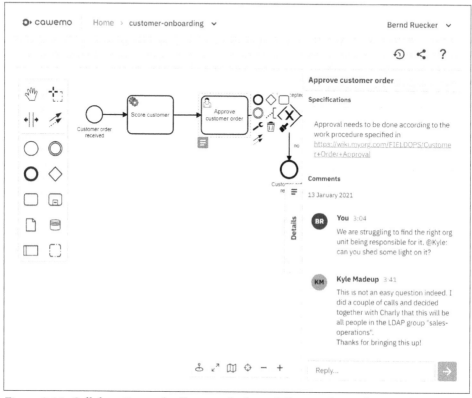

Figure 2-13. Collaboration tools allow people from different roles to share and discuss models

Collaboration tools typically have their own repositories where they store process models. It is important that these models are not treated as part of the source code of the process solution. Instead, the developer works on a process model stored in their version control system. We'll explore this topic in more detail in "The Power of One Joined Model" on page 205. For now, let's remember that collaboration tools can help in discussions around to-be process models, but they are not used to implement the process solution.

Operations Tooling

Once you've put your process solution into production, you need a tool that allows you to discover, analyze, and solve problems related to the processes, as shown in Figure 2-14.

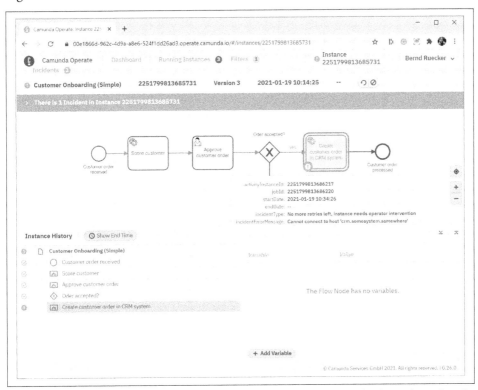

Figure 2-14. Operations tooling allows you to discover, analyze, and solve technical problems related to processes

Imagine there is a problem with the service call to the CRM system. You first need monitoring that will recognize that problem, e.g., because incidents are piling up. You will also want to send alerts or integrate with your existing APM (application performance monitoring) tool, so the right person gets notified quickly. In addition to alerting, the tool should support root cause analysis to help you understand the problem at hand (e.g., some endpoint URL has changed) and fix the issue (e.g., by updating a configuration option and triggering a retry)—and it should be able to operate at scale, because there may be a large number of affected process instances. Developers can also use these tools to play around during development.

Tasklist Applications

A process model can include tasks where a human needs to take some action. In these cases, there must be a way to notify the human that it is their turn. For this purpose, most vendors ship a tasklist application like the one shown in Figure 2-15.

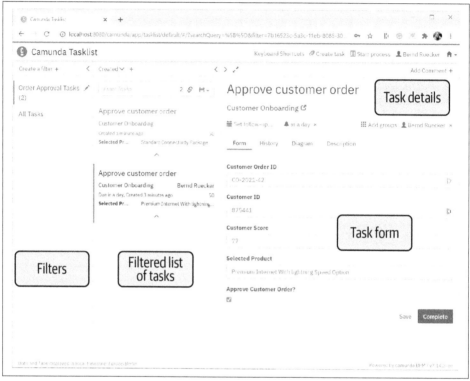

Figure 2-15. The Camunda Tasklist

These tools allow end users to see all the tasks they have to do in various running process instances. They can select a task, work on it, and let the workflow engine know when they are finished. "The User Interface of User Tasks" on page 85 goes into more detail on this.

Business Monitoring and Reporting

When your process solution is running in production, your business stakeholders want to monitor processes.

In contrast to operations, these people are much less interested in urgent technical problems and more interested in the overall performance. For example, this can be measured in cycle times, waiting times, or in-flight business value. They might also want to receive some notifications, but typically these are focused on performance indicators. For example, they need to be notified if a process instance is taking too long and thus will miss its SLA.

Business stakeholders also care about optimizing the overall process, which can be supported by analytics capabilities like a clear view on which process path is used most often, which paths are slow, which data conditions often lead to cancellations, and so forth. This information can be derived from the audit data that a workflow engine stores when executing process instances.

Figure 2-16 shows an example dashboard including different data points around a hiring process.

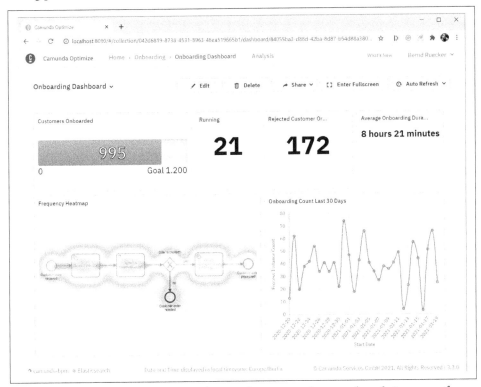

Figure 2-16. Business monitoring tools provide reports, alerts, and analytics on performance indicators

Conclusion

This chapter described the workflow engine and process automation platforms in more detail. The hands-on, executable example presented here should give you a better understanding of process solutions and workflow engines.

This equips you for diving into more detail on developing process solutions in the next chapter.

CHAPTER 3

Developing Process Solutions

This chapter:

- Introduces Business Process Model and Notation as an executable process modeling language
- Explains how to execute process models and how to combine process models with programming code
- Explores important aspects of developing your own process solutions

Business Process Model and Notation (BPMN)

After jumping right into an executable process in the last chapter, let's take a step back and explore some of the things you just saw in more detail. We'll start with the process modeling language, which allows you to design a blueprint of your process that can be executed on a workflow engine. Such a language can express a sequence of tasks and all the nuts and bolts around it, like decision points, parallel tasks, and synchronization points.

Different tools might use different process modeling languages. For this book I will use BPMN, for two main reasons: it's an adopted standard, and it's great. I will elaborate on why it's so great in "Process Modeling Languages" on page 100, but I first need to explain the basics.

Not all process models need to be executed on an engine, of course; sometimes you may simply want to draw a picture to understand or document certain behavior. While this is a valid use case, it is not the focus of this book. Still, drawing business processes for discussion or documentation can help people in your organization understand the potential of process automation with a workflow engine. Make sure you use an executable process modeling language, like BPMN.

A BPMN process can be visually expressed as shown in the example in Figure 3-1.

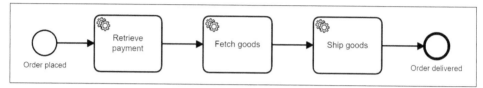

Figure 3-1. A BPMN process

The BPMN process is also an XML document. In normal life, you might never need to look at this XML. However, I'll show it to you here to reassure you that there is neither magic nor huge complexity hidden within it:

```
<?xml version="1.0" encoding="UTF-8"?>
<definitions>

  <!-- Execution semantics understood by a workflow engine: -->
  <process id="OrderFulfillment" isExecutable="true">

    <startEvent id="Event_OrderPlaced" name="Order Placed" />
    <sequenceFlow id="1"
      sourceRef="Event_OrderPlaced" targetRef="Task_RetrievePayment" />
    <serviceTask id="Task_RetrievePayment" name="Retrieve payment" />
    <sequenceFlow id="2"
      sourceRef="Task_RetrievePayment" targetRef="Task_FetchGoods" />
    <serviceTask id="Task_FetchGoods" name="Fetch goods" />
    <sequenceFlow id="3"
      sourceRef="Task_FetchGoods" targetRef="Task_ShipGoods" />
    <serviceTask id="Task_ShipGoods" name="Ship goods" />
    <sequenceFlow id="4"
      sourceRef="Task_ShipGoods" targetRef="Event_OrderDelivered" />
    <endEvent id="Event_OrderDelivered" name="Order delivered" />
  </process>

  <!-- Graphical layout information: -->
  <BPMNDiagram id="BPMNDiagram_1">
    <bpmndi:BPMNPlane id="BPMNPlane_1" bpmnElement="OrderFulfillment">
      <bpmndi:BPMNShape id="_BPMNShape_Event_OrderPlaced"
                        bpmnElement="Event_OrderPlaced">
        <dc:Bounds x="179" y="99" width="36" height="36" />
```

```
<bpmndi:BPMNLabel>
  <dc:Bounds x="165" y="142" width="65" height="14" />
</bpmndi:BPMNLabel>
...
```

The XML document contains all the information workflow engines and modeling tools need to interpret its contents. At the same time, the visual representation contains just enough information to be quickly understood by humans, including nontechnical people. The BPMN model is source code and documentation in one artifact. This duality makes BPMN very powerful.

BPMN is an industry standard for process modeling and execution. Originally created in 2004, it had a major overhaul in 2011 and was published by the International Organization for Standardization (ISO) as ISO/IEC 19510:2013. Since then, the notation has deliberately been kept stable, because a proliferation of versions could reduce some of the advantages of a standard. You can find the specification as a PDF on the Object Management Group website (*https://www.omg.org/spec/BPMN*).

Today, many companies have adopted BPMN; there are numerous books and resources about it, and it's commonly taught in university courses. Many modern workflow vendors comply with BPMN, and there is no competing standard.

I recommend that anyone entering the field of process automation learn BPMN. It will help you understand relevant patterns, even if you decide to work with a tool that uses another process modeling language. (A discussion of different modeling languages can be found in "Process Modeling Languages" on page 100.)

The following sections cover the most important patterns for process modeling in BPMN. This will allow you to understand the examples in this book and the code that is released along with it, and help you understand the mechanics and the power of executable process models.

This book does not discuss BPMN in depth; it only covers a subset of the language. There are many resources available that can teach you all the nitty-gritty details. You can find starting points on this book's website (*https://ProcessAutomationBook.com*).

Start and End Events

First things first: every process needs a starting point, which is a start event in BPMN. This is where the process flow will begin whenever a new process instance is started. End events are where a flow will end, as shown in Figure 3-2.

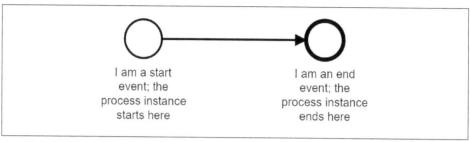

I am a start
event; the
process instance
starts here

I am an end
event; the
process instance
ends here

Figure 3-2. The start and end event of a process

To better understand a process flow, it's helpful to know about so-called *tokens*. We'll look at those next.

The Token Concept: Implementing Control Flow

According to the BPMN specification, a token is "a theoretical concept that is used as an aid to define the behavior of a process that is being performed." In essence, the token implements the control flow in BPMN.

You can think of every process instance as a token running through the process model. When a process is started, one token is spawned at the start event. With every completed step it advances along the process flow to the next task, as visualized in Figure 3-3. When a token reaches an end event, its life cycle ends.

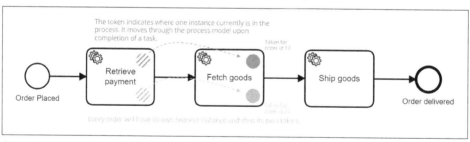

The token indicates where one instance currently is in the
process. It moves through the process model upon
completion of a task.

Token for
order id 17

Retrieve
payment

Fetch goods

Ship goods

Order Placed

Order delivered

Every order will have its own process instance and thus its own token.

Figure 3-3. A BPMN process

Whenever there is a decision point, the token needs to go down exactly one path. When the token reaches an end event, it is consumed and the process instance ends. A token is created for every process instance that gets started, so that multiple tokens flow through the model at the same time.

Workflow engines typically persist the status of these tokens, as they depict exactly where in the process a given instance is waiting.

You can compare the token concept to a car traveling along a road. At each intersection, the driver must decide whether to continue in a straight path or to turn left or right. The road system corresponds to a process model, and any particular route the car takes represents a process instance. Just note that this metaphor breaks down as soon as we hit parallel paths, as you can't easily clone a car so that it continues straight *and* left, but you can easily do this with a token in a process model, as you'll see in "Gateways: Steering Flow" on page 51.

Sequence Flows: Controlling the Flow of Execution

A BPMN sequence flow defines the order in which steps in the process happen. In BPMN's visual representation, a sequence flow is an arrow connecting two elements. The direction of the arrow indicates their order of execution.

Tasks: Units of Work

The basic elements of BPMN processes are tasks. From the perspective of a BPMN process, a task is an atomic unit of work. Whenever a token reaches a task, the token stops until the task is completed; only then does it continue on the outgoing sequence flow.

Choosing the granularity of a task is up to the person modeling the process. For example, the activity of processing an order can be modeled as a single task, or as three individual tasks to retrieve payment, fetch goods, and ship goods. What determines the right level of granularity will be discussed in "Extracting (Integration) Logic into Subprocesses" on page 211.

BPMN defines various task types, which refine what the unit of work is.

One important task type is the *service task*. When a token passes through a service task, some software functionality will be executed. Often this means calling a service, a microservice, a method, a function, or whatever is a first-class citizen in your architecture. As you saw in "An Executable Example" on page 29, you might simply connect glue code you have written in the programming language of your choice to such a service task, as illustrated in Figure 3-4.

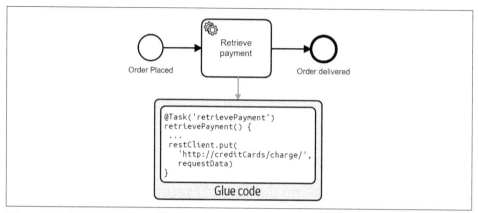

Figure 3-4. A service task will lead to functionality being executed, most probably expressed in some programming code

Another task type is the *user task*, shown in Figure 3-5. For this example, imagine a small company where fetching and shipping goods is simply done manually. The process is waiting for humans to do the described work. You could imagine that a to-do item is generated in a tasklist for the people who do the fetching and shipping. The workflow engine will wait until those folks tick off the to-do item.

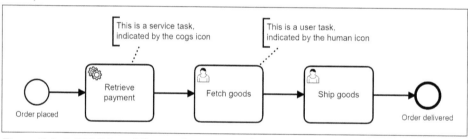

Figure 3-5. A BPMN workflow with service and user tasks

Other commonly used task types include the *business rules task*, which can involve a decision engine to evaluate a rule table, and the *script task*, where the workflow engine will execute a script in a defined scripting language.

The hard part is often defining which tasks you need and their sequence. As soon as that is clear, you might start with human tasks for rapid prototyping (to "click through" a model) and possibly also for a first iteration rolled out to production. You can then replace human labor step by step with automated tasks.

Gateways: Steering Flow

Gateways are elements that route tokens in more complex patterns than plain sequence flows. The *exclusive gateway* chooses exactly one sequence flow out of many based on data. You can see an example in Figure 3-6, where the "retrieve payment" task is only entered if a prepayment method is selected.

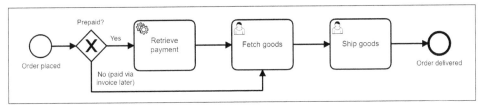

Figure 3-6. A BPMN process with an exclusive gateway that determines the outgoing flow

We won't discuss yet whether this decision should be handled by the order fulfillment process or within the payment task; you will learn more about that in Chapter 7.

The *parallel gateway* generates new tokens by activating multiple sequence flows in parallel. For example, you could decide that you want to fetch goods while you are still retrieving payment, as shown in Figure 3-7.

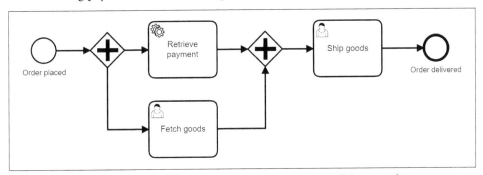

Figure 3-7. A BPMN process with a parallel gateway that parallelizes work

An important side note here is that this does not necessarily mean that the tasks run concurrently, in the sense of multithreading. Processes are about waiting, so "in parallel" basically means that you can do something else on one path while you are waiting on another.

Events: Waiting for Something to Happen

Events in BPMN represent things that happen. A process can react to events by
"catching" them. A great example is *timer events*, which simply wait for a defined
period of time to pass. In Figure 3-8 you can see two different ways to make use of
this type of event.

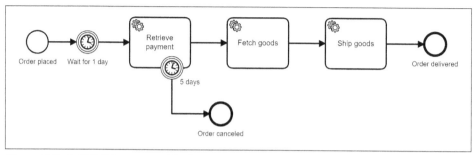

Figure 3-8. A BPMN process with timer events

The first timer is within the sequence flow, which means the process waits within that
timer event for one day (for example, for the right of withdrawal to expire).

The second timer is a *boundary event*. In this case, the process can react to this event
as long as it is waiting at that task. Here, that means we will wait five days for the
payment to be retrieved; if that doesn't happen the workflow engine cancels the task
at hand (retrieve payment) and moves on via the alternative sequence flow to end the
process (which of course might not be the best possible business approach to handling a payment delay).

Message Events: Waiting for a Trigger from the Outside

The example in Figure 3-9 introduces another important element, the message event.

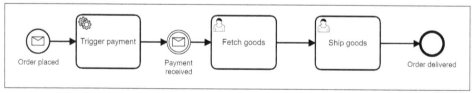

Figure 3-9. A BPMN process with message events

A message event is sent to a process instance from outside the workflow engine. This
can start a new process instance or lead to the continuation of an existing instance.

Message events sometimes lead to confusion if developers are familiar with message
brokers, as people think that they can connect the BPMN message events with their
message broker. Really, a BPMN message simply refers to a trigger from outside the

---

workflow engine. Technically speaking, this can be anything from a simple method call in your application via some REST API to a message or event in your message or event broker.

To make it even more concrete, if you want a process to react to a message in your message broker, you typically write a piece of glue code to wire this up, as shown in Figure 3-10. Of course, some vendors provide out-of-the-box connectors for common scenarios.

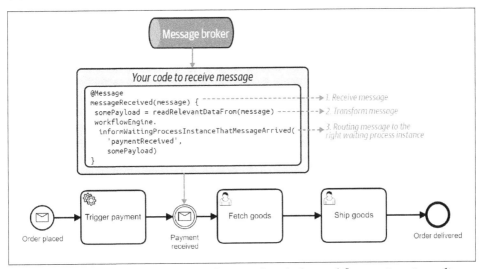

Figure 3-10. You need to connect your "universe" with the workflow engine via application code

Message events are also often used in combination with the event subprocess, which allows you to interrupt a process instance upon receipt of a message, independent of which task the process instance is currently waiting at.

Take the example in Figure 3-11. If a cancellation request comes in, this immediately interrupts the normal order fulfillment flow, whether we just started to retrieve payment or whether we're already about to ship the goods. You will learn about strategies to restore consistency in this case—for example, to refund already taken payments—in Chapter 9.

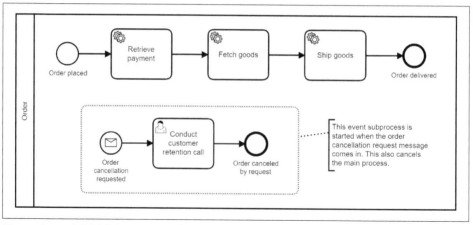

Figure 3-11. A BPMN process with event subprocess

Combining Process Models and Programming Code

As seen in the example in Chapter 2 and explained in "The limitations of low code" on page 16, you want to stay away from low-code approaches and connect process models with programming code. This allows you to embed process automation technology into proven software development practices.

There are differences between vendors in terms of how process models are combined with programming code, and different projects might use totally different programming languages and architectures. But there are three common conceptual methods for adding logic: subscribing to the process, referencing code, and using prebuilt connectors.

There is executable code available on the book's website (*https://ProcessAutomation Book.com*) showing examples of all these options.

Publish/Subscribe to a Process

Publish/subscribe (or pub/sub for short) is a mechanism known from messaging systems. Message brokers provide queues. A sender can publish messages to a queue, and recipients can subscribe to the queue and then receive messages. The recipients are not known to the sender.

Many workflow engines provide a similar pub/sub mechanism for logic in the process. In this scenario, the workflow engine itself acts as a broker; you don't need an actual message broker. Instead, you write some glue code that subscribes to the workflow engine, typically to a service task in BPMN, and executes logic whenever a new process instance arrives there.

Let's look at the example visualized in Figure 3-12, where the order fulfillment work-flow needs to call the payment service. Therefore, it contains a service task and defines a logical task type named `retrieve-payment` for it.

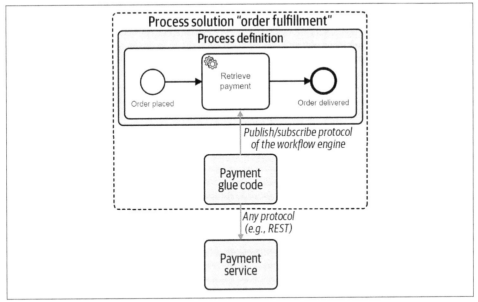

Figure 3-12. The workflow engine provides a publish/subscribe mechanism to add logic to the model, such as glue code to call external services

Let's assume this model:

```
<bpmn:serviceTask name="Retrieve Payment"
                vendorExtension:taskType="retrieve-payment">
```

Then you can imagine the following glue code (of course the exact code used will depend on the tool, the programming language, and your style) that implements the REST call to the payment service:

```
paymentHandler = new WorkflowLogicHandler() {
  public void handle(WorkflowContext context) {
    // Do input mapping of data here
    restRequest = RetrievePaymentRequest
      .paymentReason( context.getVariable('orderId') ) // ...

    // The real logic that is executed, e.g. calling a REST endpoint
    restResponse =
      restEndpoint.PUT(paymentEndpoint, restRequest);

    // Do output mapping of data here
    context.setVariable( 'paymentId', restResponse.getPaymentId()));

    // Let the workflow engine know once we are done
```

```
    context.completeServiceTask();
  }
```

Now you can open a subscription to the workflow engine, so that the handler will be called whenever a process instances reaches the service task with the task type name `"retrieve-payment"`:

```
subscription = workflowEngineClient
  .subscribeToTaskType("retrieve-payment")
  .handler( paymentHandler )
  .open();
```

Technically, this subscription might be implemented by different means. A common option is to use long polling under the hood. Somewhat simplified, you can imagine the client periodically asking for new work, but in a way that is very efficient and avoids delays in processing. This makes it easy to use common remote protocols, like REST, and limit the communication to one direction: from the client to the workflow engine. Using standardized remote protocols also allows you to write glue code in almost any programming language.

In Figure 3-12, the glue code was deliberately part of the process solution. The process model and glue code are tightly linked and belong together. This is a pretty common design, but as you'll see in "Microservices" on page 70, it's not the only possible one in a microservices architecture.

With the pub/sub mechanism the glue code is fully under your control, which offers a few important advantages.

First, it makes it easy for you to decide if you are ready to execute any tasks. If, for example, the external service is not available, you could close the subscription and wait for the service to become available again, or simply shut down the application containing the glue code. Any process instance waiting at a service task will keep waiting there for the work to be pulled and executed by the client, which might happen at any time in the future when you reopen the subscription.

Second, you can scale your glue code independently of the workflow engine itself. Assume you need to do some resource-intensive calculation in the glue code—you can simply scale up the application containing that glue code, or you can build small workers focusing on only this glue code and scale those up. It even works the other way around: if you have a resource where you have to throttle the load, you can also control that easily. A common example is optical character recognition (OCR) tools that are licensed for only one parallel OCR job at a time. Independent of the number of process instances arriving at the service task at the same time, you can create a subscription where only one task at a time is processed.

Third, your glue code can control when timeouts happen in the BPMN process. Imagine that you need to implement some logic that takes a long time to complete, like a video transcoding process. Transcoding a movie will take hours. With the pub/sub design, your glue code can start the transcoding process and only talk to the workflow engine again when it's finished. It would not be able to do the transcoding when running in the context of the workflow engine itself, because it would hit timeouts.

Referencing Code in Process Models

Another popular option is to reference code directly in a process model. This code is then executed by the workflow engine when passing through the task in question.

In pseudocode, it could look like this:

```
<bpmn:serviceTask name="Retrieve Payment"
                  vendorExtension:javaClass="io.processbook.RetrievePayment">
```

And:

```
public class RetrievePayment implements WorkflowLogicHandler {
  public void handle(WorkflowContext context) {
    // same as in last example...
  }
}
```

The big difference from the pub/sub approach is that in this case the workflow engine executes that code within its own context, meaning within the thread of the engine and probably also in the same technical transaction. While this may sound simple and straightforward, it comes with a couple of challenges:

- You have limited technology choices, as you are nailed to the environment the workflow engine runs in (e.g., Java).

- There is no temporal decoupling, as the code is called whenever the engine reaches the task in question. Coupling is further discussed in "Strong Cohesion and Low Coupling" on page 127.

- You have to work with more restrictions regarding computing time, timeouts, and transactional control.

This leads us to probably the most critical downside: the exact behavior depends not only on the engine, but also the configuration of that engine and what exactly you are doing in your glue code. This makes it hard to investigate failure situations.

Over the last decade I have contributed to various open source workflow engines. In the first few projects we started with referenced code and were super happy with the simplicity of it. But over time and with increasing adoption of the tools pub/sub turned out to be preferable in most situations, which is why modern engines focus on it. This preference is fueled even more by the trends toward cloud native architectures and polyglot teams.

Using Prebuilt Connectors

The third common possibility for adding logic is to use prebuilt connectors that come with the process automation platform. You can reference and configure them via the process model. For example, if you want to call some service via REST, you could leverage an HTTP connector as indicated by the following pseudocode:

```
<bpmn:serviceTask name="Retrieve Payment">
  <bpmn:extensionElements>
      <vendorExtension:connector type="HTTP" />
      <vendorExtension:connectorConfig key="method" value="PUT" />
      <vendorExtension:connectorConfig key="url"
                              value="http://myPayment/retrieval" />
  </bpmn:extensionElements>
```

Figure 3-13 shows this possibility.

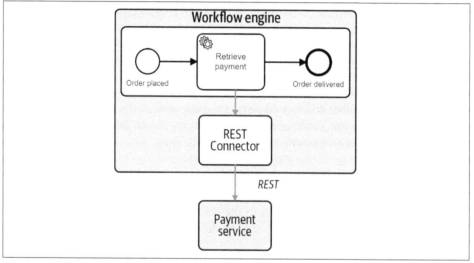

Figure 3-13. Using your workflow engine's prebuilt connectors to integrate other systems

The amount and type of connectors as well as their power differ between vendors, but there are common downsides with connectors:

- The possibilities are limited to what the vendor has foreseen. In reality, you might quickly hit a limitation of a connector, such as the HTTP connector not correctly handling multipart forms that you need for your service call. In this case the only hope you have is that your vendor extends the connector quickly enough for you to move on. As this rarely happens, you should at least have a plan B for these cases.

- Testing is often harder, as the connector is out of the scope of your process solution. You are tied to testing possibilities that the vendor has foreseen for this connector.
- The connector is proprietary to the vendor.

As you've probably figured out, connectors are not my preferred option. If I can easily write a piece of glue code in the programming language of my choice to do a REST call and attach that to the process model, I prefer to do that.

There are some situations where connectors come in handy, though. A common example is when you want to stitch together a couple of serverless functions or RPA bots, which are covered in "Serverless Functions" on page 71 and "Orchestrate RPA Bots" on page 88.

Model or Code?

So, you have different possibilities: you can express business logic in a process modeling language as well as in the programming language of your choice. You might be wondering about guidelines, and which type of logic belongs where. Obviously, neither of the extremes makes too much sense. On the one hand, you don't want to end up with a process model with one task saying, "This is where all the magic happens." And on the other hand, you don't want to do graphical programming, where each and every piece of logic ends up in a process model. There have been many attempts to push pure graphical programming in the past, but none of them took off. Writing code using normal programming languages with today's IDEs is faster and more efficient in many ways, and the resulting code is more maintainable. Not only does a model with too much detail become difficult to maintain, but also the value of the graphical visualization completely degrades, as you can't see the forest for the trees anymore.

Hence, as a rule of thumb, you can make the programming code the default for where you implement your business logic. However, there are good reasons to put certain logic into the process model. The following three questions can help you decide what to put where.

Where do you need to (potentially) wait?

If you need to wait, whether for humans to act, for external services to become available, for response messages to arrive, or for some other reason, you need to be able to store the state safely. This is exactly what the workflow engine does for you, but only if the task in question is part of your process model.

You can see process instances waiting at tasks in your operations tooling, so you can, for example, identify which instances are waiting too long and figure out why. You can also model escalation logic for tasks in the process model, for instance involving a manager when a human task is waiting too long to be completed.

The workflow engine enables this at the granularity of tasks. For instance, if the glue code attached to one task calls two remote services, you can only proceed if both calls are successful. But if you design two service tasks that make only one remote call each, the workflow engine can remember that one service call was already successfully executed and just retry the other.

What do you discuss regularly with other stakeholders?

A good rule of thumb is that everything you need to discuss with other stakeholders regularly should go in the graphical model. This might be a bit too fuzzy, as you might need to discuss complex pricing calculations regularly, and this might not be something you want to include in the graphical process model. But as a general rule it's useful, and it is definitely true for the control flow, as there are areas that are interesting to the business and others that are not.

You might also want to think about what key performance indicators (KPIs) are interesting to various people. Whatever is part of the model will lead to audit data in the workflow engine, which can be leveraged to build KPIs.

What crosses boundaries?

A more technical way to look at it is by focusing on boundaries. If you want to invoke two software components or services that cannot be joined in one technical transaction, you should separate the two invocations into their own tasks. This not only allows the workflow engine to retry failed service calls, but also developers to implement strategies around reconciling consistency. You will learn more about these topics in Chapters 7 and 9.

Example

Let's take a look at a quick example. Suppose you're tasked with developing a service that determines whether to accept a new customer. Part of that checking involves basic data validation and some scoring mechanism. Let's assume in a first iteration you program everything in Java, so a simple version of your service looks like this:

```
public boolean isCustomerDataAcceptable(Customer customer) {
  if (!verifyCustomerData(customer)) {
    return false;
  }
  int score = scoreCustomerData(customer);
  if (score >= SCORE_TRESHOLD) {
    return true;
  } else {
    return false;
```

```
      }
    }
```

So far, everything is fine. You might need to draw the logic on a whiteboard a couple of times, but it probably does not yet justify using a workflow engine.

Now assume that the scoring will be done by some external service. So instead of a local method call, you dive into REST communication and the question of whether the service is available or not. Remember "Wild West Integrations" on page 4 in Chapter 1? This could be a good moment to introduce a lightweight workflow engine to resolve the problems around waiting for the availability of the scoring service. The easiest option would be the process in Figure 3-14, with one task.

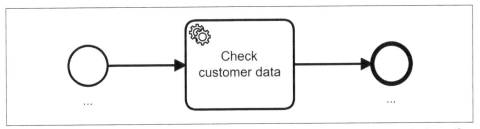

Figure 3-14. If you only want to leverage the long-running capabilities, it might be sufficient to have a very simple process model

You can then do the whole check in the glue code:

```
@Task(name="CheckCustomerData")
void checkCustomer(WorkflowContext ctx) {
  Customer customer = loadCustomerFromContext(ctx);
  if (!verifyCustomerData(customer)) {
    ctx.setWorkflowData("accepted", false);
  } else {
    int score = scoreService.scoreCustomer(customer);
    ctx.setWorkflowData("accepted", (score >= SCORE_TRESHOLD));
  }
}
```

Now assume that the scoring costs money per invocation. There are a lot of discussions around when you really need to score customers and what checks can be done beforehand. So instead of explaining over and over again how verification and scoring is done, you could simply add that information to the process, as shown in Figure 3-15.

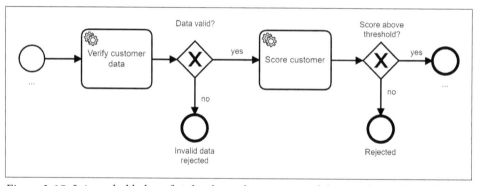

Figure 3-15. It is probably beneficial to have the sequence of these tasks visible in the graphical model

This process model answers a lot of questions for you. As a bonus, you get statistical data around your process for free; for example, the percentage of orders that are rejected because of invalid data versus the percentage rejected because of a low score.

Sometimes there are even more specific reasons to add elements to a model, like compliance, analysis, or intelligence. Be open to these requirements. It is typically easy to adjust the model accordingly, and this delivers additional value quickly, often without bloating the diagram.

Testing Processes

As process models are just another kind of source code, they deserve the same attention when it comes to testing. This is actually an area where a lot of workflow systems are more an obstacle than a help—in particular, low-code tools either don't support automated testing at all or have some very bespoke way to run tests.

A good workflow tool needs to support unit tests for processes, which should be an aspect you check when evaluating products. In reality, the best approach is that process testing just hooks into your normal testing procedure (e.g., JUnit tests if you work in Java). Some tools provide great support, even including assertions to verify that a process instance ran as expected. "An Executable Example" on page 29 showed a source code example for JUnit and Camunda Cloud.

The aim is not to test the workflow engine itself—the vendor has already done that—but rather to verify that your process model, its configuration, the corresponding glue code, and expressions for gateway decisions behave as you intend them to.

One complexity is that most processes invoke external services, but you don't want to make every process test a complete integration test. Instead, you want to mock up external systems in order to reduce the test scope to the process logic.

Hooking process testing into the test framework of your choice allows you to leverage existing frameworks in that area easily.

Versioning of Process Solutions

Processes can be long-running, meaning that one instance can last for hours, days, weeks, or months. If you want to update your process model, you face the situation that there are always running process instances in your system. By running, I mean that they are not yet finished and are paused waiting for the signal to continue, such as a human deciding on something. These running process instances are persistently stored somewhere, such as a database, and you have to deal with these instances whenever you change your process model.

Because this problem is so common, workflow engines provide versioning capabilities:

- If you deploy a changed process model, a new version is created.
- Active process instances will continue to run in the version they were started in.
- Newly created process instances will run in the new version (unless you explicitly want to start an older version).

Good tools also support migrating existing process instances to a new version.

Equipped with those possibilities, you can select between two basic strategies regarding versioning:

- Running process model versions in parallel
- Migrating process instances to the new version

Running Versions in Parallel

You can run several versions of a process model in parallel. The big advantage of that behavior is that you can deploy changed process definitions without caring about process instances that are already running. The workflow engine is able to manage running instances based on different process definitions in parallel. The disadvantage is that you need to deal with the operational complexity of different versions of the process running in parallel, as well as the additional complexity in the event that those processes call subprocesses which have different versions of their own.

Run different versions in parallel for:

- Complying with legal requirements, as some procedures need to remain stable once started
- Development or test systems for which you do not care about old instances
- Situations in which migration is not advisable, because it is too complex and too much effort when weighed against its upsides

Migrating process instances to the new version

You can also decide to migrate all process instances to the latest and greatest version you just deployed. Depending on the tool, it might even be possible to script this and hook it into your CI/CD pipeline. Do this when:

- You are deploying patches or bug fixes, so you want to stop using the old model immediately.
- Avoiding operational complexity due to different versions running in production is a priority.

Versioning glue code and data definitions

Versioning does not stop with the process model. New process models might require a change in the glue code that is linked to the model. Depending on the situation at hand, you might either reference new code or adjust your existing code to handle different process models.

For example, suppose new fields have been added to the customer object, which should be taken into account when the customer is rated. As you have saved the customer as process data, old process instances will have customers without these new attributes. First you have to make sure that you can still deserialize the data, e.g., by making the new attributes optional. Then you could simply copy code for the customer scoring and implement a new version that uses these attributes. The new process model will reference `customer-scoring-v2`, while the old model still references `customer-scoring`.

As an alternative, you could adjust your code to check if the new attributes are set and only use it then. While this makes the code a bit more complicated, it also has a clear advantage: it works without further adjustments if you migrate process instances to a new version. The drawback is that in order to avoid dead code accumulating over time you should regularly check if such code is still needed by any version and, if not, clean it up.

There is still another possibility to handle data structure changes: write some upgrade scripts that adjust the data. For example, you can add some default attributes to old instances.

Conclusion

This chapter described the elements of process solutions in detail. We looked at BPMN and how it can be used to model executable process models, and we dove into what it takes to execute these process models on a workflow engine. In the spirit of this book, it is not about low code, but about connecting process models with source code. This results in process solutions that consist of process models and additional glue code.

This chapter also described best practices to decide when to put business logic into process models or programming code, and it explored how the whole approach fits into your software development life cycle, including testing and versioning.

CHAPTER 4

Orchestrate Anything

Now we'll shift our attention to what problems process automation can solve for you. This chapter shows that workflow engines can orchestrate anything, especially:

- Software components
- Decisions
- Humans
- RPA bots and physical devices

But what is orchestration? It's a loaded term with different meanings for different people. For example, in the cloud native community, orchestration is often connected to container management, which is what tools like Kubernetes are doing. In the process automation space, orchestration really means coordination.

Looking back at the BPMN examples earlier in the book, you could say that the workflow engine orchestrates the tasks contained in the models. And as these tasks might call some external services, you could also say the process orchestrates these services. Whenever you add human tasks to the mix, the workflow engine orchestrates the humans. While this sounds a bit odd, it is actually accurate (if you prefer, you can replace *orchestrate* with *coordinate*).

In this chapter we'll use the example of a small telecommunications company. Whenever a customer wants a new mobile phone contract, the customer's data has to be saved into four different systems: the CRM system, the billing system, the system to provision the SIM card, and the system to register the SIM card and phone number in the network.

To improve the onboarding process for new customers, the company uses a workflow engine. Depending on the situation at hand, each task within the onboarding process might involve:

- Calling a software component
- Evaluating a decision using a decision engine
- A human doing the work manually
- An RPA bot steering some graphical user interface

Each of these options is discussed in more detail in the next sections.

A quick note for the impatient: Chapter 8 will dive into choreography, another approach to automating processes. You don't need this knowledge to apply orchestration, so we can safely postpone it until you understand more about process automation, but it will be handy to help you better understand the spectrum of solution approaches.

Orchestrate Software

We'll start with what we as tech folks like most: orchestrating software. A workflow engine can basically orchestrate anything that has an API.

Let's assume the onboarding process looks like Figure 4-1.

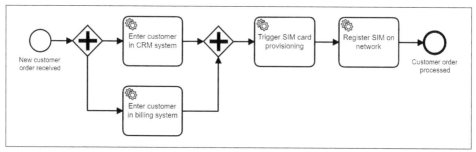

Figure 4-1. A process orchestrating data entry into different systems

Whenever there is a new customer order, a new instance of the onboarding process is started. The new customer is saved in the CRM and billing systems in parallel. Only if both are successful is the SIM card provisioning triggered and the SIM registered in the network. The service tasks are wired up to API calls, as you saw earlier in this book.

This leads to a fully automated process, also known as *straight-through processing* (STP). This has big advantages over manual processing:

- You save manual labor and reduce your operational spend on this process. At the same time, you increase your capability to scale, as the process can now handle more load.

- You reduce the potential for human error by making sure the data is always transferred correctly.

Different architecture patterns exist, which influence the way you operate the workflow engine and design your process. We'll look at the most important ones in the next sections: service-oriented architecture, microservices, and functions.

Service-Oriented Architecture (SOA) Services

A typical SOA blueprint is illustrated in Figure 4-2. These blueprints advocate for a central BPM platform containing the workflow engine, which then communicates with the services via a central enterprise service bus (ESB). This centralized infrastructure is the typical pain point and leads to a lot of problems, as described in "Centralized SOA and the ESB" on page 15.

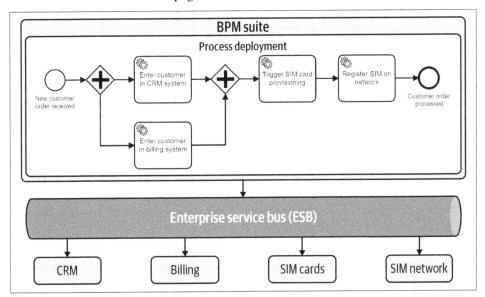

Figure 4-2. A typical SOA and BPM blueprint from around 2010

This kind of architecture is typically not the architecture of choice for new projects. Of course, there are good reasons to distribute business logic into multiple services, but ideas around microservices are the more modern way to look at it, avoiding failures of the SOA era.

If you are working in a SOA environment, you can still be successful. Make sure that you avoid the issues around centralized tooling and be extra cautious about ownership of process definitions—for example, every business process model needs to be owned by a development team that cares about business logic, and should not be owned by a central BPM team. We'll discuss this further in "Decentralized Engines" on page 117.

Microservices

The movement around microservices took a lot of lessons about SOA into account and defined what some see as SOA 2.0. Sam Newman provides a useful definition in his book *Building Microservices* (O'Reilly): microservices are "small, autonomous services that work together."

Regarding them being small, the most important thing to know is that microservices are clearly scoped and focused. A microservice is purpose-built to solve a specific domain problem. Chapter 7 will dive more into the boundaries between services and processes.

To understand the autonomy aspect of a microservice, suppose that your team is fully empowered to own a microservice around SIM card provisioning. You can freely choose your tech stack (typically, as long as you stay within the boundaries of your enterprise architecture) and your team deploys and operates that service itself. This allows you to implement or change the service at your own discretion (as long as you don't break the API). You don't have to ask other people to do anything for you, or join a release train. This will make your team fast in delivering changes and actually also increase motivation, as owning their service makes team members truly feel empowered.

Applying the microservice architectural style does have an impact on process automation. Automating one business process typically involves multiple microservices. With SOA, the view was that an orchestration process "outside" of the services was required to piece them together. The microservices style doesn't allow business logic outside of the microservices, which means that the collaboration between them is described within the microservices themselves.

For example, a customer onboarding microservice owns the business logic around onboarding, which includes the onboarding business process. The team implementing the microservice can decide to use a workflow engine and BPMN to automate that process, which then orchestrates other microservices. The decision is internal to the microservice and not visible from the outside; it is an implementation detail.

Communication between the microservices is done via APIs, and not through the BPM platform, as was the case with SOA. This scenario is sketched in Figure 4-3.

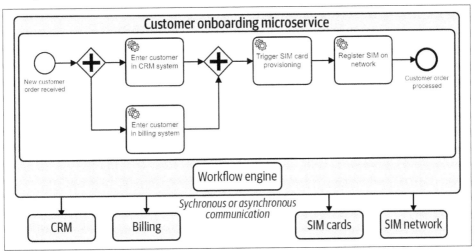

Figure 4-3. Processes are part of the business logic of a microservice; no central workflow engine is needed

In microservices communities, the argument is often made to not use orchestration, but to let microservices collaborate in an event-driven way. We'll table this question for now and discuss it in Chapter 8.

Serverless Functions

Microservices might be small, but you can disassemble your architecture into even smaller pieces: functions.

A serverless function is similar to a stateless function in your favorite programming language, but operated in a hosted cloud infrastructure. This means you don't have to provide an environment for the function to run in yourself. A serverless function takes some input and produces some output, but needs to be completely self-contained. For example, you can't hold any data that survives the current invocation (unless storing it in some external resource). Serverless is popular because it promises elastic scalability. You don't pay for computational resources when your functions aren't being used. When your traffic skyrockets, those resources are automatically scaled up to handle it.

But having a bunch of functions raises the question of how they interact to fulfill a goal. Suppose you want to use this approach for customer onboarding. You implement one function to add the customer to the CRM system, one to add them to the billing system, one for provisioning the SIM card, and so on.

The simplest way to provide the onboarding functionality would be to create a combined function that includes or calls the other functions:

```
function onboardCustomer(customer) {
    crmPromise = createCustomerInCrm(customer); // 2 seconds
    billingPromise = createCustomerInBilling(customer); // 100 ms
    // TODO: Wait for 2 promises
    simCard = provisionSimCard(customer); // 1 second
    registerSim(simCard); // 4 seconds
}  // --> 7 seconds runtime for onboardCustomer
```

While this looks simple, it has severe downsides. First, it only works if all of the functions are available and return fast results. Otherwise, you can easily end up with a customer created in CRM and billing that never gets a SIM card because the last function crashed. Additionally, this solution accumulates latency, as indicated in the previous code snippet. Even if a longer response time isn't a problem, it will add up on your cloud bill, as serverless providers charge for the computing time consumed by your function.

So, a combined function is best avoided. Instead, most projects use their cloud provider's messaging capabilities to create a chain of functions. Imagine it like this:

```
// callback function registered for message "customerOnboardingRequest"
function onboardCustomer(customer) {
    ... do business logic ...
    send('createCustomerInCrmRequest');
}
// callback function registered for message "createCustomerInCrmRequest"
function createCustomerInCrmRequest(customer) {
    ... do business logic ...
    send('createCustomerInBillingRequest');
}
// callback function registered for message "createCustomerInBillingRequest"
function createCustomerInBilling(customer) {
    ... do business logic ...
}
```

This way, you get rid of the one expensive combined function and make your code more resilient. The message queue will remember what to do next even if a function's code fails.

But now you may end up with problems similar to those associated with batches and streaming: you don't have end-to-end visibility of your chain, you have no single point where you can adjust it, and it is hard to understand and resolve failures. To mitigate these problems (which will be explained in more detail in "Limitations of Other Implementation Options" on page 93), you can use a workflow engine to orchestrate your functions. To do this, you will need a workflow engine that runs as a managed service. This means that the workflow engine itself is also a serverless resource for you.

In the onboarding example, the team responsible for developing the customer onboarding function can also define the process model, as visualized in Figure 4-4. In this process model, every service task is glued to a function call. How this is technically done depends on your exact cloud environment; typical examples are native function calls, HTTP calls via an API gateway, or messages. Your workflow engine of choice might also provide prebuilt connectors you can use (one of the examples where connectors, introduced in "Using Prebuilt Connectors" on page 58, make a lot of sense).

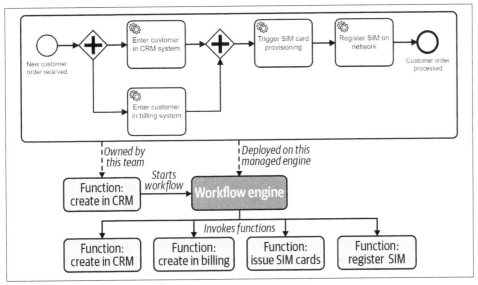

Figure 4-4. A process can orchestrate functions

Whenever the team deploys the onboarding function, it also needs to deploy the process model on the workflow engine, which can probably be automated.

Every major cloud provider today has stateful function orchestration capabilities in its platform (AWS Step Functions, Azure Durable Functions, GCP Cloud Workflows). Unfortunately, they all miss important workflow engine functionality as described in this book. Specifically, none of them uses BPMN, which leads to limited language power (see "Workflow Patterns" on page 101) and no or very poor visualization capabilities (see "Benefits of Graphical Process Visualizations" on page 102).

So there is additional value in leveraging BPMN-based workflow engines to orchestrate functions, which is a very promising area to explore. You'll find an executable example using Camunda Cloud and AWS Lambda on the book's website (*https://Proc essAutomationBook.com*).

Modular Monoliths

Not every company is able or willing to dump its monolith in favor of fine-grained systems like microservices or functions. In fact, there is even a growing trend toward embracing the monolith for some of its advantages. Because a monolith is not a distributed system, it doesn't have to constantly fight with remote communication or consistency issues. And you can still apply modularization strategies so that any changes only affect small parts of the code.

A monolith can be perfectly fine if it solves your problem, which often has a lot to do with your internal organization and size. A development team of 10 people might very well master a monolith, but struggle with the added complexity around working on 100 microservices. On the other hand, an organization with a thousand developers might not be productive if it builds and releases one single monolith.

The interesting observation with regard to processes is that you can still apply the practices described in this book within your monolith. You will (hopefully) structure your monolith in a meaningful way, for example by forming components, sorting the code into packages, and creating interfaces for important services. To design executable processes, you simply orchestrate these internal components—for example, this might translate to using local method calls instead of remote calls. The workflow engine itself can be embedded as a library into your monolith. Process definitions simply become one additional resource in the source code of the monolith. This is visualized in Figure 4-5.

This way, you can add the benefits of using a workflow engine (long-running capabilities with state management, visibility of the process) without losing the benefits of a monolith (not having a distributed system). Adding a workflow engine typically does not have much impact on performance. Of course, this depends on the tool you choose and the architecture you set up, but even with a workflow engine operated as its own service, the overhead can be minimal (like with a database, which is also a remote service that is consumed).

Furthermore, having a workflow engine might give you the possibility to deploy changed process models without redeploying the whole monolith. That alone is sometimes enough motivation for introducing a workflow engine to a large monolith.

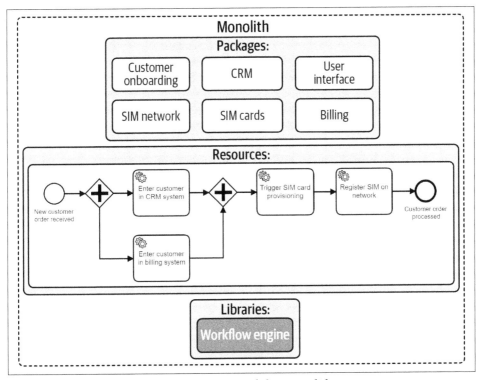

Figure 4-5. Orchestrating components in a modular monolith

Deconstructing the Monolith

While a modular monolith can be a valid solution, many companies are on a migration path, moving away from monoliths and toward a more fine-grained architecture. Process automation can help with this journey. Imagine you have the telco monolith from the last section in place, but want to change the customer onboarding procedure. Instead of squeezing the process into your monolith, you can instead take the opportunity to create a (micro)service to do the onboarding.

To do this, you have to create APIs for the services required, which means that you start to add facades to your existing monolith. At the same time, you have to remove hardwired connections between components; for example, the CRM component should no longer directly call the billing component for new customers, as you want to control this connection via the new (micro)service. Figure 4-6 visualizes this approach.

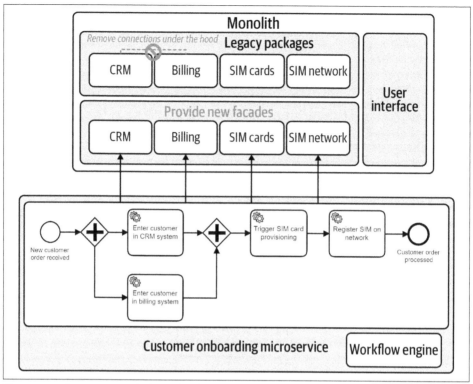

Figure 4-6. Processes can help to slowly remove unfortunate connections under the covers

These projects are typically not easy to tackle. And while this might feel like putting lipstick on a pig, it is a first step in the right direction toward deconstructing the monolith and increasing agility. If you keep doing this for every process you touch, you will decrease the monolith's footprint slowly over time, in favor of a more fine-grained architecture. The most successful architecture transformation I've seen did exactly this: the developers did not do a sudden transformation, but kept migrating, one step at a time, with discipline and endurance. The first steps were hardly visible, but after five years, a huge difference could be seen.

Orchestrate Decisions

Let's extend the onboarding example to first validate the customer order by invoking some decision logic or business rules. The resulting process is shown in Figure 4-7.

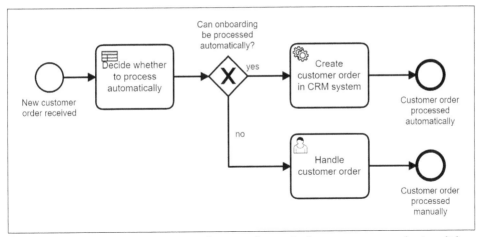

Figure 4-7. A process orchestrating a decision about whether a customer order is valid or not

A decision involves deriving a result (output) from given facts (input) on the basis of defined logic. While this decision logic could be executed by a human, it often makes sense to automate it, especially in automated processes. Of course, it could simply be hardcoded, but there are certain characteristics that justify the use of specific tooling.

First, decision logic is important business logic and needs to be understood by business stakeholders. And compared to process control flows, decision logic changes much more rapidly, so it is vital for business agility to be able to easily change this logic. Whenever you learn about a good reason to not validate certain customer orders, you want to adjust the decision logic right away before you onboard more customers with high-risk profiles. You definitely want to avoid situations where nobody really knows the decision logic because it is buried in tons of code that was written years ago.

On top of that, you gain visibility into decision instances, so that you can understand why a certain customer order was successfully validated or not.

This is the domain of decision automation. The core software components here are *decision engines*, which take decision logic expressed in a model and apply it to make decisions based on the given input. These engines typically can also version decision models and store a history of decisions that have been made. You might recognize some similarity to workflow engines, but decisions are not long-running; they can be made in one atomic step.

Decision Model and Notation (DMN)

As with BPMN for business processes, there is a globally adopted standard available for decisions: Decision Model and Notation (DMN). It is close to BPMN, and they're often used alongside one another.

Let's take a quick look at what DMN can do. The two concepts I want to focus on in this book are:

Decision tables

> These are used to define decision logic. Years of experience with various formats has shown that tables are a great way to express decision logic and business rules.

Expression language

> In order to automate decisions, you have to express logic in a format the computer understands. At the same time, you want to end up with decision logic that can be read by non-programmers. This is why DMN defined FEEL, the friendly-enough expression language that is executable, but also human-readable. As mentioned in Chapter 2, some workflow engines also use FEEL within BPMN processes, for example to decide which path to take in a process flow.

Let's look at an example. Assume you want to decide if you can onboard the customer automatically. For this, you create the DMN model visualized in Figure 4-8.

Automatic Processing Applicability			Hit Policy: First	
When	**And**	**And**	**Then**	
Payment Type	Customer Region Score	Monhtly Payment	⊕ Manual Check Necessary?	⊕
"prepaid","invoice"	long		long	boolean
1 "prepaid"	-	-	false	
2 "invoice"	<50	-	true	
3 "invoice"	>= 50	< 25	false	
4 "invoice"	>= 50	>= 25	true	
+	-	-	-	

Figure 4-8. A DMN decision table to find risks

You will use certain data points as input: namely, the payment type, some scoring for the customer's neighborhood, and the monthly payment associated with the contract. This will result in an output, which in this example is one Boolean field that indicates whether a manual check is necessary.

Every row in such a table is one rule. The cells on the input side contain the rules or expressions and will resolve to `true` or `false`. Checks included in this example are `paymentType == "invoice"` and `monthlyPayment < 25`. These expressions are created by some information in the header of the table and the exact cell value.

Most examples in real life are as easy, as shown here, but it is also possible to create more sophisticated expression logic using FEEL. To give you some examples, the following expressions are all possible:

```
Party.Date < date("2021-01-01")
Party.NumberOfGuests in [25..100]
not( Party.Cancelled )
```

In a DMN table you can have as many input columns as you want. The expressions are connected using a logical AND. If all expressions resolve to true, one says the rule "fires."

A DMN table can control what happens in this case. This is the hit policy you can see at the top of Figure 4-8. In the example, it is "first"; this means that the first rule (starting from the top of the table) that fires will determine the result. So in this case, if a customer selected "prepaid," the result is clear in the first row: a manual check does not need to be performed. Other hit policies could be that you expect only one rule to fire because there is no overlap, or that you sum up the results of all firing rules, e.g., to sum up risk scores.

While the example table has only one output column, you can have as many as you want.

Under the hood, a DMN decision table is stored as an XML file, like a BPMN process. Typical decision engines parse that decision model and then provide an API to make decisions, as shown in the following pseudocode:

```
input = Map
 .putValue("paymentType", "invoice")
 .putValue("customerRegionScore", 34)
 .putValue("monthlyPayment", 30);

decisionDefinition = dmnEngine.parseDecision('automaticProcessing.dmn')
output = dmnEngine.evaluateDecision(decisionDefinition, input)

output.get('manualCheckNecessary')
```

This pseudocode uses a decision engine in a stateless way. It parses a file and then evaluates the decision directly. While this is very lightweight, you might want to leverage some further capabilities of a decision engine, like versioning of the decision models or keeping a history of decisions. So your code might look more like this:

```
input = Map
 .putValue("paymentType", "invoice")
 .putValue("customerRegionScore", 34)
 .putValue("monthlyPayment", 30);

output = dmnEngine.evaluateDecision('automaticProcessing', input)

output.get('manualCheckNecessary')
```

Decisions in a Process Model

Decision engines can of course be used standalone. While there are good cases for doing that, this book focuses on decisions in the context of process automation. In that context, decisions can be hooked into a process.

In BPMN there is even a specific "business rule" task type available for this. It is called a business rule task instead of a decision task for historical reasons, as these tools were called *business rule engines* at the time BPMN was standardized; today, the industry speaks of decision engines.

While the business rule task defines that a decision shall be made by a decision engine, it does not specify what this means on a technical level. So, you can write your own glue code to invoke the decision engine of your choice.

An alternative is to use vendor-specific extensions. For example, Camunda provides a BPMN workflow engine and a DMN decision engine, and has integrated them under the hood. This means that you can simply refer to a decision in the process model. In operations, audit information about why a decision was made is then also available directly from the history of the process instance.

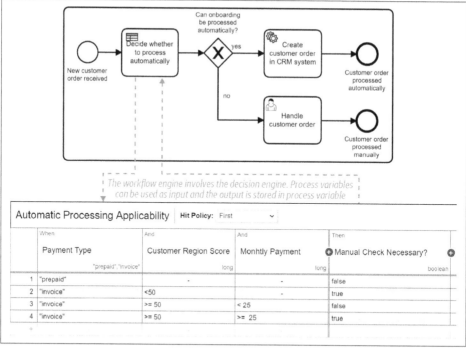

Figure 4-9. A BPMN process can invoke DMN decisions

Decision automation with DMN is a great way to improve business–IT collaboration and increase agility as decision logic gets easier to change. DMN is a great supplement to BPMN, as automating decisions helps to automate tasks within processes.

Orchestrate Humans

Of course, not every process is fully automated, even if most companies try to automate their processes to the highest possible extent. There are three typical reasons to let humans work on tasks:

- With automation, you often need to have human task management as a fallback. Humans can easily work on the 10% of nonstandard cases that would be too expensive to automate, or deal with exceptional situations.

- Human task management is often a first step toward automation. It allows you to quickly develop, roll out, and verify a process model, perhaps with only human tasks. Then you can increase automation by "replacing" humans with machines task by task.

- Humans continue to play a role in more creative areas of processes, such as handling rare cases or making decisions. Removing repetitive tasks by automating them will not only increase their capacity for doing this, but will also remove friction between manual and automated work.

Please be aware that your business department is unlikely to talk about "orchestrating humans"; the more common (and psychologically acceptable) term is *human task management.*

A process using human task management for the onboarding process could look like Figure 4-10.

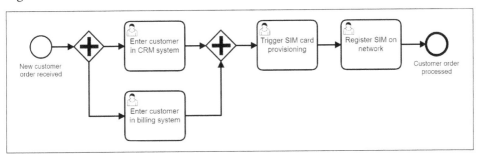

Figure 4-10. A process orchestrating humans

Even if the tasks themselves are not automated, using the workflow engine to automate the control flow still has a lot of benefits, especially if you compare it with the most likely alternative—passing around new contracts via email, with different people adding data to all these systems manually. For example:

- You can make sure that no customer order gets lost or stuck, thereby increasing reliability in your services.

- You can control the sequence of tasks. For example, you could parallelize entering the CRM and billing data, but still make sure that both need to finish before anything is provisioned. This speeds up your overall processing time.

- You can make sure that the right data is attached to a process instance, so everybody involved always has everything they need right at hand.

- You can monitor cycle times and SLAs, making sure that no customer order hangs for too long. You can also analyze more systematically where you can make improvements, which helps you increase efficiency.

- You will get some KPIs around your processes, for example about the number of customer orders, types of contracts, and so on.

Business departments might not talk about workflow engines, orchestration, or human task management at all, even if this technology is working in the background. For example, take the approval of incoming invoices. Maybe a manager has a user interface to see all open invoices where they can approve them easily so that they get paid. Someone else will do the actual paying. This is a user experience you might be familiar with from accounting tools. But in the background, there might still be a workflow engine with a process model at play, so maybe the list of invoices to be approved in reality is a list of human tasks created from process instances. In this case, neither the process model nor the human tasks are obvious from a business perspective.

We'll discuss some interesting aspects of human task management in the next sections.

Task Assignment

One important question is who should perform a particular task. Most workflow products provide a life cycle for every human task out of the box, like the one shown in Figure 4-11.

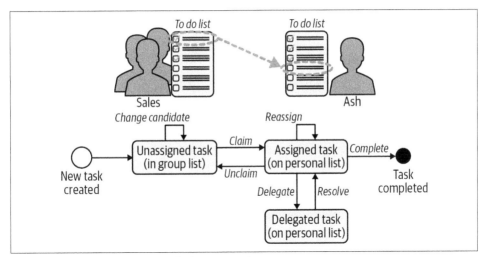

Figure 4-11. Typical life cycle of a human task

This example allows you to differentiate between candidate people and assigned people. Any candidate might do the task, like "somebody from the sales team" or "Joe, Mary, Rick, or Sandy." The first of these candidates to start the work claims the task, and only then is it assigned to them personally. This claiming avoids two people working on the same task by coincidence. A task can be *delegated* when the assigned person wants somebody else to resolve (part of) the work. When they finish, it is passed back to the assignee. This is different from *reassigning* the work, which means handing over the task to another person, who then is fully responsible for completing the work at hand.

As a general rule, you should route human tasks in your process to groups of people instead of specific individuals (e.g., "the sales team"). This not only eases assignment rules, but also accommodates new hires, departures, vacations, sick leave, etc. Of course, there can be exceptions, like if a certain region has a dedicated salesperson assigned to it.

Please note that not all humans in your process have to be employees of your company. You can also assign work to customers—for example, asking them to upload missing documents.

In BPMN, the assignment of people is controlled by attributes of every user task. Here is an example:

```
<bpmn:userTask id="Check payment"/>
  <potentialOwner>
    <resourceAssignmentExpression>
      <formalExpression>sales</formalExpression>
    </resourceAssignmentExpression>
```

```
        </potentialOwner>
    </userTask>
```

Additional Tool Support

Some tools provide additional capabilities around notifications, timeout handling and escalation, vacation management, or replacement rules. These capabilities can typically be configured as attributes of tasks and are as such not graphically visible in the process model.

It is a good idea to leverage these capabilities and not manually model these aspects into each and every process. So while you might be tempted to model an email reminder about work that has been waiting in the queue for too long via BPMN, please avoid it if your tool can do that out of the box using a simple configuration option. This will make your models easier to create, read, and understand, as you can see in Figure 4-12.

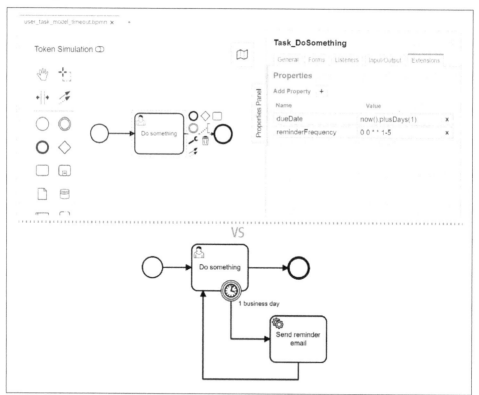

Figure 4-12. Don't model aspects the built-in life cycle of user tasks can address for you

Supporting human task management is its own challenge for workflow engines. In addition to the vendor needing to provide graphical user interfaces for end users, the engine also needs to support extensive capabilities around filtering and querying of tasks.

While this might sound easy at first, it can become quite complicated if you need to deal with thousands of employees working with millions of tasks on a daily basis. You also face the challenge of providing flexible query possibilities without allowing single users to bring the performance down for the whole company. How this is implemented varies between vendors, but it is definitely a very different type of workload than microservices doing task after task after task.

The User Interface of User Tasks

The workflow engine is controlling the process. It knows for every process instance what the next activity is that the human needs to perform. But the human needs to know this too! So the workflow engine needs a way to communicate with real people.

One approach is to use the tasklist application provided by your vendor, as introduced in "Tasklist Applications" on page 42. These tools often allow end users to filter tasks. This means they might need to blend in business data, as end users not only want to see the task name, but also business data like order IDs, products applied for, or the applicant's name.

Another important aspect is what kinds of task forms are supported. Some products allow the creation of only basic forms, by defining simple attributes. Others provide their own form modeler. Some allow you to embed HTML or to use custom forms like a one-pager in your custom web application, or a form created by a dedicated form builder application. Keep in mind that you'll often need to blend data from the process with domain data from entities referenced in the task, in a single form, as shown in Figure 4-13—this results in better usability for your users.

Using your workflow vendor's tasklist application can be a good way to get started quickly. You can immediately build a prototype for your process and click through it, probably even to verify the process model with business stakeholders. Most people are much better at understanding a process model if they can role play using real-life forms, instead of reading a formal model.

But there are also situations where you have requirements for a more customized way of involving humans. For example, you might use email, chat, or voice interaction. The workflow engine could send an email to a person who needs to do something. This email contains all relevant information for that person to do the task at hand. When they are finished, they can indicate that either by replying to the email or by clicking a link in the email.

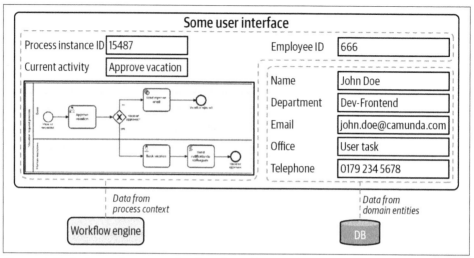

Figure 4-13. In forms for user tasks, data from the workflow engine often needs to be blended with domain data

Two other common scenarios are using a third-party tasklist application and developing a completely customized user interface. Let's briefly explore both options.

Using an external tasklist application

The workflow engine can invoke the API of an external application, as visualized in Figure 4-14. This might be a tasklist app that is already widely adopted in the company, from the likes of SAP or Siebel, or some very broad application like Trello or Wunderlist. I've also seen one customer using screens on the mainframe to handle open tasks, as this was the way all clerks did their daily work. Tasklists might also be referred to as job lists, to-do lists, or inboxes.

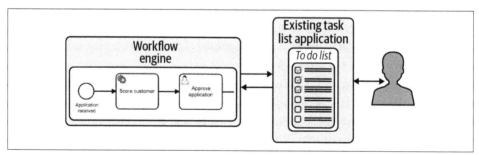

Figure 4-14. User tasks lead to to-do entries in a tasklist application

Whatever form it takes, this application gives the user possibilities to see all open tasks, to indicate that they've started working on a task, and to mark tasks as completed. The status gets reported back to the workflow engine. When implementing such an integration, you will need to take care of:

- Creating tasks in the tasklist application whenever a process instance enters a user task
- Completing user tasks in the workflow engine and moving on in the process when the user is finished
- Canceling tasks, triggered either by the workflow engine or the user in the UI
- Transferring business data to be edited into the to-do application, and vice versa

It's also proved to be a good idea to think about a problem detection mechanism just in case the two systems diverge, for example because of inconsistencies caused by failures with remote calls.

Using a third-party app is often when there is an existing tasklist application that is already rolled out to employees, as it allows them to continue using the known application. They might not even recognize that a workflow engine is at play or that a product is replaced under the hood. In that case, issues of authentication and authorization are often already solved.

Building a customized tasklist application

If you need a more customized experience than the vendor's tasklist application can deliver, you can develop a bespoke application yourself. This can be adapted to your needs without compromise. You have freedom of choice among development frameworks and programming languages, and tasks inside your custom application can follow your style guide and usability concepts. This is often done if you embed workflow tooling into your own software product, or if you want to roll out your tasklist to hundreds or thousands of users and efficiency in the UI is important.

This approach also allows you to satisfy very special requirements. For example, you might face a situation where you have several user tasks that are heavily interdependent from a business point of view and should therefore be completed in one step by the same person. Imagine a document input management process where you decided to manage each document with a separate process instance, but present mailings consisting of several such documents as a bundled task to the user. An example is shown in Figure 4-15.

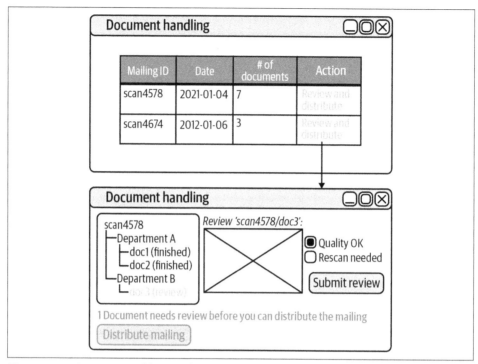

Figure 4-15. A custom tasklist can hide complexity and improve efficiency

In one real-life project I was involved in, this approach allowed an organization's employees to work much more efficiently. This kind of grouping is no problem with a customized tasklist, but might not be doable with out-of-the-box applications.

Orchestrate RPA Bots

Let's switch our attention from orchestrating humans to orchestrating bots—robotic process automation (RPA) bots, to be precise. RPA is a solution for dealing with legacy applications that do not offer an API, as many older systems were developed at a time where there was not such a big need for connectivity. RPA tools automate the control of existing graphical user interfaces. Big topics are screen scraping, image processing, OCR, and robots steering GUIs. It's like the Windows macro recorder on steroids.

RPA has experienced rapid growth recently, and become a huge market, recognized by analysts.

Suppose your billing system is very old and does not provide any kind of API. You can use the RPA tool of your choice to automate the data entry for your onboarding process. In RPA lingo this is called a *bot*. How this bot is developed depends on the specific tool, but typically you record GUI interactions and edit the steps the bot needs to take in the RPA's GUI, like "click this button" and "enter text in this text field." An example is shown in Figure 4-16.

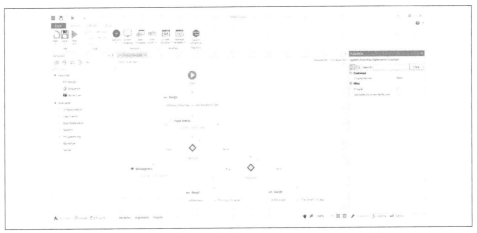

Figure 4-16. Example of a typical RPA development environment and flow

It is important to note that the bot should implement one function only. In terms of the BPMN process, the bot is just another way to implement one service task, as shown in Figure 4-17.

Of course, bots are always much more brittle than a real API call, so whenever possible you should prefer to use an API. But unfortunately, real life is full of obstacles. The system might not provide the API you need, or you might be facing a shortage of development resources. Suppose entering data in the billing system is getting delayed because of people being overloaded with onboarding work. The business department needs to solve this problem quickly, as customers are starting to cancel their orders due to the long delays (which causes even more manual work, leading to a very unfortunate downward spiral). But IT is buried in other urgent work, so they cannot do this integration right away.

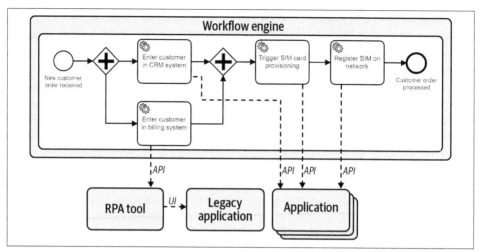

Figure 4-17. A process also orchestrating an RPA bot

Developing an RPA bot can be a good way for the business department to move forward quickly without the need for IT, which is beneficial for the company at this stage. But you need to keep in mind that bots are hard to maintain and depend on user interfaces that might change quickly—and if the RPA solutions and bots are not governed or operated by IT, this can lead to architecture problems down the road.

So in this example, you should directly plan for replacing the bot with a real API. I've even seen organizations that require projects to report technical debt whenever they introduce a new RPA bot to make sure this is addressed later.

You can tackle some of the problems around the brittleness of bots by keeping human tasks as a fallback in case there are errors within the RPA bots. This allows you to concentrate on automating the 80% of cases and route the exceptions to a human, as shown in Figure 4-18.

Now, there is one risk you should be aware of. As you saw in Figure 4-16, an RPA flow is also a kind of process model. This can lead some companies to try to automate core business processes with RPA tools, especially if they suffer from limited bandwidth in IT. Unfortunately, this does not work out.

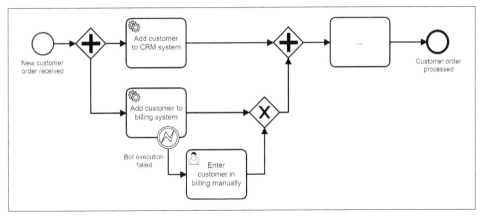

Figure 4-18. A process orchestrating a bot with humans as a fallback

 RPA is not meant to automate core business processes. Using the RPA tool as a low code process automation platform is a trap. Using RPA flows to automate whole business processes has severe downsides and risks. All the disadvantages of low-code apply here, and additionally RPA flows quickly become a wild mix of granularities, containing business process flow logic as well as control sequences for the user interface.

The workflow engine should always be the primary driver that controls the overall process, and calls RPA bots whenever it needs to integrate with a resource that cannot be called via an API for whatever reason.

RPA is applied in one step of the process. As soon as you can switch to an API, you should do that. The beauty of this architecture is that you might not even need to change your process model: simply call the API instead of the RPA bot.

Orchestrate Physical Devices and Things

But let's not stop with RPA bots. We can also orchestrate physical devices, like real lab robots (*https://oreil.ly/WRBb2*).

Technically speaking, orchestrating devices boils down to orchestrating software, as devices are integrated via APIs. Still, there are some specific nuances to it. In particular there is a common pattern with regard to emerging use cases around the Internet of Things (IoT), where a myriad of devices connect to the internet and produce data. This data can lead to actions, which then might involve orchestration.

Let's understand that by looking at a use case around airplane maintenance. Assume that an airplane produces a constant stream of sensor data—for example, the current oil pressure. A stream processor could derive some actual knowledge out of that measurement, such as an oil pressure that is too low. This is another stream of data. But now we have to act on that insight, and schedule maintenance at the next possible opportunity. This is where a process starts, because now we care that the mechanic looks into the insight within a defined time frame, decides how to handle the issue, and schedules the appropriate maintenance actions. This is visualized in Figure 4-19.

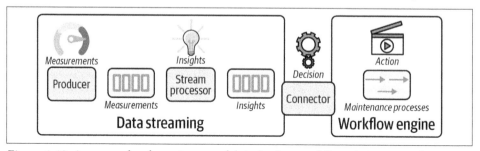

Figure 4-19. An example where streams of data lead to workflows being started

The transition from a passive stream to a process reacting to data in the stream is very interesting. In a concrete real-life project, a stateful connector might be developed that starts a process instance for a mechanic only once for every insight. If the oil pressure keeps being reported as too low for the same hardware, this does not start additional process instances. If the oil pressure goes back to normal, this insight is routed to the existing process instance, so that this process instance can take action. For instance, it might simply be canceled as the maintenance is no longer necessary.

Conclusion

This chapter demonstrated that workflow engines can orchestrate anything, from software to decisions to bots and devices. This should help you understand what kinds of problems process automation can solve. Of course, in real life the use cases overlap, so processes typically involve a mix of components. To implement an end-to-end process you might need to orchestrate humans, RPA bots, SOA services, microservices, decisions, functions, and other software components, all within the same process.

Note that some people do not talk about orchestration, but rather about *human task management* and *straight-through processing*. This is a subtle point based in the psychology of terminology.

CHAPTER 5

Championing Workflow Engines and BPMN

This book concentrates on using workflow engines and BPMN to automate processes. Of course, there are other ways of automating processes in the developer's toolbox. Also, BPMN is not the only process modeling language you can use.

This chapter gives you the background on why I've made these choices. This knowledge will hopefully not only convince you, but also help you in discussions with your company or organization about why certain scenarios can benefit from a workflow engine and BPMN. Feel free to skip this chapter if you simply want to move ahead and learn more about process automation; you can always come back to it later. This chapter:

- Explains alternatives to using a workflow engine, and the trade-offs you should be aware of
- Describes different options for process modeling languages and explains why I consider BPMN to be the best choice
- Briefly touches on process automation with blockchain, as it often comes up as a topic that nobody really understands

Limitations of Other Implementation Options

There are many common ways that developers use every day to automate processes. Each of these implementations has its own shortcomings, and all of them could benefit from the adoption of a workflow engine. Let's explore how the typical alternatives work.

Hardcoded Processes

Hardcoded process automation was covered in "Wild West Integrations" on page 4. There is not much to add, but I wanted to include the headline here for completeness.

Batch Processing

Batch processing is a very popular option to automate processes. Let's start by exploring what a batch job is and how you automate processes with a bunch of batch jobs.

Have you ever taken a crowded elevator in a hotel? This is a good analogy for a batch job. All the items (in this case, you and any other passengers) have to wait until the elevator arrives; then they're all packed inside together and processed (in this case, elevated to various floors).

In a skyscraper hotel, you might even have to switch elevators, so after the first successful batch job (elevator ride), you have to wait in line for the next batch job. If somebody uses the emergency stop, nobody in the cabin will move on.

The process happening here is you moving from the hotel lobby to your room, and it is implemented by multiple batch jobs. A single job typically does not really know about the overall process, even if some architect has hopefully thought about the whole journey to your room.

The metaphor is friendlier than typical IT batch jobs are. Elevators react to you pressing a button, so the waiting time for your batch job to run is relatively short. Most real-life batch jobs are time-controlled; assuming there are multiple elevators, elevator A could go up at 8 a.m., elevator B at 9 a.m., and so forth. In this scenario, the whole journey might take a very long time.

So, one batch job only focuses on one task in the process, but the whole process is implemented by multiple batch jobs in a row. Batch processing is actually *orthogonal* to the real processes.

A real-life example of batch processing is shown in Figure 5-1. Here, customers request an update of their credit limit online. This request is not processed right away (referred to as *online processing*), but instead waits in a queue until the next batch is run, which typically happens at a specific time of day. Then, all the items waiting in this batch are processed at once.

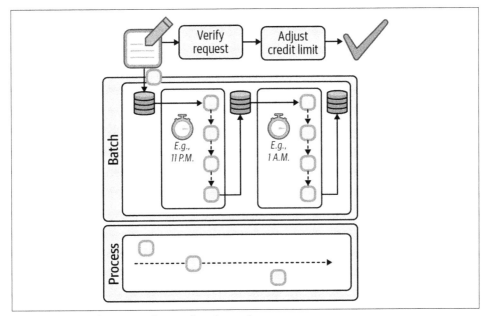

Figure 5-1. Batches are orthogonal to the real process

Batch processing is a very popular approach because this is how computers functioned when they were first created. At the outset, computers could only run one program at a time, read data from sequential memory like tapes, and so on. Today, mainframes are still optimized for batch processing and can process large quantities of data, even in one transaction, very efficiently and quickly. But these orthogonal batches have severe shortcomings for process automation:

- Batches *add processing latency* to the individual unit of work, which slows down process cycle times. While this behavior was often tolerable in the era of sending letters by mail, it no longer meets customer expectations in the era of smartphones. Some organizations try to reduce latency by running batches more frequently—even to the point where one batch job starts before the previous one has finished, leading to all sorts of weird concurrency issues.

- *Failure handling* gets harder, for three reasons. First, an error can often stop the whole batch job, and not all batch jobs can be restarted from the exact position where they stopped. This leads not only to additional latency for all items, but also to possible double processing. Second, failures don't expose any context. An operator might simply see a failure in the batch job and the record that caused it, with no indication of how this record came to be there, why it contains that strange data, what will actually happen with that record downstream, and so on. And third, it is typically unclear how to clean up a failed batch job and revert to the original state to restore consistency. In short: operators don't know about the overall process. This makes it very hard to analyze or fix problems.

- *The process is not visible*, as it is hidden in the connections between batch jobs. Companies need to invest a lot of effort in scheduling to make sure batches run in the right order. They have to do archaeology to understand the process. The whole construct gets brittle and hard to change.

A lot of enterprises have launched "unbatching" initiatives, where they begin phasing out batch processing to avoid these shortcomings. One recent example I saw was a big car insurance company that began to replace a couple of batch jobs around contract renewals for corporate fleets. They designed one end-to-end process for the whole fleet renewal of one customer, and started subprocesses for each contract. By doing this, they not only brought down the overall processing time, but also reduced the problems surrounding failed batch jobs. Whenever there was a failure in one contract, an incident in the single failing process instance was created, which made it easy to identify the failure and understand, resolve, and continue the process. While resolving the incident, the whole renewal process could still continue, so failures would not affect other contracts or customers.

 There are use cases where you need to look at data from all records, such as when computing totals. In these scenarios the batch job is not orthogonal to the process, but rather one task in the process. This is less problematic from a process perspective.

Data Pipelines and Streaming

Data streaming has become increasingly popular in recent years. The idea behind data streaming is to move away from "data at rest" that is stored somewhere and processed by large, time-controlled batch jobs, and toward sending data in a steady stream that is constantly flowing—typically through queues or immutable logs. The data is processed by so-called *stream processors* as it arrives. This reduces waiting times (latency) and increases processing speed.

A good example to illustrate this is the detection of double swipes for credit card payments, where a merchant swipes the card twice in order to get an additional payment. While this was traditionally detected by nightly batch jobs that catch the double data, it can be now discovered in real time by using a streaming architecture. This allows a notification to be sent to the customer immediately, hopefully even while they are still in the shop, as illustrated in Figure 5-2.

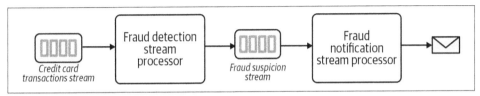

Figure 5-2. Data streams put data in motion, reducing latency

Streaming architectures go hand-in-hand with reactive systems, as stream processors are reactive—they simply react to new data coming in. (Note that some tools in this market speak of *data pipelines* or *data flows* instead of *data streams*, while others refer to *events* rather than *data*.)

Streaming can be used for a wide variety of use cases. One common example is extract, transform, load (ETL) jobs that pump data from one database to another, such as from your production systems into your data warehouse or data lake. Another canonical example is the use of serverless functions to create a thumbnail for every picture uploaded to some kind of storage.

The line between data streaming and process automation can become thin, as you can implement a process by a couple of stream processors in a row, as shown in Figure 5-3 for an order fulfillment process.

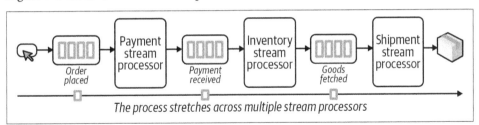

Figure 5-3. Implementing a process using streams

Using streaming for process automation shares most shortcomings of traditional batch processing, except the latency aspect. You lack visibility and your ability to change the process is limited. It is hard to operate such a system and diagnose failures, and it is hard to query the current state. Let's briefly look at these shortcomings in more detail.

There is a lack of visibility into the process as it is implemented by the topology of stream processors. Process instances only exist virtually because there is data flowing through queues. You have no way to inspect how the overall process really works. The behavior emerges during runtime, which makes it hard to understand, especially in contrast to an approach where process logic is explicitly defined. I recently heard the term *pinball machine architecture*, coined by Neal Ford, and think that captures it very well.

You also have limited ability to change the process, mainly because it is really hard to change what you don't understand. But let's assume you do a good job with the archaeology and manage to get a clear picture. You still can't make certain changes without changing multiple stream processors at the same time, which probably requires a coordinated deployment. This eventually leads to a degree of coupling you'd prefer to avoid.

Chapter 8 discusses this subject in more depth and explains what are good and bad use cases for event-driven communication and streaming architectures. You will see there that streaming is great in some cases, but it can also degrade your architecture.

Typical tools only allow models that are acyclic, which means you can't loop back. While this is a reasonable decision for ETL jobs, it does limit the possible use cases of these tools for automating processes. In general, you have operational loops in many processes. For instance, a customer may change their mind about an order, a payment might bounce, a forklift might drive over your nice little parcel—a lot of things can happen that mean you have to go back in the process and start over.

To address problems around visibility, some tools allow you to model data flows graphically. But even with these graphics, it is still hard to operate the solution you've built because the state of the overall business process is distributed amongst data flowing around in streams, and probably even state in the stream processers themselves. If you need to query the current state of one process instance, you can't ask a single component but potentially have to puzzle together pieces of data from various sources.

This becomes even more challenging if there are failures in the processing. You can't simply stop processing one specific instance, capture the problem, and alert somebody to resolve the problem. Instead, you have to write the poisoned data item into some kind of dead letter queue to indicate a fault.

The Actor Model

The *actor model* is one approach for tackling concurrent computing. It's based on messaging: the basic idea is to have a single responsible software component, the so-called actor, that processes each and every message of a certain type and thus can fully control threading and the level of parallelism. Actors communicate with each other—or even with themselves—only via messaging. This allows you not only to leverage queues but to scale the overall system, as typically parallel processing is limited to a single actor.

Actors are allowed to have local persistence. Some frameworks explicitly know the concept of persistent actors, so you can easily build one actor that implements a process, communicating with other actors to fulfill certain tasks.

Projects often hardcode their process into such a persistent actor. This has some nice upsides, especially that the process definition is put in one place where it is easy to find and change. But it also has severe shortcomings that you should keep in mind:

- There is no modeling language that supports patterns you need for long-running behavior (described in "Workflow Patterns" on page 101). This means you have to code all that behavior yourself.
- The process logic is buried in source code and not visible, making it hard to understand for all stakeholders.

An important observation about the actor model is that there is limited adoption in the industry, which is more of a practical concern. Even if some tools have advocated heavily for the actors approach for some time, and the concept is arguably beneficial for some scenarios, there aren't many companies that have adopted the approach at a large scale. Particularly because you would need to go all-in with your architecture to have an ecosystem of actors to leverage the benefits, this is a rare scenario.

If you apply actors, there is an interesting combination possible: you can build one actor that implements the process but leverages a workflow engine for handling the details. This mitigates the downsides and is a great fit. You can find a link to an example on the book's website (*http://ProcessAutomationBook.com*).

Stateful Functions

Modern streaming and cloud environments provide a concept called a *stateful function* (e.g. Azure Durable Functions). Such a function can be long-running and persist its state between executions. This is somewhat comparable to the persistent actors described in the last section.

While this functionality can also be used to automate long-running processes, it has severe drawbacks compared to using a dedicated workflow engine:

- There is no modeling language that supports patterns required to express long-running logic. (Process modeling languages will be covered in detail in the next section.)
- There is no graphical representation of the process logic, which makes collaboration between business, developers, and operations harder. Overall, these frameworks solely target developers and do not look at other roles.
- The support around scheduling and versioning is very limited. So, for example, functions cannot easily run different versions of the same orchestration code, or can do so only by using workarounds.
- The surrounding tooling, e.g., for operations, is very basic.

Note that there is currently innovation happening in this area, especially around serverless architectures. So while the preceding statements are true at the time of writing, things might have changed slightly by the time you're reading this. Therefore, it might be worth double checking on these limitations if you're considering using durable functions to automate processes.

Process Modeling Languages

So far you've been exposed to BPMN as "the" process modeling language. But there are various other options out there, and I regularly participate in heated discussions around which one to choose. Very often these conversations are not based on expressing facts, but rather opinions and personal preferences. One time, I had a discussion with a big Silicon Valley–based company, and the architect told me that they couldn't work with BPMN because it is serialized as XML: "XML is legacy, you know." So is electricity, but we still use it!

Making decisions based on gut feeling without backing arguments is simply not a good approach. Instead, try to understand what problems you are trying to solve and what trade-offs you encounter with the different solutions. In the case of process models in XML, the common critiques are about problems with diff and merge. What if a colleague changed the process model at the same time as I did? While it may seem complicated to do this with XML files, it is actually not such a big problem in reality. It's rare that two people change the same elements within the model; changes are more often far away from each other, even if they are in the same XML file. So, diffing and merging XML as a text file is normally easy, especially if you comply with some basic rules. Most importantly, you should not touch elements you don't want to change, or just redo the layout without a good reason for it. This is the same as how you should treat source code: you don't reformat the whole file without a good reason, because that makes spotting real differences harder.

Overall, the two arguments against XML—that it is old and that it is hard to merge—don't stand up to a proper test.

But let's take a step back and inspect the really important aspects when choosing a process modeling language. In the next sections we'll consider these questions:

- What behavior does the language support? This defines the overall maturity and will determine if you will encounter situations that can't be modeled with the language of choice.

- What value does a graphical representation bring to the table? Should you use a graphical modeling language, or is a text-based language sufficient?

Workflow Patterns

In order to judge if a process modeling language provides the functionality you need, you can refer to the patterns defined by the Workflow Patterns initiative. According to the website (*http://workflowpatterns.com*), the research done by this initiative (which has been around for over 20 years):

> Provides a thorough examination of the various perspectives (control flow, data, resource, and exception handling) that need to be supported by a workflow language or a business process modelling language. The results can be used for examining the suitability of a particular process language or workflow system for a particular project.

Workflow patterns simply define the patterns, not any kind of implementation. BPMN implements most of these patterns. Other languages, such as the Amazon States Language which is used in AWS Step Functions, implement only some of them. This can help you judge the power of the process modeling language of your choice.

If you are a pattern type of person, you might even find it useful to read through all the pattern descriptions online. This will definitely foster your understanding of why you need a properly designed process modeling language, and why you should not code your own workflow engine.

You might wonder what such workflow patterns look like. Table 5-1 shows some basic control-flow patterns and how they are expressed in BPMN.

Table 5-1. Some workflow patterns from http://www.workflowpatterns.com/patterns/ mapped to BPMN

Pattern number	Pattern name	BPMN element	Description
1	Sequence		A task in a process is enabled after the completion of a preceding task in the same process.
2	Parallel Split		The divergence of a branch into two or more parallel branches, each of which executes concurrently.
3	Synchronization		The convergence of two or more branches into a single subsequent branch such that the thread of control is passed to the subsequent branch when all input branches have been enabled.
4	Exclusive Choice		The divergence of a branch into two or more branches such that when the incoming branch is enabled, the thread of control is immediately passed to precisely one of the outgoing branches based on a mechanism that can select one of the outgoing branches.

Pattern number	Pattern name	BPMN element	Description
5	Simple Merge	◇⊗◇	The convergence of two or more branches into a single subsequent branch such that each enablement of an incoming branch results in the thread of control being passed to the subsequent branch.
...			
14	Multiple Instances with a Priori Run-Time Knowledge	Do something "for each" ‖‖‖	Within a given process instance, multiple instances of a task can be created. The required number of instances may depend on a number of runtime factors, including state data, resource availability, and interprocess communications, but is known before the task instances must be created. Once initiated, these instances are independent of each other and run concurrently. It is necessary to synchronize the instances at completion before any subsequent tasks can be triggered.
...			

Custom process modeling languages often come with the promise of being simpler than BPMN. But in reality, claims of simplicity mean they lack important patterns. Hence, if you follow the development of these modeling languages over time you will see that they add patterns once in a while, and whenever such a tool is successful it almost inevitably ends up with a language complexity comparable to BPMN, but in a proprietary way.

This is why I have never understood the motivation to use a custom modeling language when there is a mature and usable standard like BPMN available.

Benefits of Graphical Process Visualizations

The benefits of graphical process visualizations are prominent. Of course, it's all about the visibility and comprehensibility of the model, and how easily it can be discussed with different stakeholders.

With regard to business stakeholders, graphical models are a great tool to use when discussing requirements before and during implementation. This can remedy a continuous frustration for many developers that requirements are "obviously incomplete" and "clearly never going to work." Graphical models can help to identify potential problems much earlier, probably even by the business stakeholders themselves.

Graphical models can also be leveraged by operations, for example to mark problems in a process instance. They allow people who are not developers to get a rough idea about what is going on, which would be impossible with programming code.

It is noteworthy that graphical models even align developers with other developers. Close your eyes (metaphorically speaking) and think of the last time a colleague of yours explained to you some process, algorithm, or other complex piece of software. Did they actually show you a wall full of code? Did they walk you through a long document containing prose? Or, rather, did they draw a picture on the whiteboard to explain the core concepts? I bet it was the latter.

 There are even arguments for graphical models from the field of psychology of perception. The saying "A picture is worth a thousand words" captures this well. The geekier version is that for recognizing visual patterns you can use your brain's GPU, but for reading you have to use the CPU. Having graphical models helps to reduce CPU utilization and makes room for thinking about the content of your models. Of course, this only applies after you've learned a graphical modeling language and have it ready to be used in your brain, but the core elements of languages like BPMN are boxes and arrows, and as such they can be intuitively understood by most people. So, graphical models free up some of your brain's CPU to actually develop better models. Isn't that great?

Let me add a short personal story to reinforce the value of a graphical model that is in sync with the real implementation. Remember in the Preface, where I told the story of how my friend started his own business, setting up a specialized retail store for graphics cards? That was also the first time I learned about process modeling. I started drawing processes with Microsoft Visio to discuss them with my friend and the handful of employees he had. While Visio was far from providing a good modeling experience and the resulting pictures were pure documentation, I benefited from this exercise.

As I was intrigued by process models, I started to search for workflow engines that could directly execute them. I finally found an open source project that could handle that, and the process model eventually went live.

Twenty years later, I was astonished to see that the software at my friend's company was still in production. And amazingly, the graphical representations of the executable process models are still being used, even as the company continues to evolve (because graphics card modding is no longer a thing) and as new employees are onboarded. These models help people to understand the business processes of the company as well as the behavior of the software.

I am a huge fan of graphical models that are executable artifacts. The Visio diagrams I created are totally outdated now, but the executable models are source code and still show exactly what is really executed.

There are two ways to achieve a graphical process visualization. The obvious approach is to create a process model that includes graphical information, as is done with BPMN. Keep in mind that proprietary symbols limit the value of the visuals for collaboration with other roles, so BPMN is really a good choice.

The other approach is to auto-generate visuals from a process model that might even be in a textual form, as discussed in the next section. Unfortunately, auto-generation produces visualizations that are often hard to comprehend.

Textual Process Modeling Approaches

In contrast to graphical process models like those created with BPMN, there are also textual models. How can you create such a model? The most common approach is to use some JSON or YAML to define a process model, as shown in the following example taken from Netflix Conductor:

```
{
  "name": "sample-workflow",
  "version": 1,
  "tasks": [
    {
      "name": "task_1",
      "type": "SIMPLE"
    },
    {
      "name": "someDecision",
      "type": "DECISION",
      "decisionCases": {
        "0": [
          {
            "name": "task_2",
            "type": "SIMPLE"
          }
        ],
        "1": [
          {
            "name": "fork_join",
            "type": "FORK_JOIN",
            "forkTasks": [
              [
                {
                  "name": "task_3",
                  "type": "SIMPLE"
                }
              ],
              [
                {
                  "name": "task_4",
                  "type": "SIMPLE"
                }
              ]
            ]
          }
        ]
      }
    }
```

```
          ]
        }
      },
      {
        "name": "task_5",
        "type": "SIMPLE"
      }
    ]
  }
```

The sequence of task definitions in that JSON file also defines the sequence of tasks in the process. Allowing a different sequence requires you to define explicit transitions, often by referring to the IDs of elements. This is actually not that different from the XML serialization format that backs BPMN models.

Typically, the problem with textual modeling is the lack of modeling tools. It is really hard to express complex workflows in a JSON file like the one just shown, especially if you add loops or parallel paths.

Another option is to express process models via programming code, as illustrated in the following example with Spring State Machines:

```
public void configure() {
    states.withStates()
        .initial(States.START)
        .state(States.RETRIEVE_PAYMENT, new RetrievePaymentAction())
        .state(States.WAIT_FOR_PAYMENT_RETRY)
        .end(States.DONE);

    transitions.withExternal()
        .source(States.START)
        .target(States.RETRIEVE_PAYMENT)
        .event(Events.STARTED)
        .and()
        .withExternal()
        .source(States.RETRIEVE_PAYMENT)
        .target(States.DONE)
        .event(Events.PAYMENT_RECEIVED)
        .and()
        .withExternal()
        .source(States.RETRIEVE_PAYMENT)
        .target(States.WAIT_FOR_PAYMENT_RETRY)
        .event(Events.PAYMENT_UNAVAILABLE)
        .and()
        .withExternal()
        .source(States.WAIT_FOR_PAYMENT_RETRY)
        .target(States.RETRIEVE_PAYMENT)
        .timer(5000l);
}
```

This can be directly coded in your IDE, and your compiler can do some checks. Still, it is not easy to express processes that do not run in a straight sequence. Imagine the process in Figure 5-4, where invoices are sent in parallel to charging the credit card. This is hard to express in understandable text.

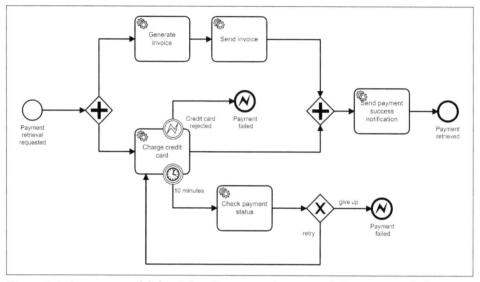

Figure 5-4. A process model that is hard to express in a textual domain-specific language

In short, all but easy models are hard to express in a textual form. But some tools, including Camunda, allow you to generate a BPMN XML file from models expressed in programming code. This allows you to switch to graphical modeling later, for example if the process gets more complicated.

When giving presentations, I often leverage this functionality and start with Java code to define a simple process model. This way, the audience can clearly see that there is no hidden magic behind some modeling tool. I could also do that using a BPMN XML file, but code is typically easier to digest than an XML file at first. In the background, the workflow engine generates a BPMN process model, including graphics, with auto-layout.

Typical Concerns About Graphical Modeling

So why isn't the world simply going all-in with graphical process modeling and making graphical models first-class citizens? Good question! In my experience, some developers are not overly fond of graphical modeling languages. Here is a summary of some common concerns:

They contain hidden magic

After giving a lot of conference talks and live demos, I have learned that developers feel uncomfortable if they think they are missing important pieces of the solution. And as graphical modeling tools often hide certain logic and configuration in property panels or wizards, users who don't know the tools get the feeling that they are missing something crucial. Even if no secret magic is used (and there is nothing magic about it), they are never fully confident in these tools.

In contrast, source code does not hide things (OK—it probably does behind method calls or frameworks—but I do understand the argument). An easy solution can be to toggle between the graphical view and the serialized file in XML. In that file, nothing is hidden. Another handy strategy is to start with coding the process model in the beginning, as described earlier, and switch to a graphical modeling approach as soon as it gets more complicated.

They degrade the developer experience or development speed

Developers know how to handle text files very well. They are experts in using their version control systems of choice and diffing and merging source code in complicated scenarios. Platforms like GitHub support the typical use cases out of the box and IDEs offer code completion and sophisticated templates to increase developers' productivity, so they're good places to work in.

Then, the conception is that along comes something strange (the graphical model) that does not fit into their tooling landscape. This is partly true, as you might lose some capabilities of the IDE, such as code completion for known classes and methods, when editing the model. But it is also partly wrong, as we saw earlier: you can easily diff and merge the serialized format of a graphical mode (the XML file), which is simply stored in your version control. Some tools even allow you to do graphical diffing on top of BPMN.

But more importantly, this concern is mostly irrelevant. "Combining Process Models and Programming Code" on page 54 showed that you can express logic either in process models or in code and simply combine them, so the process model expresses "only" the sequence of tasks and all other logic is still contained in normal programming code.

They threaten the developer's self-image

I've come across another reason for rejecting process models that took me a while to understand. Some developers actually don't embrace the fact that normal human beings can understand what they are doing. They are artists, and of course there must be some mystery behind a working program. This also guarantees them job security, or so they think. But having this mindset in your project will obviously lead to big problems in the future, and you definitely have to address it.

Software engineering has changed a lot over the last few decades, and developers often invest the vast majority of their time into discussing requirements and sketching the right solution, just to change it again tomorrow. Agile approaches and collaboration are everywhere, and graphical process models are one important piece of that puzzle.

Another concern is that once you have understandable graphical models, business stakeholders will interfere with the development all the time and want to join all conversations around the solution design. I have seen this happen. But the solution is not to avoid graphical models, but rather to learn to apply them correctly. This is mostly about respecting the different roles in a project. An executable process model is also source code. It is part of the solution design and thus under the responsibility of the people who build the solution (i.e., the development team). They need to have the last call on the design choices, and if there are good technical reasons to change a model they need to be empowered to do this. Of course, they also need to be able to explain their reasons to other stakeholders. Similarly, the process model needs to be included in the software developers' toolchain and CI/CD pipelines.

Executable process models are also source code and must be owned and governed by the software development team.

Graphical Versus Textual Approaches

In summary, visuals are beneficial to understanding process logic, for all stakeholders (including developers themselves). They help to get everybody on board when discussing the process and during operations.

The easiest way to create a visual model is to use a graphical modeling language. This will also help ensure that even complex processes are understood.

Remember that only the sequence of tasks itself is expressed in the process model graphically, and this is then connected to programming code for other logic. This gives you the best of both worlds.

Process Automation with Blockchain?

I wanted to include a section about blockchain in this book, because there is so much confusion around it. Blockchain is often described as a technology that will radically change business processes. Let's quickly examine what that means for process automation. Spoiler alert: it will not change much for automation of the processes within a company. It "only" influences the collaboration of multiple parties.

But let's take this step by step. We'll start with an example. A couple of years back I had to buy a car. So I went to the internet portal of my choice, searched for a car, and bought it via email. The platform was just a broker; the buying process was handled by the dealer directly.

In this scenario, there are two parties who don't trust one another: I do not trust the car dealer (a noble profession, but for some weird reason I always think car dealers want to shaft me) and the car dealer does not trust me, basically because they don't know me. At the same time, a car is expensive enough that both sides care about trust.

This is a stalemate situation: I don't want to transfer money before getting the car's documents, and the dealer does not want to send the documents before receiving the money. And you can be sure that I don't want to get into any solution that involves packing the money in a suitcase.

Partners doing business without mutual trust is the optimal setting for blockchain use cases. In these situations, the classic approach to solve the problem of lack of trust is to introduce a trusted intermediate, like a bank, a notary, or some dedicated service. Blockchain technology can make this intermediary unnecessary.

Blockchain establishes trust without the intermediate party by providing a database where all data is distributed to everybody joining, and adding some clever cryptography to make it impossible to change or fake data once it is in there. This leads to a database everybody can trust, as there is no single party in control.

It is possible to implement so-called "smart contracts" in a blockchain. Smart contracts are automated and long-running programs in the blockchain. Their data as well as the current state is secured. In a way, a smart contract can be seen as a kind of a workflow engine with persistence in the blockchain. A specialty is that the process model and all instances are publicly visible.

A smart contract allows automation of the public parts of the car buying process—but only the part both parties need to agree on. All aspects of the process that are specific to one party will still be either handled manually (in the case of the car customer) or automated, probably using process automation as described in this book (in the case of a big car dealer). This is visualized by the collaboration model in Figure 5-5.

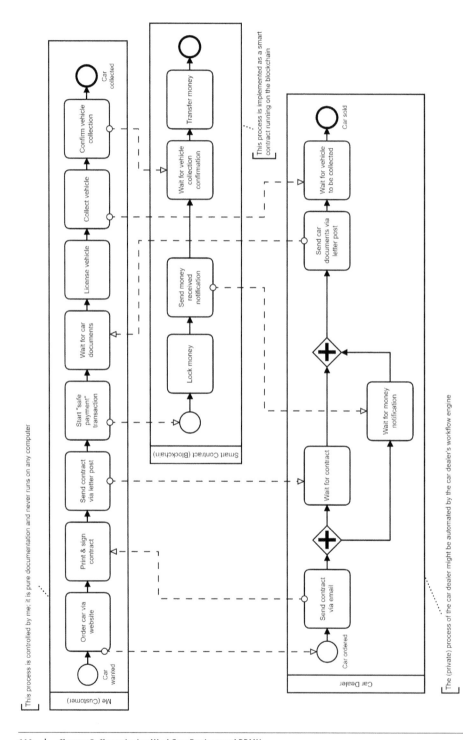

Figure 5-5. Smart contracts in blockchains can be seen as a workflow engine for the public parts of a process between partners

Collaboration models will be introduced in "The Power of One Joined Model" on page 205. In short, they allow us to model the processes of different participants and express how they collaborate; in this example, the buyer (me), the car dealer, and the smart contract all have their own processes.

Because you can get rid of intermediaries, reduce paperwork, and increase trust with smart contracts, I am convinced that blockchain has the potential to revolutionize many business processes. But it is hard to predict when bigger disruptions will happen, because there are a lot of hurdles along the way—the biggest being that it requires radical changes to the way business is done, and no party can start such initiatives alone.

Also, note that even with blockchains all over the planet, you will still use workflow engines to automate the private processes of each party.

Conclusion

This chapter explained alternatives to a workflow engine to automate processes. You should have a better understanding of their shortcomings and the value a workflow engine brings you.

It also introduced some other process modeling languages, showed the advantages of graphical ones, and underlined the importance of BPMN.

PART II

Process Automation in the Enterprise

Process automation is just one piece in the overall enterprise architecture puzzle, and it needs to support a complex balancing act. If your organization is successful, it needs to scale. To develop more features faster, it wants to add development teams. To allow this, you need to cut your applications into smaller pieces and assign teams to these pieces. This is what is currently happening with microservices, to name the most prominent approach at the time of writing.

But the customers don't care about all that—they just want to have their desires fulfilled (e.g., an order to be shipped as fast as possible). The customer cares only about the end-to-end business process.

Your job is to allow for the modularization that you need to survive as a company, but at the same time to make sure that the overall end-to-end business process runs smoothly and can be understood. This includes fitting the processes within the boundaries of the right modules and making these modules as decoupled as possible.

Sound easy? Yeah, kind of. This part of the book equips you with some important guidelines to survive this mission:

Chapter 6
> This chapter discusses typical architectures and trade-offs, which will help you to sketch your own architecture.

Chapter 7
> This chapter talks about modularization, cohesion, and coupling. The goal is to equip you with the basics to understand how to define the boundaries of your services, and how that influences process automation.

Chapter 8

   This chapter (re)defines orchestration and choreography as command-driven
   and event-driven communication. This allows us to discuss a good balance
   between commands and events.

Chapter 9

   As typical architectures favor distributed systems, you will need to solve certain
   challenges around remote communication. This chapter describes how a workflow engine can help with these by enabling long-running capabilities.

Chapter 10

   This chapter discusses the value of graphical process models for collaboration in
   enterprise IT projects. You will learn about different stakeholders that may be
   interested in these models and how you can get them all on board.

Chapter 11

   Learnings in the previous chapter are a good basis for looking at how to enable
   process visibility, which we do in this final chapter in this section.

CHAPTER 6

Solution Architecture

By now you should have a better understanding of how to design and execute process models, and what problems a workflow engine solves. It's time to think about its place in your architecture.

This chapter:

- Gives some guidance on when to use a workflow engine
- Covers the most important questions to ask to define your architecture
- Helps you start your own evaluation endeavor

When to Use a Workflow Engine

Now is a good time to come back to a question that I skipped in Chapter 2: when does it make sense to use a workflow engine?

The way I think about it is visualized in Figure 6-1.

The two main advantages of a workflow engine are that it adds long-running capabilities to your application or service, and that you make the process logic visible. Depending on what you want to do with the workflow engine, these capabilities are of different value for you.

For example, if you want to orchestrate an end-to-end business process (maybe as part of your microservices endeavor), you will definitely benefit very much from long-running capabilities and visibility. If you need to implement business transactions in distributed systems, as will be described in "Transactions and Consistency" on page 183, these will also be of value, although maybe slightly less so. When you simply leverage the long-running capabilities to solve very technical challenges, as will be described in Chapter 9, there is limited value in visibility, but still this use case makes a lot of sense.

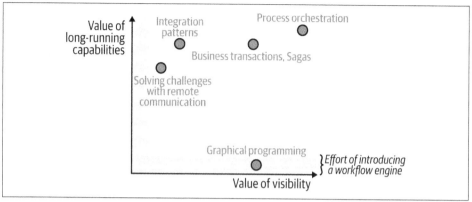

Figure 6-1. The value a workflow engine brings might differ for different use cases, but as long as the return exceeds the investment it is typically worth introducing it

As long as the value (the return) exceeds the effort of introducing the workflow engine in the first place (the investment), a workflow engine will have a positive impact on your architecture. The exact threshold depends very much on how easy it is to introduce the selected tool. I expect that this barrier will drop further over the next few years, as tools get more and more lightweight or are made available as managed services. This will increase the applicability of workflow engines for a wider range of problems.

Still, of course there are use cases that do not make much sense. An example would be using BPMN to do graphical programming, meaning you simply express programming code in the graphical model without the need for state handling or collaboration with other roles.

The return on investment depends on both the return *and* the investment. If the investment is low, you can apply workflow engines to a bigger range of problems.

Architecture Trade-Offs

Deciding on a solution architecture involves a number of trade-offs, as the answer to the question of which architecture is best is always "it depends." It depends on your goals, your architecture and stack, and the tool of choice. And there are no right or wrong architectures, but rather some that might work better for your situation than others.

This section will give you a basic understanding of which questions need to be clarified and the implications your decisions might have.

Running the Workflow Engine

The first and most important question is: how do you run the workflow engine itself? Is it a managed service? Is it a Docker container that can run side-by-side with your microservices? Or is the workflow engine an embeddable library that will be part of your application?

Some other questions you should consider are:

- Is it easy to provision in your environment?
- What resources does it need to run, like databases or application servers?

Make sure your engine of choice fits into your situation. If you're building a serverless application, of course you would look for a managed service. If you're building a cloud native application, Kubernetes support might be vital. If you run mostly human task workflows, maybe a standalone workflow server is the easiest option. If you're building a monolith, an embedded library may work well.

You also need to understand the level of flexibility of the tools. Some cloud services are only available with certain cloud providers, and you have no idea how they work behind the scenes. Some other tools have different distribution options, such as a self-assembly open source, as a standalone distribution, and as a Docker image, while also being available as a managed service in the cloud. A certain level of flexibility might be an advantage, especially if your requirements change over time.

In this entire decision process, you must also take the experience of your team into account. If the team has never touched Kubernetes or Docker, don't force introducing these just to leverage process automation.

Decentralized Engines

One of the most important discussions that always comes up concerns how many workflow engines should be operated. Does a company run the workflow engine as a centralized platform? Or does every team that requires a workflow engine run its own in a decentralized manner? Guess what: it depends.

If you embrace microservices, you'll want to give teams a lot of autonomy. A team should be able to act independently of other teams and make changes as required. Also, each team should be isolated in a way that ensures that another microservice going crazy does not affect its ability to operate normally. In this setting, the default is to have decentralized engines—one workflow engine for each microservice that needs one. This ensures that every team can stay independent, for example when they want to update or reconfigure a workflow engine. Each team can likely even decide for itself which tool it wants to use. This setup also enforces the designed boundaries, as nobody outside of the current microservice can access the workflow engine.

The clear advantages are autonomy and isolation, but the cost is that every team has to evaluate and operate its own engine. The complexity of this very much depends on the technical stack. For example, using a managed service is easy if you are already using the cloud, or a Kubernetes operator can make it easier to spin up workflow engines if you are already fully committed to using containers.

A remaining challenge is how to gain central visibility over decentralized engines. Chapter 11 will dive into this very interesting topic. A decentralized engine deployment is visualized in Figure 6-2.

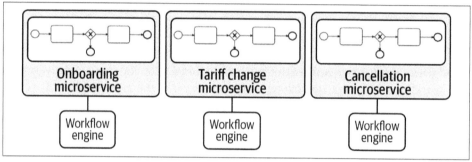

Figure 6-2. Decentralized workflow engines provide isolation

Sharing Engines

If you want to simplify operations, you can run a central engine as a service for the whole company, or at least one engine per department, as visualized in Figure 6-3.

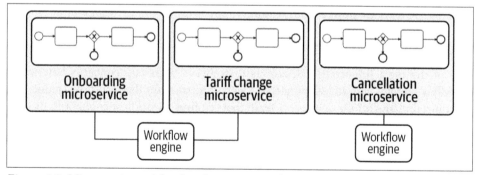

Figure 6-3. Microservices might also share engines; they still own the process model and you might still operate multiple engines

The workflow engine is a remote resource that applications can connect to in order to deploy and execute processes. While this is typically easy to set up, it comes with the downside that you lose isolation of the services, not just in terms of runtime data but also in terms of product versions. A central workflow tool also needs to be scalable and resilient to avoid hitting a bottleneck, or a single point of failure.

Ownership of Process Models

There is one really important thought to keep in mind here: there is a difference between ownership and physical deployment location. You can deploy process models from different teams to a central engine. If these models are still owned and governed by the various team, this is not too big of a problem. If it means that all models need to be governed by one central team, it is. This is comparable to a centrally operated in-house cloud platform, where each team still owns, configures, and provisions its own resources.

Actually, if the deployment is properly integrated into your CI/CD pipeline, teams might not even notice where their processes are physically deployed. This is comparable to relational databases. Many companies still share a database installation among different applications, with each of them getting their own schema and being responsible for the table structure. This works relatively well, but still, one application going mad can bring performance down for everybody.

Using the Workflow Engine as a Communication Channel

A very different option in a microservices environment is to let different microservices directly pub/sub to a central workflow engine, as shown in Figure 6-4. In my experience, this design polarizes people's opinions. I'll discuss why in a minute, but let's understand this option first.

As shown in the figure, you don't need glue code to call the payment service from within the order fulfillment service. Actually, there is not even any additional communication channel, like messaging or REST calls, between the services for order fulfillment and payment.

Instead, the payment service directly subscribes to service tasks with the type name `retrieve-payment`, and the shipment service subscribes to tasks with the type name `ship-goods`. As the task type name is the connection information, the pub/sub mechanism still decouples the two services. Payment doesn't need to know anything about order fulfillment; it simply knows that it will execute all `retrieve-payment` tasks.

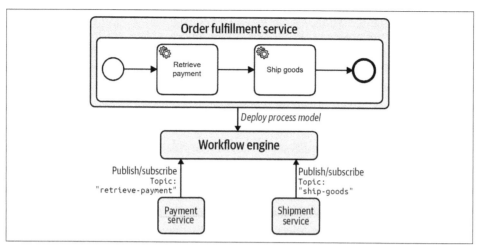

Figure 6-4. Different microservices can publish and subscribe to a central workflow engine

Now the workflow engine becomes a shared system, like the messaging system is in other architectures. There are pragmatic companies that love the simplicity of that approach, as they don't have to introduce an additional messaging system, but still can benefit from the temporal decoupling of pub/sub. There are also companies that don't want to see a workflow engine in such a central position. If these companies want to leverage the power of pub/sub, they run an additional message or event bus.

Chapter 7 dives a bit more into the reasoning around that question. For now, you can simply remember that both are valid possibilities that come with trade-offs.

In-House Workflow Platforms

The current industry trend is that companies leave as much freedom as possible to development teams, so they can, for example, choose the tooling they like. At the same time, most companies want to provide central guidance around process automation to save effort and to share knowledge. You'll learn more about this later, in Chapter 12; it might involve providing a curated list of vendors so that the number of tools in use remains manageable, sharing best practices or success stories on the company's wiki, or even establishing a center of excellence that can support teams with questions related to process automation.

However, some companies go a step further and start to prebuild their own software components and platforms on top of specific vendors' workflow engines. At its simplest, this might involve creating a facade in order to reduce the dependency on the vendor. In this scenario, developers program against a bespoke facade, and the workflow engine API is only wired in under the hood. At the other extreme, companies might assemble a whole SOA or integration stack with a couple of components from different vendors. The motivation here is to avoid vendor lock-in and to provide some predeveloped additional functionality.

All of the initiatives like this that I've seen have struggled. It's one thing to set up a bespoke platform, but quite another to keep this platform up-to-date with new version releases, to fix all bugs that are reported internally, or to make all of the workflow engine's features available via a custom-built facade. And users of that platform will still hit dead ends, because its capabilities typically won't match those of the underlying workflow engine. What's more, you can't research problems in your own bespoke platform via Google like you can for well-known commercial products or open source projects.

Overall, it's really not worth the effort—especially not to avoid vendor dependencies. "Dos and Don'ts Around Reuse" on page 254 will look into a more meaningful way to achieve reusability. I strongly recommend that you skip the undertaking of building a custom platform. I have seen it fail even with very smart teams that tried hard. Unless you are a process automation company, don't build a process automation platform.

Performance and Scalability

An important angle to consider when looking at a workflow engine concerns performance and scalability. Does the workflow engine satisfy your requirements? To judge this, look at your workload's characteristics and get clarity on questions like:

- What kind of throughput do you need? For example, how many process instances are started per second or day?

- What cycle time is acceptable for single tasks or the complete process? For example, how many milliseconds is a fully automated process with 10 tasks allowed to take? This might also affect latencies if you need to offer synchronous facades.

- How volatile is your load? Some companies start 90% of their monthly process instances in the same hour of the month. So, while you should of course look at your average load, you also need to understand what peaks you need to expect. The ability to handle those peaks is the more crucial requirement.

So, to determine the characteristics of your workload, it is important to look at how many process instances are started, how many service tasks need to be executed, how many events need to be routed to the workflow engine, and so on. Examining these "actions" is typically more important than looking at the total number of process instances that are waiting somewhere. Waiting often boils down to records in a database, which seldom hits limitations.

It is advisable to do a load test with a representative workload in the target architecture. Such a load test is often easy to set up, especially if you can leverage modern cloud environments. This will help you get a feeling for whether the workflow engine can serve your needs. It is especially important not to wait for the production environment to be ready, which is something I often see customers do. Spin up something that is close enough as early as possible; that's typically more than sufficient.

Many developers still think that workflow automation tools are mainly designed for low-throughput scenarios like human tasks. And of course, humans don't process tasks within milliseconds. But some process automation tools can also be applied to high-performance use cases, like in the financial industry where payments or trades must be processed at scale within super-short time frames.

And I have seen big data use cases that really benefited from process automation—especially the visibility and failure handling parts, where the teams initially never thought the workflow engine could handle hundreds of thousands of events per second.

Developer Experience and Continuous Delivery

In order to judge if a specific tool fits your development approach, you need to look at how process solutions will be implemented. Process solutions not only include the process model, but also all the glue code needed to transform data or to invoke services, as described in "Combining Process Models and Programming Code" on page 54. Furthermore, the workflow engine API and the availability of client libraries will determine whether your developers can work in their preferred environment and programming language, and use the frameworks they are productive with.

This will directly influence:

How you can develop user interfaces
Some tools allow you to use your preferred UI technology. Others want you to use something the vendor chose or invented, which may provide convenience features.

How you can deploy process definitions
Can the deployment be hooked into your CI/CD pipeline easily? While this sounds obvious, there are tools that require manual deployments of process models, which is of course not what you want.

How you can test processes
Some tools allow local unit tests, as you saw in "Testing Processes" on page 62. Other tools force different ways to test process models, and some cannot do automated testing at all.

How you can store and version process models
Some tools allow you to store process models as files in your normal Git repository; others force you to have a separate repository for models, which then needs to be synced with the tags in your version control system for code.

Selecting the process automation tooling will have significant impact on the developer experience. It is super important to keep a close eye on these factors, as they not only influence the amount of effort needed to implement a process, they can torpedo your whole software development approach and demotivate your developers.

Evaluating Workflow Engines

Now that you're aware of the trade-offs, let's turn our attention to selecting a workflow engine. Unfortunately, I can't give you a shortlist of tools here, for three basic reasons: it won't be fair, because I might miss some tools; it will become outdated as I write it; and it might be too long to be useful. On the book's website (*https://ProcessAutomationBook.com*), you'll find a curated list of tools to use as a starting point.

Unfortunately, the boundaries of the workflow engine category are blurry. There are very different types of tools available. Some real workflow engines are called "orchestrators," whereas other tools are called workflow engines but actually do something else. Let's first explore the different categories.

Foremost are the tools that fit the definition used in this book, meaning they can handle persistent state and thus enable long-running processes. I categorize them as:

- Developer-friendly workflow engines or workflow automation platforms (e.g., Camunda), which are discussed in great detail in this book.
- Managed orchestration or workflow engines (e.g., AWS Step Functions or Camunda Cloud).
- Homegrown orchestration and workflow engines that are made available open source (e.g., Netflix Conductor). These open source projects are close to the lightweight workflow engine category, but they are typically very opinionated and come without any guarantees.
- BPM suites (e.g., Pega), as discussed in "Misguided BPM suites" on page 16.
- RPA tools (e.g., UiPath), as introduced in "Orchestrate RPA Bots" on page 88.
- Low-code platforms (e.g., Zapier), which target end users looking to automate tasks within office-like workflows without any software development.

Additionally, there are tools that don't provide state handling out of the box and thus don't qualify as workflow engines. Still, they are often taken into consideration when workflow tools are evaluated. These include:

- Data pipeline tools (e.g., Apache Airflow) allow data pipelines to be modeled graphically, but they lack important features, as discussed in "Data Pipelines and Streaming" on page 96. These tools don't have their own implementation of persistence; the state of a process instance is the data item flowing through the pipe.

- Integration tools (e.g., Apache Camel) can solve certain integration problems very well. Integration logic can also be chained together to implement a business process, with the downsides noted in "Data Pipelines and Streaming" on page 96.

Finally, there are categories of tools that are in the realm of process automation, but focus on the visibility aspect. For example:

- Distributed tracing tools (e.g., Jaeger) can visualize how requests flow through the system on a technical level. This might help you understand emergent behavior, which will be introduced in "Emergent Behavior" on page 150.
- Process mining tools (e.g., Celonis) can help you understand how processes are implemented by the current ping-pong of legacy systems.

You need to clearly understand the category a tool falls into. The website for this book (*https://ProcessAutomationBook.com*) gives some more guidance on this.

This book focuses on workflow engines, so the first category. When selecting such a tool, I recommend specifically that you look at:

- The vision and road map of the vendor. The vision tells you where the tool is headed; it drives direction and future actions.
- The extensibility of the platform. Extension points allow you to stay on top of things, even if you go beyond what your vendor had in mind. Hitting dead ends in later projects is often a very painful experience, and it can kill whole projects.

Both aspects, vision and extensibility, are actually more important than specific features. The concrete feature set is always subject to change, but you might stay with a vendor for a long time. However, this mindset is the exact opposite of what I've observed in countless tenders or requests for proposals (RFPs) in the past.

Be Cautious with RFPs

Very often, requests for proposals are super-long spreadsheets where vendors tick boxes if they support a feature. From that spreadsheet, customers derive a score, and the tool with the highest score is selected. While this approach sounds fair and objective, it actually is not.

The biggest problem is that vendors often optimize for this buying process. Many features are simply developed to tick a box, and not to be used in real life. That means that you will hit limitations very soon in your project, which is not at all reflected in the spreadsheet. And to add insult to injury, these features make the whole product more complex and harder to maintain, which will lead to even less usable features in the long run. I don't want to blame the vendors, though; they are often forced into this by their prospects.

And in many RFPs the decision is made up front anyway. The spreadsheet is tuned to select the tool of choice. This is actually more of a positive thing than it sounds, as it is often a good way to select tools based on their vision when the company requires a formal spreadsheet evaluation.

My personal highlight was a customer calling me up to discuss my answer to an RFP. They went through the whole spreadsheet with me. On many lines they told me answers from our competitors and said: "Look, they said yes here. But I know their out-of-the-box feature, it will be unusable for us. You said no as you don't have that feature. But you have an easy-to-use extension point that allows us to code that feature ourselves. This is much more valuable to us. Do you agree that we can switch your answer to a yes here?"

But of course, you also need to perform a concrete assessment to build your shortlist of tools. The following list of questions can be used to check the most important aspects. Keep in mind that the whole endeavor is meant to find the engine that matches your needs, so you don't need a "yes" to all questions, but only to the ones important to you. Your evaluation criteria should include:

Integration possibilities
How can you combine process models with code? Can you use the programming language of your choice? Do you get the prebuilt connectors you need? Do you need to use proprietary connectors or can you code everything you need? Can you integrate with all the technologies you need? Is the platform extensible?

Deployment options and supported environments
How can you run the engine itself? Can you consume it as managed service in the cloud? Is it a Docker container? Can you run it on Kubernetes? Is it a library, like a Spring Boot Starter? Does it need some specific environment, like an application server? Does it need other resources to run, like a database?

Tooling
Does it have all the tools you need (as discussed in "Typical Workflow Tools in a Project's Life Cycle" on page 38)? Is the platform still lightweight? That is, are these tools optional when using the core workflow engine?

Process modeling language
Which modeling language is used (as discussed in "Process Modeling Languages" on page 100)? Is BPMN supported? Does the tool cover the BPMN symbols you need (as some tools have severe gaps)?

Scalability and resilience
Can the engine provide the performance and scalability you need for your use case? How complex is it to set up the engine to operate in a fault-tolerant way?

License and support

> Is there support available for the tool? Can you access the source code (just in case)? What guarantees are there for the future development of the tool (e.g., a vendor depending on the revenue stream, so it cares about the tool and its users)? Do you get all the legal guarantees you need (e.g., contracts, SLAs, specific open source licenses)?

My recommendation is to create a shortlist of tools based on the assessment of these aspects. Then start on proofs of concept (POCs) as soon as possible, as described in "Proofs of Concepts" on page 250. Modern tools allow to automate your first process within hours. This allows you to do POCs with more than one vendor. If necessary, you can partner with a consulting firm you trust that has some experience with different vendors; they can help you get started. The hands-on experience of such POCs will massively help you shape your direction.

Conclusion

Designing a solution architecture and selecting the stack requires careful consideration of a lot of factors. It's not an easy task, but on the other hand it is seldom rocket science.

This chapter equipped you with a basic understanding of architecture questions to ask. This should be sufficient—to start your journey, and you can learn along the way. Every architecture is slightly different, and so is every journey. It is impossible to design the perfect solution up front, and if you try, you will face a high risk of getting stuck in endless discussions and evaluations right at the beginning.

Autonomy, Boundaries, and Isolation

Modern systems are composed of many smaller components, like microservices. Microservices architectures value autonomy and isolation of the services. Every service is focused and follows the Unix philosophy: "Do One Thing and Do It Well." This raises important questions on how to set the boundaries of a service. What functionality goes into one service or another, and how many services do you design? How do you achieve decoupling between these services?

These questions, or more so the answers to them, influence process automation, which is why it is important to cover these topics in this book. This chapter:

- Introduces domain-driven design and its ideas around coupling as important basics
- Describes how business processes can help you in designing boundaries
- Examines how boundaries affect your processes
- Discusses how workflow engines can run decentralized to respect boundaries

Strong Cohesion and Low Coupling

Let's start with some basics around cohesion and coupling, which are opposite forces and need to be balanced carefully. You should aim for what is known as Constantine's law (*https://en.wikipedia.org/wiki/Larry_Constantine*): "A structure is stable if cohesion is high, and coupling is low."

Cohesion has to do with how code is organized and how strongly the code in each component is related. As Sam Newman puts it in his book *Monolith to Microservices* (O'Reilly), "the code that changes together, stays together." The idea is that one desired change in business functionality should lead to changes in (ideally) only one component.

Coupling generally means that components need to change together. There are different forms of coupling. The categories and their names vary a bit between different sources, but in this book we'll use the four categories Sam Newman defines:

Implementation coupling
> If a second component uses internal implementation knowledge of your component, you will end up with implementation coupling. A very common example is if another component looks into your database structure, making it hard for you to change that structure later.

Temporal coupling
> With synchronous communication in distributed systems, you are dependent on the current availability of your peer. This is temporal coupling. Messaging systems typically mitigate that, as the recipient of a message does not have to be available at the moment you send the message.

Deployment coupling
> In order to run software, you have to build deployment units, which can contain additional libraries, resources, or process models. A deployment unit always has to be redeployed in one chunk, even if most of the artifacts are unchanged. Another example of deployment coupling is release trains, where you force multiple projects to deploy in one bigger effort. An example of this is if your company does only two big releases a year.

Domain coupling
> Some coupling between components is unavoidable when creating a meaningful business capability for your end customer. For example, even if your shipment services do not care about payment details, you still have to make sure only paid orders are shipped.

You might be able to avoid implementation, temporal, or deployment coupling, and it is often advisable to do so, but domain coupling cannot be eliminated unless you change your business requirements. Still, you can design your component boundaries thoughtfully to reduce potential problems. Domain-driven design can help you define these boundaries, so let's explore this a bit further.

Domain-Driven Design, Bounded Contexts, and Services

Let's take a look at domain-driven design (DDD) and its ideas around bounded contexts. The basic concept is that you need to apply sharp boundaries to any model to make it focused and unified. This increases your chances that the model is correct and useful.

This methodology became popular at a time when many companies developed and deployed software as monoliths, where databases were used to integrate different parts of applications. In these systems, dependencies often grew to the point where they became unmaintainable—a small change in one part of the system could lead to unpredictable side effects in other parts of the system. When such a system grew big, changes became risky and expensive to deploy, so companies became incapable of adjusting their IT systems. This was a pain DDD addressed, and bounded contexts are one of the core ideas in that context.

Let's discuss an example around order fulfillment. A mail order company might have five core bounded contexts: checkout, payment, inventory, shipment, and order fulfillment, as shown in Figure 7-1.

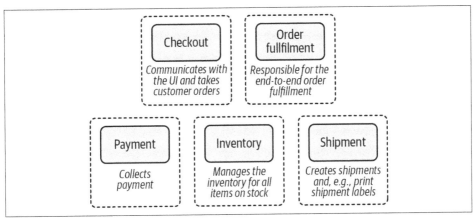

Figure 7-1. A mail order company might end up with these core contexts

DDD advocates for a ubiquitous language shared by different stakeholders, in particular domain experts and software developers. But with DDD the agreement on language, terms, and concepts is valid only within one bounded context, which is contradictory to a lot of enterprise architecture approaches where an attempt is made to define a common language for the whole company, or at least to business units larger than appropriate. The focus in DDD ensures that terms can be defined consistently within a single bounded context, even if they may mean different things within different contexts.

For example, an "order" is a concept that's known in different contexts, but whose meaning might differ. In the checkout context an order relates to the shopping cart being filled by a customer. This order can easily be changed. In the order fulfillment context, an order is an exact instruction of what to charge and send, and it is immutable. And in the inventory context an order is something very different: it involves reordering goods from a supplier to fill up the stock.

Another example is the customer. Most contexts care about this concept, but they care about different aspects of it: in order fulfillment you only need to know the customer's identity, in shipment only the address, and in payment only the payment details. So, different contexts may have different definitions of customers and orders, even if they use the same terms.

Of course, the design can be different. If the mail order company uses an off-the-shelf online shop that already can handle payments, inventory, and packaging labels, you might have one context for that shop, but no separate payment or inventory one. In this case you also have one bounded context, and terms are not allowed to overlap anymore.

DDD can help you define your service boundaries. One or more services implement one context. It doesn't have to be a one-to-one mapping, but no service is allowed to span multiple contexts.

Boundaries and Business Processes

All of this discussion is interesting, but why am I writing about it in a process automation book? Excellent question! Contexts and boundaries massively affect your business process design, and vice versa, for the following reasons, that are examined in more details in the following sections:

- Many end-to-end business processes will touch multiple contexts during their lifetime. A typical order fulfillment scenario will involve retrieving payments and shipping goods. Still, you need to avoid designing an omniscient process model that needs inside knowledge of different contexts in order to function. Instead, process models must be owned by exactly one context. Process models are domain logic and thus should be contained within the service implementing the respective context. And as process models are especially visible to many stakeholders, it is very important that they apply the ubiquitous language of their context.

- Modeling and discussing business processes, especially on an end-to-end level, helps you find boundary candidates, understand the resulting responsibilities, and thus finally decide about your boundaries.

- Having workflow engine capabilities available in a context allows you to acknowledge the long-running nature of many problems. This will help you to defend your boundaries.

Respect Boundaries and Avoid Process Monoliths

In the book *Real-Life BPMN* (CreateSpace Independent Publishing Platform), which I coauthored, we used the order fulfillment example shown in Figure 7-2. Whenever you process an order, you first check if the item is in stock. If it is not, you trigger the procurement for that specific item. This is done using a BPMN call activity that basically invokes another process as a subprocess and waits for it to finish. The procurement process could report delays or unavailability to the order fulfillment process, which then catches these events and takes action, e.g., to delete unavailable items from the product catalog.

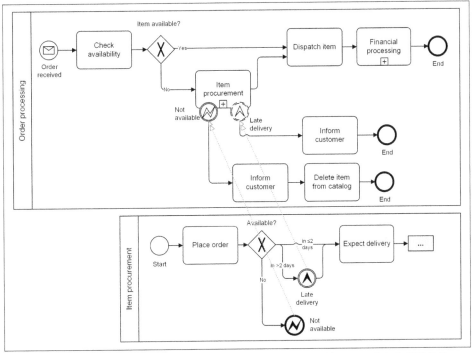

Figure 7-2. A process model mixing different responsibilities (from Real-Life BPMN)

The example was a good one to explain various BPMN symbols and their semantics in that book. However, the process design is problematic with regard to the boundaries.

Let me elaborate. This process design only works well in one scenario, which is most likely not the one you are facing: a scenario where you fulfill specific orders with customized products that you have to purchase explicitly for each customer order. In this case, you could decide to put order fulfillment and item procurement in the same context, and probably even the same service.

But in reality, it is much more likely that you build an order fulfillment service that expects items to be in stock. If they are not, the order fulfillment process might need to wait, but that service will definitely not be responsible for procurement or catalog management. Rather, the inventory service is responsible for monitoring stock and forecasting demand in order to procure items when needed, probably even independent of concrete customer orders.

In this case, process models like the one sketched earlier, become process *monoliths*. Figure 7-3 visualizes such a monolith for the order fulfillment example. This process model violates the boundaries and thus the ownership of the involved services. It shows details of different contexts that should never be combined within one model. For example, it contains many internal details from payment.

You will not find a single person in your organization who can own that whole model. Instead, you will need to call meetings with multiple teams to discuss changes, or to sync on rollout plans. Additionally, you face a situation where you have to update this process model with every relevant change in one of the services (or vice versa). And as you saw earlier, you might also get in trouble with the ubiquitous language if you mix different contexts in one model, as the same term may mean different things within different contexts.

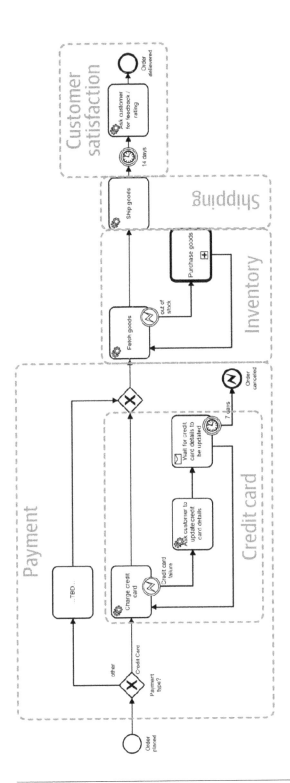

Figure 7-3. Avoid process monoliths like this

A process like this is clearly something you want to avoid. Instead, you need to cut the end-to-end process into appropriate "pieces" that fit into the different services. Figure 7-4 shows an example for order fulfillment, payment, and inventory. In this example, every process model can be clearly and fully owned by the team responsible for the respective service.

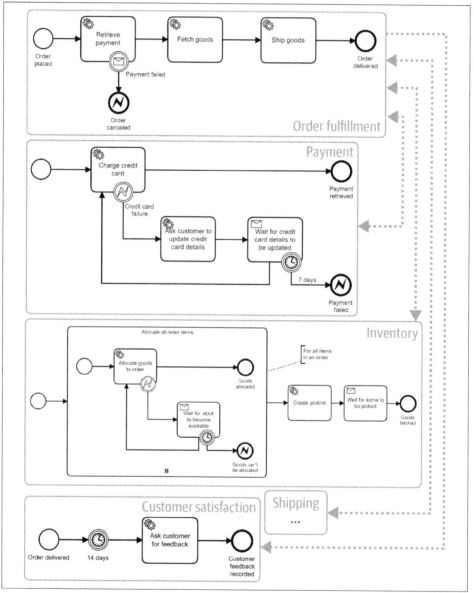

Figure 7-4. Different services collaborating; each clearly focuses on its own responsibility having local processes

It is worth pointing out that cutting the process into pieces means more than just adding some structure to the process model, like you could do with subprocesses in BPMN. You need to distribute responsibilities to different services to achieve a level of isolation that allows scaling development, as described earlier. For example, your order fulfillment process does not need to care about any details of payment; it can rely on the payment service to provide a final result (paid or payment canceled).

How you divide things essentially boils down to the question of "who to blame" if something does not work. While this is a bit exaggerated, and I really hope you don't have a culture that is based on blame, it conveys the essence of responsibility and accountability. In the preceding example, the order fulfillment business owner will rely fully on the capabilities and performance of the other services. There is no need for them to think too much about how payment works, but they might want to monitor SLAs, as a low-performing or faulty payment service might affect the overall order processing time, which they are responsible for.

How responsibilities are divided should be in harmony with your organization. This means that there is no universal answer. Take the example of payments: I know companies where this is one service, and others where it's divided into multiple services. You might still have one service that is ultimately responsible for payments, but that relies on other services that handle credit cards, vouchers, or other types of payments. Any of these services might have its own process model.

The idea of having multiple process models often gets connected to the question of whether you run one central or multiple decentralized workflow engines (an architectural decision we considered in "Decentralized Engines" on page 117). However, I want to emphasize that the two decisions do not need to be connected. You can properly design process models that are owned by different teams and still deploy them on a central engine, just as many companies deploy multiple schemas in a central database. This does not lead to the same level of isolation, but it is still doable and manageable.

 Respecting the boundaries of services when designing process models is a must: don't let this goal be torpedoed just because your organization is not yet ready to run decentralized workflow engines!

Foster Your Understanding of Responsibilities

You need to think about the business responsibilities of every service in your organization. Important questions to ask are:

- What is the business output that this service is responsible for?
- What are the SLAs it needs to provide?

Thinking about end-to-end business processes is a great help in understanding boundaries and responsibilities. You need to clarify what the different services are doing and how they communicate to complete the process. This results in a better understanding of how a business capability comes to life.

In BPMN, you can model collaboration diagrams to visualize this logic. These diagrams will be discussed further in "The Power of One Joined Model" on page 205; they allow you to visualize different participants and how they work together.

Figure 7-5 shows an example for the order fulfillment example. You can see when the user pushes the Dash button, that the button then communicates with a checkout service via HTTP. This service does some verification and passes a message via AMQP to the order fulfillment service, which kicks off a process instance. When order fulfillment is finished, this leads to an event that will be read by a notification service which in turn sends an email to the customer.

Collaboration diagrams show how the various actors interact, making them a great tool to think through certain designs and their implications. They are useful for validating whether your ideas about responsibilities and APIs hold true, even and especially for failure scenarios.

Please note that these diagrams are mainly of help during the design phase. They should be thrown away afterward, as they are typically incomplete and it's not worth the effort to keep them up-to-date. In typical customer engagements, we create these models for certain scenarios that are currently under discussion and do not aim to make them entirely accurate; doing so would inevitably make them too large to visualize. So, in Figure 7-5, some processes are missing details or are hidden. Other processes are not 100% accurate with regard to their internal workings. That is all OK if the model serves its purpose.

It might happen that your peers in your company reject BPMN collaboration models as being too complicated. In this case, you still need to discuss and capture the same information as you would in the models. Techniques like Event Storming, Storystorming, and Domain Storytelling might help you discover that information. I am not covering these techniques in this book and recommend you search the internet for an introduction if you are interested. The important thing is that at some point in time you have to gain a deep understanding of business processes and certain collaborations. At this point, you not only need discovery techniques, but also an analytical tool to verify whether your ideas will really work. It's definitely beneficial to invest the time to sketch out collaboration models in appropriate detail.

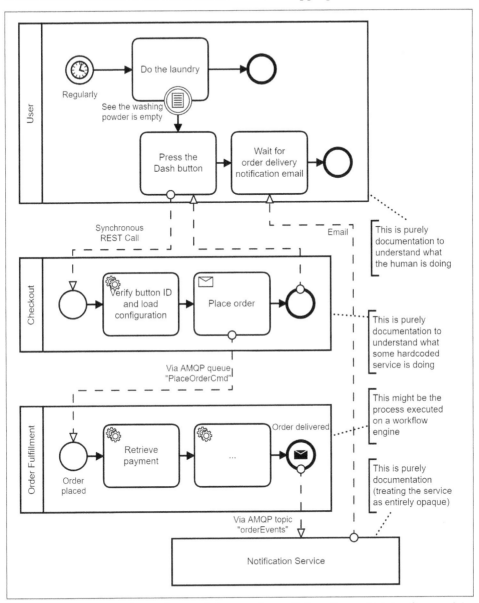

Figure 7-5. BPMN can be used to model a complete collaboration, which is often useful to model scenarios that help to understand how the services play ping-pong

This is also a useful way to check that exceptions are dealt with in the right context, as you can see if problems "over there" need to be handled "here" or not. This can help you improve your boundaries.

Long-Running Behavior Helps You Defend Boundaries

Having a workflow engine available will help you to defend your boundaries. To illustrate this, think back to the example from "Wild West Integrations" on page 4. The payment service needed to talk to a flaky credit card service under the hood. In the first step, the service did not store any state, which meant the only possibility in the event of a problem was to hand over that problem to the client—in that case, the order fulfillment service.

Without the possibility to store persistent state, the payment service could not send the user an email and wait for a week until they enter the right data. So the payment team might be tempted to simply hand over the problem to order fulfillment. This is what I call the *hot potato* antipattern—you simply try to get rid of any problems as quickly as possible. Unfortunately, this leads to payment concepts leeaking into the API and ultimatively also to the client.

For example, in Figure 7-6 the order fulfillment service needs to know about credit cards—but this shouldn't be the case. If your payment service can be long-running, you can provide an API that simply lets you know when a payment goes through or fails, as shown in Figure 7-7. A workflow engine is a simple way to enable this long-running behavior in a service without Wild West integration.

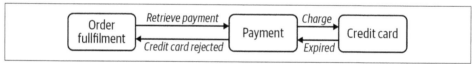

Figure 7-6. If a service cannot be long-running, it has to rethrow certain problems to its client, leading to internal concepts leaking into the API

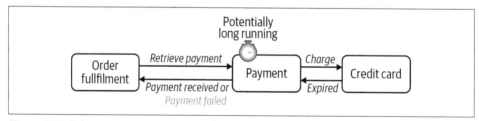

Figure 7-7. A long-running service implements everything it is responsible for and provides a better API

If you do *not* have long-running capabilities available in your services, it is hard to implement certain requirements. This can lead to internal concepts leaking into your API, which in turn will increase coupling between your services. A workflow engine helps to mitigate this risk.

Let's add another perspective to the same example, as the need for long-running capabilities can also come from business requirements. Sometimes credit cards are expired or locked, so they can't be charged. In these scenarios, business stakeholders want to inform the customer and ask for new payment details. This is especially important in situations where the customer does not enter the payment data online, for example, because automatic renewals simply leverage stored payment data from the account. This also requires the payment service to become potentially long-running.

How Processes Communicate Across Boundaries

There are two basic options for interprocess communication:

Call activities
Use a BPMN construct to leverage workflow engine capabilities to invoke other processes.

API calls
Call a normal API to another service that internally starts a process instance. Consumers of the API don't even know that a workflow engine is at play.

Which approach you select will influence the degree of coupling of different services.

Let's explore this with a small example. Recently, I had a meeting with a customer that applied a workflow engine throughout the whole company. They had an outdated document management system (DMS) with a very brittle API, which they wanted to hide from processes that needed to store or update a document.

The customer went ahead and created a BPMN process to communicate with the DMS. This was a good idea, as the communication was asynchronous and involved a lot of waiting and retrying. Now they wanted to make this process available for the whole company.

Let's explore the two options for this example.

Call Activities: Handy Shortcuts Only Within the Boundary

BPMN supports *call activities* that can directly invoke other processes. The calling process (the parent) will wait until the called process (the child) has finished. A child process can raise specific events, like errors or escalations, to communicate with its parent process. Most workflow platforms support call hierarchies in their operations tooling, for example, by showing the process hierarchy or by dealing gracefully with cancellation of processes that are part of a hierarchy. In this case the tooling needs to also cancel all of the process's children and decide what needs to happen with its parent.

Figure 7-8 shows an example for the document process. In this case, the workflow engine will take care of all the nuts and bolts. You can define input and output data mappings, so the call activity to the document storage process is like an API.

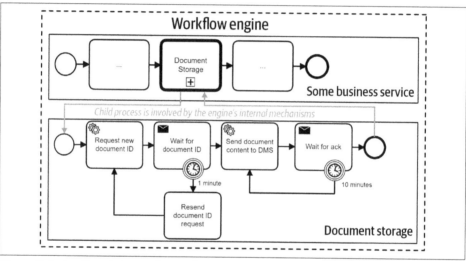

Figure 7-8. A call activity can be used to invoke a process deployed on the same workflow engine

The great thing about this solution is that it is simple to develop and operate. Invoking the process is as easy as specifying the name of the process definition you want to call.

But like everything in life, it comes with a price. In this case, the API technology is your workflow engine. That means you can only use this mechanism if your business service also uses BPMN. Furthermore, you can only use this mechanism if your business service runs on the same workflow engine as the document service. This should only be the case if they run in the same boundary.

In short: if you want to extract the details on how to invoke the document workflow from your main business process, this solution is great. If you want to reuse the document storage workflow from different business processes within one service, this is also OK. But if you want to reuse the document storage process across boundaries in different services, you should not do it.

Crossing Boundaries Is an API Call

When you cross the boundary between services, you should not limit the communication technology to your workflow engine. This is typically too narrow for communicating across boundaries. You should use common API technologies instead, such as REST, SOAP, messaging, or whatever the communication standard in your company is.

Figure 7-9 shows the same example, but with the document storage process deployed as a separate service and the business service communicating with it via an API. The business service doesn't even have to know that the document storage uses a workflow engine. If in the future you want to change the document storage implementation then you are free to do so, as long as the API remains backward compatible.

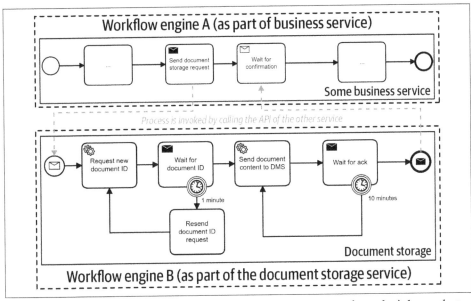

Figure 7-9. You can invoke another process behind an API, even if you don't know that a workflow engine is at play on the other side

While this is definitely the best approach in theory, in the customer scenario with the outdated DMS there was one additional practical challenge. I want to describe it here as a good example of why reality might not follow the textbook.

The customer used SOAP to communicate. Asynchronous responses, like the responses from the document storage service, required a SOAP callback. While conceptually easy, the customer dismissed this approach for very practical reasons: every SOAP callback required firewall rules to be configured, which was not a nice process to go through. As document storage was needed by a lot of services, this would have required too many cyclic communication links. So, they switched to a polling approach, where the business service asked every minute if the document storage service was finished. Waiting a minute was totally OK in this scenario, as the latency did not matter at all. Also, the load of the additional polling was no problem. As a result, all communication was made one-directional toward the document storage service.

But now the polling logic itself yielded some long-running complexity (poll, wait for a minute, poll again, and so on). Every process talking to the document storage service needed to add that polling logic. To prevent this from polluting all the business processes, they extracted the polling to a separate process: the document storage adapter process. This process could then be invoked from the business processes via a call activity, as shown in Figure 7-10.

To avoid needing to copy and paste that adapter process into every project's own codebase, the customer packaged the adapter workflow as a library and embedded this in every business service deployment that needed to talk to the DMS.

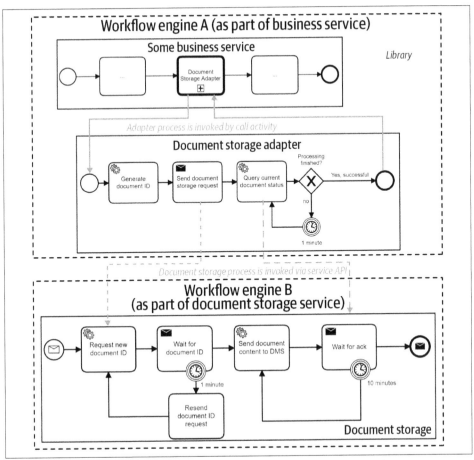

Figure 7-10. Extracting technical aspects of document storage into an adapter process

Technically, this means that the business service deploys its own document storage adapter process, but the process model is taken from the library, as visualized in Figure 7-11. This library also contains the glue code necessary to do all the remote calls and data conversions. This solution turned out to be very successful for the customer, but note that this flexibility in terms of packaging and deployment is not possible with every workflow engine.

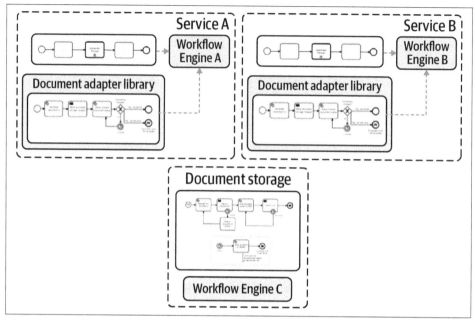

Figure 7-11. The adapter process is individually deployed on every workflow engine, but comes from a library to reduce duplicate effort

Of course, this solution has the downside that the library needs to be updated in all clients using it if there are important changes. In this case, this level of deployment coupling was tolerable, as the library simply implemented a small piece of polling logic to overcome obstacles with the SOAP callback in the architecture. The main DMS logic was still kept in the document storage adapter. But if possible, you should prefer simply using the API of the separately deployed document storage service.

Decentralized Workflow Tooling

In his famous article on microservices, Martin Fowler wrote (*https://martin fowler.com/articles/microservices.html*):

> When building communication structures between different processes, we've seen many products and approaches that stress putting significant smarts into the communication mechanism itself. A good example of this is the Enterprise Service Bus (ESB), where ESB products often include sophisticated facilities for message routing, choreography, transformation, and applying business rules.
>
> The microservice community favours an alternative approach: *smart endpoints and dumb pipes*. Applications built from microservices aim to be as decoupled and as cohesive as possible—they own their own domain logic and act more as filters in the classical Unix sense—receiving a request, applying logic as appropriate and producing a

response. These are choreographed using simple RESTish protocols rather than complex protocols such as WS-Choreography or BPEL or orchestration by a central tool.

Even though this article is from 2014, it is still relevant. And of course, it basically expressed a common feeling after doing SOA and centralized BPM, as described in "Misguided BPM suites" on page 16. One result of this is that you will find many people out there, especially in microservices communities, who instantly connect the term *process automation* or *orchestration* to centralized tooling. They picture a central spider in the web (I often literally hear this term), which goes against the microservice values around isolation and autonomy. It introduces single points of failure and adds organizational friction because everybody has to talk to "the BPM team."

Reading this far in the book, you should already have gained a better understanding that process automation does not have to be centralized at all. As you've seen:

- Business processes should be designed according to the bounded context and service boundaries (see "Boundaries and Business Processes" on page 130). Process monoliths can thus be avoided.

- Process models are also domain logic, contained in their boundary alongside other domain logic that is probably expressed in programming code.

- Workflow engines can be operated in a decentralized manner, which means that every service team can make its own decisions and operate its own workflow engine (see "Decentralized Engines" on page 117), or even decide to not use one at all. An important mind shift is to disconnect the term *process automation* from *centralized tooling* in your brain.

Conclusion

This chapter introduced bounded contexts and service boundaries. You have to find these boundaries with the domain in mind. There is no right or wrong solution, but there are different design possibilities.

Business processes often touch multiple contexts and services. This is fine, but you need to make sure that every executable process is clearly owned by exactly one service, and that you avoid process monoliths. Having a workflow engine available within your services helps you to deal with long-running requirements in those services, which will allow you to defend these boundaries. Sketching end-to-end processes can help you find or validate your boundaries.

The chapter also discussed that while you can use BPMN mechanisms (the call activity) to invoke subprocesses in the same workflow engine, this capability should not be used to invoke processes from another context. For such a scenario, a normal API between services should be used.

This is a great foundation for looking at how processes are automated when multiple contexts or services are involved, which is the topic of the next chapter.

CHAPTER 8

Balancing Orchestration and Choreography

Connected to the rise of microservices are *event-driven architectures*. In these architectures, services emit events whenever something substantial happens; other services can then react to these events. This is known as *choreography*.

You might ask yourself why you need to read about this in a book about process automation. It's such a good question that it will take this full chapter to answer.

This chapter:

- Introduces events
- Explains how processes can be implemented solely by choreography and event chains
- Discusses the trade-offs of event chains when automating processes
- Describes how orchestration differs from choreography and how both communication styles can be balanced
- Explains the role of workflow engines in these architectures
- Debunks common myths around orchestration and choreography

Event-Driven Systems

Event-driven systems have become increasingly popular over the last few years. The main reasons to build event-driven systems are the desire for team autonomy and the need to build decoupled systems.

Let's look at an example in order to understand how this can be achieved. Think back to the order fulfillment example introduced a couple of times in this book already.

Assume there is a requirement that customers should receive notifications if anything of interest happens, like the order having been placed, accepted, or shipped.

All microservices can publish events. Events refer to things that happened in the past. These can be technical events, like "mouse moved" or "mouse clicked" events in user interfaces, or they can be about domain events that carry business domain knowledge. In the order fulfillment example, the order status events are domain events.

You can now build an autonomous notification service that listens to these domain events and sends customer notifications at its own discretion. This is shown in Figure 8-1.

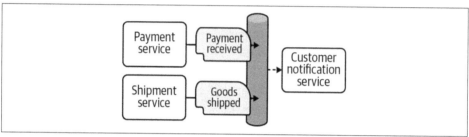

Figure 8-1. Events can be used by an autonomous microservice to implement notifications

This is great, for two reasons. First, during implementation the notification team does not have to talk to any of the other microservice teams. It can simply use the specifications of the events other services emit.

Second, no other microservice team has to think about sending notifications. For example, the payment service does not need to decide when to send a notification, and it does not need to know anything about how to send notifications to customers.

So in this situation, using events enables more autonomy in your architecture.

Another example is visualized in Figure 8-2. Assume that the checkout service should give feedback to the user if the ordered item is in stock and can be shipped right away. In order to answer the question of whether something is in stock, the checkout service can ask the inventory service about the amount of that item in stock, awaiting some response (as shown on the left). This leads to at least a temporal coupling, as the checkout service cannot answer that question if the inventory service is not available.

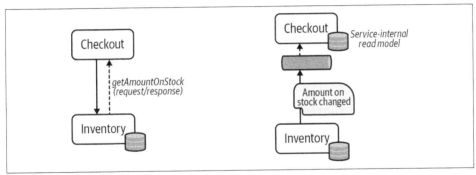

Figure 8-2. You can use events to avoid request/response calls

In the event-driven alternative (shown here on the right) the inventory service publishes any change to the amount of in-stock items as an event. For example, these events may be broadcast to a company-wide event bus. The checkout service can listen to these events and use that information to calculate and store the current amount of an item that is in stock itself. This allows it to answer any in-stock questions locally, without requiring a remote call. This reduces temporal coupling, and it might even result in a more fortunate load distribution toward the inventory service, since the company's website can use the same mechanism—which means if you have millions of page views, you don't have to request the amount that is currently in stock millions of times.

Again, like everything in life, this comes with a price; here the costs are basically increased storage requirements and eventual consistency. Storage gets cheaper almost by the hour and is typically not such a big concern, but eventual consistency can really bite you. In this example, the data on the amount in stock might be milliseconds or seconds old, as some events may not have been processed yet. This can lead to inconsistencies, such as promising fast delivery for something that just went out of stock. Some degree of potential inconsistency is typically tolerable and a necessary trade-off in distributed systems, but still, you have to be aware of it.

The most important characteristic of an event is that the component emitting the event does not know who reacts to it, or why. And it should not care, either.

For example, the mouse driver definitely does not care if a mouse click leads to a reaction in the user interface. A sensor does not care if a detected movement leads to an action. The payment service should not care what happens when it emits a payment received event. And the inventory service sends its "stock changed" events without any expectation that somebody is using them.

This will be explored further in "Designing Responsibilities" on page 165.

Emergent Behavior

Event-driven systems consist of components emitting events that do not know what will happen with them, and components reacting to those events. A very important property of these systems is *emergent behavior*. This is behavior that is only visible during runtime through observation. It is not necessarily designed up front, but emerges out of reactive components at play. This does not have to be bad, and choosing an event-driven architecture is often a deliberate decision to move in that direction.

But it comes at a price that you need to understand. There are situations where you can leverage the flexibility it gives you, but there are also situations where you need to avoid the chaos it can cause. That chaos can lead to a scenario where you don't understand your system anymore. Understanding where this tipping point is can mean the difference between success and failure. As Martin Fowler (*https://martinfowler.com/articles/microservices.html*) warns, "While many pundits praise the value of serendipitous emergence, the truth is that emergent behavior can sometimes be a bad thing."

We as an industry still need to fully understand what a healthy level of emergent behavior is. Earlier in this chapter, you saw use cases where emergent behavior can be considered good practice. Let's also look at some examples where emergent behavior is problematic. This is basically the case if there are chains of events that implement a business process, as in the next section.

Event Chains

In the order fulfillment example, domain events could also be used to implement the order fulfillment business process. In this case, the payment service could listen to order placed events from the checkout service, retrieving payments for each placed order. Processing a payment would lead to a payment received event, which the inventory service would listen to. This scenario is visualized in Figure 8-3.

At first glance, it seems that this would increase autonomy, as the different microservice teams can each work on their own and the end-to-end order fulfillment functionality emerges out of the interaction of the microservices. But this scenario is different; there is a relationship between the event subscriptions, resulting in an *event chain*.

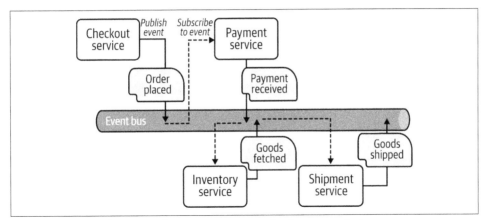

Figure 8-3. Multiple event subscriptions in a row lead to event chains

An event chain is a series of event subscriptions that really implement a logical flow or business process, so that these event subscriptions are not independent.

In this case you want the tasks to happen in a certain order, e.g., to make sure you receive payment before you actually ship anything. But there is no place where you can understand or even control this sequence.

You also want somebody to be responsible for the end-to-end fulfillment, for example to make sure every order is delivered within the promised SLA. This is a very important observation: there is someone within the organization who cares about order fulfillment, and it is very likely that this person is responsible and held accountable for meeting the SLA. From their perspective, it is completely inappropriate that the implementation of the business process emerges and thus relies on events being picked up by the right service at the right time.

These characteristics lead to some severe challenges with event chains, as Martin Fowler (*https://oreil.ly/mHUl6*) has described:

> Event notification is nice because it implies a low level of coupling, and is pretty simple to set up. It can become problematic, however, if there really is a logical flow that runs over various event notifications. The problem is that it can be hard to see such a flow as it's not explicit in any program text. Often the only way to figure out this flow is from monitoring a live system. This can make it hard to debug and modify such a flow. The danger is that it's very easy to make nicely decoupled systems with event notification, without realizing that you're losing sight of that larger-scale flow, and thus set yourself up for trouble in future years. The pattern is still very useful, but you have to be careful of the trap.

Changing the chain affects multiple components

Assume that a business department wants to fetch the goods from the warehouse before payment is received. The reason could be that they want to make sure the goods are really in stock and can be fetched as expected before taking the customer's money.

This requirement affects the sequence of tasks. This is a worst-case scenario for an event chain, as such changes cannot be made locally in one service. Instead, you have to change multiple microservices, which is exactly what you want to avoid in a microservices architecture that emphasizes the autonomy of single services.

Now the payment service must not listen to the order placed event (or at least it must not retrieve the payment when it first receives that event). Instead, it needs to listen to the order fetched event. At the same time, the inventory service must fetch goods as soon as the order placed event is received, but it needs to ignore the payment received event. And finally, the shipment service needs to listen to payment received instead of goods fetched. The two event flows are visualized in Figure 8-4.

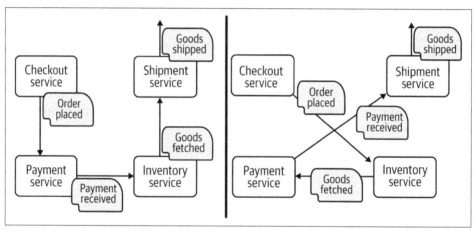

Figure 8-4. A simple change in the sequence requires three services to change (left: old; right: new event flow)

And not only do you have to understand and make these changes, but you also have to coordinate their deployment. In essence, this means that three microservice teams need to get together to discuss this change, come up with a joint time plan, and finally agree on a collective deployment (or a plan to evolve versions incrementally). If this reminds you more of a monolith than microservices, I agree.

On top of that, you also have a distributed versioning problem to solve. For every order flowing through your system, you will need to know if it was started for the old or new sequence. And especially if orders are long-running and stay in the system for a couple of hours or days, you will have orders circulating when you deploy changes.

Of course, you could probably design the event chain differently: perhaps so that the shipment service listens to both events (payment received and goods fetched), or so the inventory and payment services both listen to order placed in the first place. These chains could be a bit more fortunate and lead to fewer changes. But keep in mind that there are often business reasons to have a certain sequence, and that it's also not easy to oversee these dependencies. Also, you often don't design event flows; they emerge.

I have seen one pattern occur at various startups that dealt with a handful of microservices and a comprehensible number of events at the beginning. The events and the event bus helped them to develop the various microservices independently. One microservice could add new functionalities based on the available events, making this quick and easy. They created event chains on the way.

But after some time, the tide turned. When the company needed to change existing functionality, they had a hard time figuring out how to exactly do this. They often did not know where this or that event was used and what ripple effects a change might cause. During incidents you heard people saying that "this cannot be done by our system" or "this functionality was never implemented that way."

 Events might make it easy to add new functionality, but this comes at the price of making it much harder to make changes to an event chain.

Of course, you can consciously decide to build upon event chains to gain development speed in an early stage, being fully aware of the downsides in the long run. Just be sure you keep track of the technical debt.

Lack of visibility

Event chains are hard to understand, basically because of the lack of visibility into these chains. As the interaction of the microservices is decentralized, it is scattered across multiple codebases. You have to reason over all of them to understand the big picture.

Many projects actually do this. They run a workshop and draw a picture that is completely detached from the real codebase—and thus it is outdated the moment it is finished.

There are also tools that focus on examining the runtime behavior, and tracking the events flowing around. Tools in this category with a focus on the business process are just starting to emerge. Chapter 11 looks into this topic in depth; for now, let's just assume that the lack of visibility into how processes work in general is a challenge in event-driven systems.

There is a specifically important aspect to visibility when it comes to operating such a system, however. Whenever something goes wrong, you need to diagnose and fix the failure. In a choreography, this becomes difficult because of the missing context. A failure in one microservice cannot easily be traced back to where the event chain originates. If you have malformed data, it can take a lot of effort to understand why it is there. And you might not be aware of what next steps are currently blocked by these incidents, making workarounds very hard. These kind of problems will be further described in "Poisoned and Dead Messages" on page 181.

The Risk of Distributed Monoliths

While systems are typically designed in an event-driven way to reduce coupling, you can accidentally end up with *increased* coupling. Let's look at a real-life anecdote, where applying a dogmatic event-driven approach led to a distributed monolith.

This project was building a document management system. As part of their domain, they had pages and attachments. But they also had to clarify authorizations: every new page that got created required authorization entries to be created, to name an example.

They started with an event-driven setup. The page microservice simply published a page created event, and the authorization service could pick it up and create the required authorization entry, as shown in Figure 8-5.

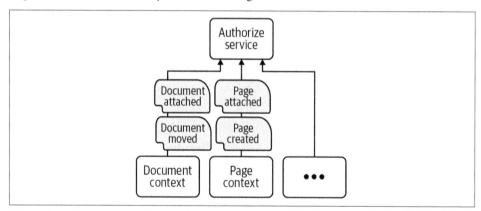

Figure 8-5. The central authorization service needs to know many concepts from other contexts

While this looks nicely decoupled, it means that the authorization service has to know about page created events, document attached events, and so on.

The result was that the microservices were coupled in an unfortunate way. They ended up in a situation where they had to redeploy the authorization service whenever they made changes in other parts of the system, as this led to new event types that the authorization service also needed to understand. This is known as a distributed monolith, where you have a codebase that needs to be treated as one, but it's kept and deployed in a distributed way. This is not a nice place to be in.

They finally refactored the system so that the authorization service provided a clear API that all other microservices have a responsibility to call if they need to propagate changes to the authorizations. This is visualized in Figure 8-6.

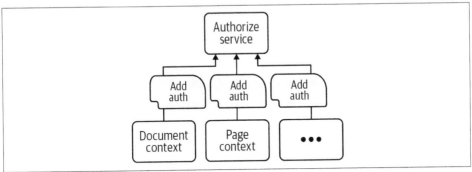

Figure 8-6. The authorization service provides a stable API and the other contexts are responsible for using it

You still have coupling, but this design leads to a very stable authorization service. The decisions about which actions need to be taken based on which event are moved to the microservices with the domain knowledge; e.g., the one that cares about pages.

Contrasting Orchestration and Choreography

The API of the authorization service mentioned in the last section is command-based. This seems to be something different from an event. Let's explore this a bit further to shed some light on the difference between orchestration and choreography.

Introducing Commands

To recap: an event is something that happened, a fact. Component A emits the event to let the world know, but it does not have any expectations about what needs to happen based on this event. Component B might or might not decide to react to the event.

In contrast, component A can also send a command to component B. That means that A wants B to do something. There is a clear intent, and B is not able to simply ignore that command.

An event does not know who picks it up or why. The component emitting the event should not even care. If it wants something to happen, what it sends is not an event, but a command.

I often use the metaphor of a tweet to explain this distinction. If you tweet that you just got hungry, this is an event. It is broadcasted to the world, and it might lead to some action, maybe even having a real impact, such as a follower bringing some food to you (if you're luckier than me). But more likely, it is totally ignored, and maybe not even read by anyone. This is OK for an event.

The situation is different for a command. Imagine that you send an email to your favorite local restaurant to order a food delivery. Now you have a clear intent: you expect them to prepare and deliver your food. You would not use a tweet to order something at a restaurant.

Note that this is independent of the communication protocol. With both Twitter and email we use asynchronous communication, but we have very different expectations of what will happen. And the same difference can be observed with synchronous communication. If you pick up the phone and call someone (synchronous communication), you can say, "Hey, I'm hungry" (event) or "Hello, I want to order something" (command). The type of content is independent of the communication channel.

For some people, the term *command* suggests that a command cannot be rejected. This is not true, as the restaurant could very well respond with a rejection of your order (perhaps because your favorite dish is out of stock today). The important aspect is that they need to respond, and they cannot ignore your order.

This points out another aspect of commands, which is that most often there is a feedback loop, like an acknowledgment of the command or even a response. While this is not a necessity for every command, there is a simple logic behind this: if you want another component to do something for you, you want to make sure it receives the command and eventually handles it. You don't feel good if you don't get any feedback if the command arrived.

To resume the example of ordering lunch: when you send the order via email, you might not feel very confident that it will have the desired outcome, unless you get an email response. Or it also feels better if you order via some shop interface that confirms your order right away. But in both scenarios, the feedback loop is not the final response, you are only happy if the meal is really prepared and delivered to you.

Messages, Events, and Commands

Events and commands have very different semantics, but they are both payloads of some communication, typically a message. It is important to note that events and commands are characterized by their semantics, not the technical protocol. For example, you can implement commands via REST, but you can also use REST feeds to implement events, even if this is rarely done in real life. You can also send commands via asynchronous messages—typically messages put in a queue for a dedicated recipient—whereas events are typically messages distributed via topics to an arbitrary number of recipients.

Now it is really important to be precise what you are talking about, whether it is the means of transport (message) or the type of payload (event or command). With the rise of event broker technologies like Apache Kafka, I saw many companies struggling with mixing up terms.

This is happening because in Kafka itself, there is no notion of messages: Kafka stores *records*. The term *record* is used instead of message because the records are stored persistently, in contrast to messaging systems that pass on the messages and then forget about them. But a lot of developers are not precise in their language and use the term *event* instead of *record*, as they think of Kafka as an *event bus*. This means you will face two different definitions of *event* in these companies, as visualized in Figure 8-7.

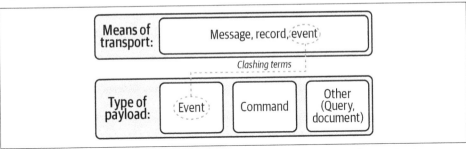

Figure 8-7. When people say "event" they might be referring to a real event in the payload or the message containing the event; this can cause confusion

This can lead to the belief that everything is an event and Kafka cannot handle commands. But this is not true; you can certainly write a command as a Kafka record.

There is a related risk of the anti pattern called *commands in disguise*. If developers believe that everything needs to be sent as an event, commands are shoehorned into (disguised as) events. If you see a "The Customer Needs to Be Sent a Notification About Their Order Event," it is clearly not an event, as the sender wants something to happen. The sender has an intent. It is a command and should be treated as such. Using "Send Message" would be much clearer.

Terminology and Definitions

The discussion of events and commands paves the way for defining *orchestration* and *choreography*. Unfortunately, there isn't a single concise definition of these terms from a globally accepted source. As misunderstandings can lead to wrong conclusions and bad decisions, let's define these terms in the context of this book:

- Command-driven communication = orchestration
- Event-driven communication = choreography

Chapter 4 covered orchestration in great detail and described how a workflow engine can orchestrate anything, from humans to IT systems and services. In this sense, orchestration really means coordinating activities or tasks. This is not limited to workflow engines. Generally, you speak about orchestration if you have a component that coordinates one or more other components. This means that the component sends commands.

In a choreography, components interact directly with each other in an event-driven way in order to get something done.

An important consequence of this definition is that it focuses on a single communication link and not on the system as a whole. This means that it seldom makes sense to say that you designed a "choreographed system." Still, I hear these oversimplifications too often.

In a good architecture, you will find both communication styles: orchestration and choreography. Very often it is a wild mix and you might not even realize that you are using orchestration, for example when you "just" call this one other service.

I often prefer to talk about event-based or command-based interactions, as the terms orchestration and choreography can add more confusion than they resolve.

Avoiding Event Chains by Using Commands

Let's revisit the fulfillment example from the beginning of this chapter and try to improve the architecture and solve the challenges around the event chain.

In particular, we need to address the responsibility of the overall business process to fulfill an order. Designing responsibility is a common theme; this chapter will explore it in more depth soon. In this specific example, it is very likely that this leads to a separate order fulfillment microservice, as the responsibility does not fit into payment, inventory, checkout, or shipment.

It might be OK for the checkout service to emit an order placed event, as the checkout team is not at all responsible for making sure an order is delivered. The order fulfillment microservice can subscribe to that event, but from there it is responsible for taking all actions that are required (see Figure 8-8).

The order fulfillment microservice first has to make sure that the payment will be retrieved for this order. Having an intent translates to a command. So the order fulfillment service sends that command and waits for payment to be received, probably indicated by the payment received event mentioned earlier. Then the order fulfillment microservice can send a command to the inventory microservice, telling it what goods to fetch from the warehouse. This way, the order fulfillment microservice can control the sequence of things.

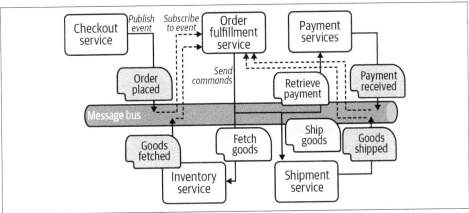

Figure 8-8. All important responsibilities need a home, like the overall order fulfillment

Note that the responsibilities are clearly defined. The order microservice is responsible for the order fulfillment, and it will command other services on its journey. The reason for this is that it cares about payment being retrieved, goods being fetched, and so on.

The payment service is "only" responsible for safely and reliably collecting money. And by listening to a certain command, the pament team is not forced to understand events like "order placed." They don't need to know what exactly they are retrieving payments for or when exactly this has to happen in the overall process.

This is also a beneficial design once there is another client retrieving payments. For example, say that your company also offers some subscriptions, or sells downloadable assets instead of physically shipped goods, as visualized in Figure 8-9.

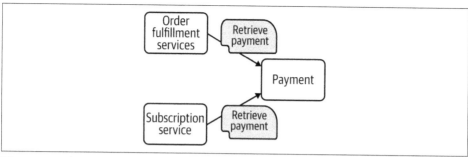

Figure 8-9. The payment team does not need to know who is retrieving payments; its responsibility is collecting the money reliably when commanded

This change does not need the payment service to adjust at all, whereas an event-based API would require a change in the payment service. Taking this thought to the extreme, can you imagine a SaaS payment provider offering an event-based API, where you even have no guarantee about what happens with that event?

> The more general a component is, the less it should be required to change if other services need to communicate with it. A command-based API is typically preferrable in this case.

A very different example is the sending of order notifications mentioned at the beginning of the chapter. In this case, the order fulfillment team might not be responsible for whether or not the order notification emails are sent out correctly. Exaggerating a bit, they don't care.

Hence, event-based communication is great for this. The notification service takes responsibility for sending notifications to the customers. It will take care of data security concerns and the customer's preferred way of communication. This frees all other services of this responsibility.

But if you design a company-wide notification service that can send any type of notification, like about orders, payments, subscriptions, news, and so on, this service should probably not know about events from order fulfillment. So, you might need an additional order notification service responsible for translating the events into the right commands, as shown in Figure 8-10.

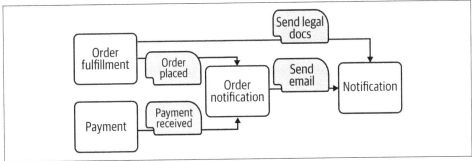

Figure 8-10. Notifications can be event- or command-driven, based on their scope and designed responsibilities

As you can see, you need to understand your organization and the different components' responsibilities to decide whether to use events or commands for a certain type of communication.

The Direction of Dependency

Every communication between two services involves some degree of coupling. An interesting aspect here is that you can choose the direction of dependency, and thus decide which components are coupled to which other components. This is shown in Figure 8-11 for aspects of the order fulfillment example.

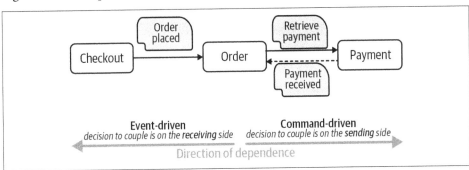

Figure 8-11. With events you couple the receiver, with commands the sender

When a service listens to an event, the receiver is "domain-coupled" to that event. This means it knows on which channel the event will be received, what the event means, and probably the schema of the data attached to it. The direction of dependency is from the receiver to the sender. As you saw earlier in this chapter, this is a good choice for some situations, but it is not a good choice in others.

In contrast, one service could send a command to another. In order to do so the sender has to know what the command means, which channel to send it to, and probably what data to attach to it. The direction of dependency is from the sender to the receiver; the sender is "domain-coupled" to the receiver.

A certain degree of domain coupling is unavoidable if different components need to interact, but you can deliberately decide if it is on the sending or the receiving side. This decision determines whether you will use events or commands.

Finding the Right Balance

You will need to apply events *and* commands, so choreography *and* orchestration, in your architecture. Therefore, you have to find the right balance. As complicated as it sounds, this basically means making a conscious and rational choice about using events versus commands for every single communication link between microservices. Let's explore this.

Deciding Whether to Use Commands or Events

A good litmus test is to ask if it is OK with the component omitting an event if that event is ignored. If so, then it really is an event; if not, you probably have a command in front of you. I am not saying that reactions to events are not important. In the order fulfillment example, sending notification emails is important, and not getting them might be annoying for the customer. Still, it is not a huge problem if this happens, and more importantly, the event approach means that it is not the problem of the order fulfillment team.

This might be different if you have notifications that are required by law. The order fulfillment team might be responsible (and held accountable) for that notification in this case, which motivates using commands.

Of course, you could also design this responsibility differently, but the communication type must match your decision. If order fulfillment is responsible, they should use a command for the notification. Alternatively, you might lay out the responsibilities differently and make the notification team responsible, in which case an event will serve you well.

Mixing Commands and Events

Let's extend the example of the customer onboarding process to find a more balanced view. In his book *Building Microservices* (O'Reilly), Sam Newman also uses that example, but basically he looks at the steps after a customer has been created, as you can see in Figure 8-12.

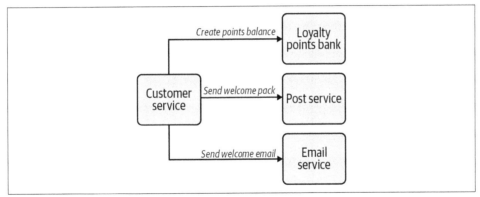

Figure 8-12. Post-customer creation process using orchestration (from Sam Newman: Building Microservices)

He notes that:

> The downside to this orchestration approach is that the customer service can become too much of a central governing authority. It can become the hub in the middle of a web, and a central point where logic starts to live. I have seen this approach result in a small number of smart "god" services telling anemic CRUD-based services what to do.

Sam further advocates using an event to notify other systems that a customer has been created, as visualized in Figure 8-13.

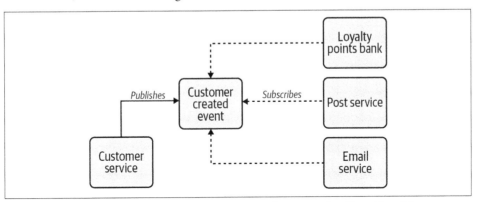

Figure 8-13. Post-customer creation process using choreography (from Sam Newman: Building Microservices)

While I can agree that events might be preferable once a customer is registered, this might not be the case for the pre-checks. Figure 8-14 shows one possible solution for the overall customer onboarding process, visualized as a BPMN collaboration diagram.

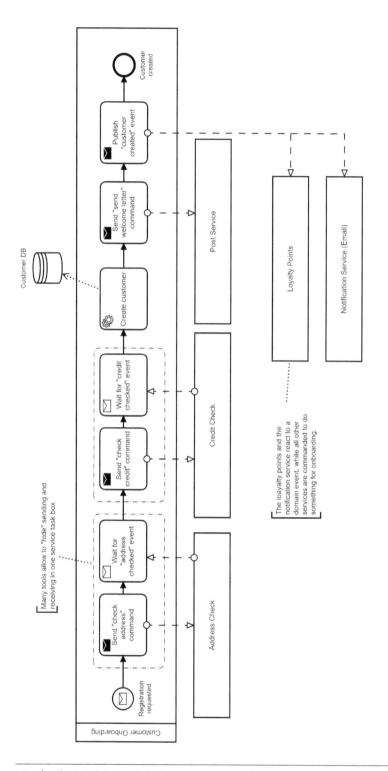

Figure 8-14. The final customer onboarding process can mix orchestration and choreography

Collaboration diagrams will be discussed in more detail in "The Power of One Joined Model" on page 205; they allow you to model the collaboration between different components in your system in one big diagram. The onboarding process itself is most likely implemented in the customer microservice, but possibly also in a separate customer onboarding microservice.

Some parts of the process are best designed using orchestration, whereas others can benefit from choreography. The process commands the address and credit checks, which is clearly orchestration. In a later stage of the process, the customer-created event leads to relevant actions in other microservices, as proposed by Sam. You have to think about events versus commands for every communication at hand.

Designing Responsibilities

This chapter showed that you really need to think about the responsibilities of each component when designing communication links. You should omit events in situations where the sender is not responsible for what happens next, and use commands when the sender is and needs to ensure that something is going to happen.

Let's explore the customer welcome letter in the customer onboarding example a bit further. As you can see in Figure 8-14, this is done by sending a command. Why is this? Why is the service that sends the welcome letter not also listening to the customer-created event?

In this case I assume that the customer onboarding team is responsible for ensuring that this letter is really sent. This might boil down to a legal requirement, which is not uncommon. It is not something the customer onboarding team can "let emerge," meaning they simply assume it will be sent by some component reacting to the right event. They are responsible. Your CEO can approach that team at any time and ask why a certain welcome letter for an important customer was not sent, and they can't point to anybody else who may not have picked up their event; it was their responsibility. Responsibility and accountability go along with the need to control certain communications. Only if they send a command can they pass on the responsibility to the notification service; once that service has received the command, it's then that team's fault if the letter isn't sent.

By contrast, sending the notification email and registering the customer in the loyalty points program might not be the responsibility of the customer onboarding team. This allows that team to maintain its focus. In that case, events would be a great way to go, as the onboarding process does not need to bother about loyalty programs at all. Instead, the loyalty program team develops its solution independently. If a customer is not getting enrolled correctly, your CEO will approach that team, not the customer onboarding folks.

You need to understand how the responsibilities are assigned to the different components. In other words: you need to know which team is held accountable for a certain requirement. This will guide you not only to good boundaries, but also to decisions about events versus commands. If the sending side is responsible, then it cares that something is happening, which means you need to use commands. If the sending side does not care but the receiver is responsible for taking action, you can typically use an event.

Responsibilities are never fixed. You or your organization can design them, and definitely need to do so. This is very much related to designing the boundaries of your microservices. Determining whether to use events (choreography) or commands (orchestration) is simply a result of taking the responsibilities into account.

If you ignore responsibilities, you will end up with teams that can't control what they are held accountable for. This can lead to fingerpointing and frustration.

If you don't design responsibilities correctly, you will build systems that require a lot of discussion and coordination between teams, as you will often have to change multiple parts together. This is exactly what you want to avoid when using microservices.

Evaluating Change Scenarios to Validate Decisions

In order to better understand the differences in coupling, it is helpful to discuss change scenarios. This allows you to predict effects when you need to make changes later. Suppose that for a customer project, you're comparing an orchestrated with a choreographed customer onboarding process.

Initially, the project team strongly believes that the event-driven alternative is less coupled. They want to implement the event chain shown in Figure 8-15, where the registration requested event triggers the credit and address check services. Both of them will eventually emit their results as events, and the customer service will wait for both to happen in order to create the customer.

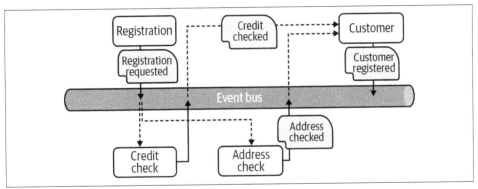

Figure 8-15. Event chain to implement a customer onboarding process

Your observation is that the decision to go down this route was based on lobbying work and the personal conceptions of some key people. It was definitely not backed by proper investigation. To stimulate a good discussion, you find a change scenario that is realistic in this context: adding an additional check to the process. We'll call it a criminal check. Figure 8-16 visualizes the change in the event flow and the microservices that need to be changed accordingly.

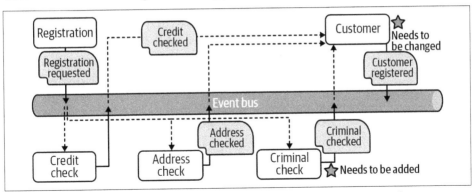

Figure 8-16. Changes required to add one additional check in a choreography

As you can see, in addition to deploying the new check as its own microservice, you also need to adjust and redeploy the customer microservice. This microservice now needs to wait for the new criminal check to provide a result. Of course, you could introduce a separate customer onboarding microservice that handles all of that logic, but that simply moves the problem to another place in the architecture.

In contrast, an orchestrated version of that process is visualized in Figure 8-17. In this case, the customer microservice (or a specific customer onboarding microservice if you prefer) reacts to the registration requested event, but then commands the other checks to do their work.

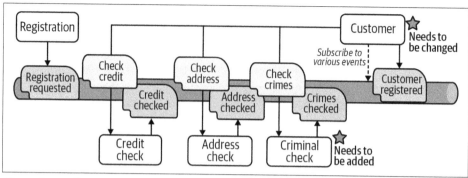

Figure 8-17. Changes required to add one additional check in an orchestration

In order to add the check here, you will have to deploy the new microservice and adjust and redeploy the customer microservice—which are exactly the same changes as in the choreography. This means that the event-driven process is not more decoupled. And in the orchestrated version, you will have a clear location to get visibility into the overall process, whereas in the choreography scenario, that knowledge is spread across the various microservices that are involved.

Note that this example is still overly simplified. In real life, the onboarding process is more complicated, requiring a certain sequence of steps when doing all of these checks. For example, you wouldn't do a credit check if the address were invalid, especially given that credit checks cost real money. A more realistic sequence will increase the number of microservices you have to touch when implementing such a change. Just remind yourself of the example of Figure 8-4, where the fetching of the goods should be done before retrieving the payment. It is hard to change the sequence of an event flow.

Debunking Common Myths

I am regularly confronted with myths about why orchestration should be avoided or why choreography is the way to go. These stories are so common that it is worth taking a quick look at them, not only to be aware of them, but also to understand why they are myths.

Commands Do Not Require Synchronous Communication

A common myth is that commands require you to communicate synchronously, and this leads to temporal coupling (which we touched on in "Strong Cohesion and Low Coupling" on page 127).

But this is not true. As "Messages, Events, and Commands" on page 157 explained, commands (and events) are independent of the communication protocol. The choice between them is not connected to the decision of whether or not to use synchronous or asynchronous communication. Hence, you can mitigate temporal coupling by using asynchronous communication. Now component A can send a command in a message to component B, even if B is not available at that moment. The message will simply wait in the queue.

It is important to understand that temporal coupling results from synchronous communication alone, not from choosing to use commands.

I have even seen one other flavor of this myth: orchestration means that there is one component that coordinates multiple others by using a chain of synchronous blocking requests. Figure 8-18 shows an example, where an order fulfillment service orchestrates by invoking synchronous blocking calls to other microservices.

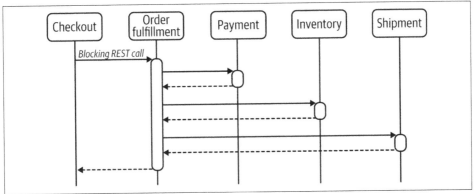

Figure 8-18. A misconception of orchestration: one component handling a lot of synchronous blocking calls

Implementing such a synchronous call chain has severe downsides. First, you will experience latency creeping into your service calls, meaning all the latencies and processing times for the various service calls will add up. This makes the checkout a rather slow experience for the user.

Second, you can see that the availability of order fulfillment erodes, as all required services need to be available at the exact time this call is triggered.

But once again, this problem is not related to the order fulfillment service orchestrating other functionalities; it is rooted in using synchronous communication chains.

 Orchestration does not introduce temporal coupling; synchronous communication does. The problem can be solved by going asynchronous. Orchestration is independent from communication protocols.

Orchestration Does Not Need to Be Central

Following up on the discussion in "Decentralized Engines" on page 117 and "Decentralized Workflow Tooling" on page 144, I want to emphasize once more that orchestration does not need to be centralized in the context of this chapter. You really have to disconnect the terms *orchestration* and *central* in your brain. It sometimes helps to use terms like *local orchestration* or *distributed orchestration* to emphasize this aspect.

Orchestration simply means commanding (or coordinating) another component. Every component can do this; it is not about having a central orchestrator.

Additionally, orchestration is not connected to specific tooling. A workflow engine is a great help to implement long-running orchestration processes. However, a component sending out a command using programming code is also coordinating others, and thus also performs orchestration.

If you succeed in having more open discussions about what orchestration really means, what role events and commands play, and whether tooling in fact needs to be central, then you will have a much better foundation for making great decisions.

 Orchestration is not centralized, even if it was advocated like this back in the SOA days. You can implement it locally in a microservice, probably using a workflow engine.

Choreography Does Not Automatically Lead to More Decoupling

This chapter already described why every communication link between two components leads to coupling. Still, there is a myth that coupling is massively reduced in event-driven architectures.

As a generalization, this is nonsense.

When you use events, you decide to couple on the receiving end of the communication, which of course can be beneficial in some situations. But in others, it is not. You need to make this choice on a case-by-case basis to create a great architecture.

The Role of Workflow Engines

Workflow engines play a vital role in your architecture, independent of whether you use choreography or orchestration. This might be surprising at first, because workflow engines are typically connected to orchestration. Sometimes they are even seen as being in opposition to choreography. But in fact, this is not true. Let's explore how workflow engines can also help out in event-driven systems.

Workflow engines can subscribe to events and start new process instances once a specific event arrives. Alternatively, they can let existing process instances wait for events to happen. For example, suppose you want to wait for two events to happen in a certain time frame, but you need to take action if one doesn't arrive, as visualized in Figure 8-19.

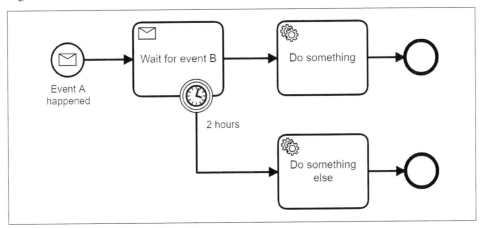

Figure 8-19. A process can react to events

Truth be told, this scenario could also be implemented using event streaming approaches that offer a query language that can take time windows into account. However, not everybody has these technologies at their disposal. And even then, it is often harder to express complex requirements in these declarative approaches than it is to describe a process model. In most situations, you will also need long running-capabilities anyway.

Figure 8-20 shows an example that is typical in real life. The process model reacts to events, but also issues commands. It simply does both. This relates closely to the definitions of orchestration and choreography given in "Contrasting Orchestration and Choreography" on page 155, as the decision is not a global decision, but very much local to every communication link.

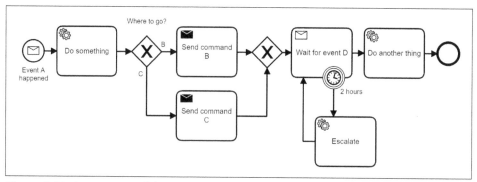

Figure 8-20. A process model can react to events as well as issue commands

Conclusion

This chapter looked at how events can be used to communicate between components. You saw that chains of events can be used to automate processes, which leads to a couple of challenges. These can be better solved with commands.

This led to modern, clear, and precise definitions of orchestration (command-driven communication) and choreography (event-driven communication). Orchestration means coordinating others by using commands, and choreography relates to reacting to events. This is independent of communication protocols and technologies.

You cannot decide whether to use orchestration or choreography on a global level, but need to make the choice each time components need to communicate. The difference comes down to the direction of dependency and the resulting responsibilities of the individual components. Either way, you will have some domain coupling; this is unavoidable.

It is not true that choreography always leads to less coupling than orchestration. While it might be true in some situations, it can also lead to additional coupling and distributed monoliths. This means you need to learn to balance both communication styles.

CHAPTER 9

Workflow Engines and Integration Challenges

Modern systems are typically designed in such a way that components are located on different computers, virtual machines, or containers. Connecting these components requires remote communication, which introduces a lot of new challenges.

This chapter will describe how workflow engines can be applied to some of these challenges. In this context, it:

- Examines communication patterns for service invocations, specifically looking at long-running and asynchronous communication
- Explores consistency problems and transactional guarantees
- Emphasizes the importance of idempotency to make all of this work

Even if you don't plan to use a microservices architecture, reading this chapter will still be valuable, as almost every system has some remote calls somewhere. The concepts described here apply even if it's just one simple REST call.

Communication Patterns for Service Invocation

There are different possible communication patterns when you invoke services from your process. Let's first have a look at synchronous communication before we dive into asynchronous communication.

Synchronous Request/Response

The typical example of synchronous request/response is a REST call. In order to invoke such a REST call in a BPMN process model, you leverage a service task, as introduced in "Business Process Model and Notation (BPMN)" on page 45 in Chapter 3. The process will wait in this service task until the REST call returns a response as indicated in Figure 9-1.

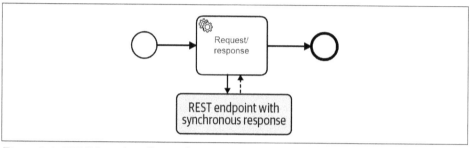

Figure 9-1. BPMN can handle synchronous communication with service tasks

This simple service call can hide quite a bit of complexity under the hood. Remote communication is inherently unreliable, as illustrated by the fallacies of distributed computing (*https://oreil.ly/1BrI9*) as described by Peter Deutsch and others at Sun Microsystems. Remote services might not be available, or might respond very slowly. This quickly imposes a requirement to make your own service long-running, as you have to wait either for those services to become available or for the responses to arrive. This is often forgotten in reality, leading to architecture smells.

In order to explain this, let's start with a real-life example. I was getting ready to fly to London. When I got the check-in invitation, I went to the airline's website, selected my seat, and hit the button to retrieve my boarding pass. This triggered a synchronous REST call in the background. It gave me the following response: "We are having some technical difficulties at the moment, please try again in five minutes."

Let's assume for a moment that the airline uses separate services for all the parts of this process, as shown in Figure 9-2. Let's further assume that these services communicate via REST calls. That means the check-in service will block its thread waiting for a barcode service to return. But what happens if the barcode service does not respond? The sketched design offloads failure handling to the client; in this case me. I personally had to do the retry. In fact, I had to wait until the next day before the problems were resolved and I could get my boarding pass. That meant I had to use my own tooling to persist the retry (my calendar) to make sure I did not forget.

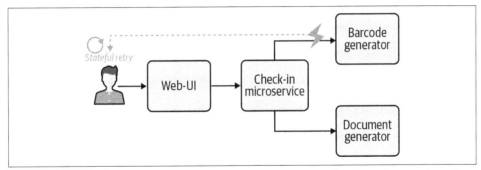

Figure 9-2. Errors are often propagated to the first service in the chain that can handle state; in the example of issuing a boarding pass this is the human making the request

Why wouldn't the airline just do the retrying themselves? They know the customer's contact data and could send the boarding pass asynchronously whenever it was ready. That would not only be much more convenient but also reduce the overall complexity, by minimizing the number of components that need to see the failure.

Whenever a service can resolve failures itself, it encapsulates important behavior. This makes the lives of all clients much easier and the API much cleaner, as Chapter 7 already described. Of course, the behavior of passing errors on to the client can be just fine in some cases—but it should be a conscious decision that is made according to business requirements.

That's not what I observe in real life. It is much more often the case that teams understand that this kind of failure resolution requires state handling, and they don't want to introduce this complexity, as discussed in "Wild West Integrations" on page 4.

In the boarding pass example, a stateful retry should happen in the check-in service to keep the error local. Using a workflow engine within that service is one possible solution to handle that state, as well as the scheduling capabilities to trigger additional retries. As explained earlier in this book, the state will be held in the workflow engine that is logically owned by the service.

Making services stateful helps to keep problems local. And while the behavior for retrying is not baked into the BPMN language, vendors typically provide extensions that make it easy to handle. You might end up with a very simple processes like the one in Figure 9-3.

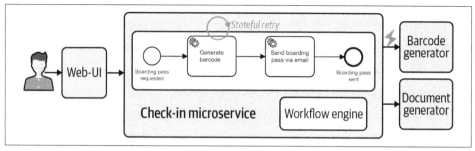

Figure 9-3. Having the responsible service handle retries

You might have recognized that I slowly introduced asynchronicity here. If a service call to the barcode generator is retried for several minutes, the check-in service can't return a synchronous response. If you look at the source code on the book's website (*https://ProcessAutomationBook.com*), you will see that the check-in service will return an HTTP 202 status code in this case, which means that the service accepted the request and will process it some time later.

So this is already asynchronous communication, which will be described in the next section. Later in this chapter you'll also see that you might still be able to keep a synchronous facade wherever you need it.

Asynchronous Request/Response

Asynchronous communication refers to nonblocking communication; the service sending a request does not wait for a reply but is happy as long as the sending worked. Although the REST example in the last section might qualify, asynchronous communication is typically the domain of messaging systems.

Messaging systems can make systems more robust, as they remove temporal coupling. If services need to wait for replies, the API of a messaging system makes it clear that waiting for that reply message can take time. This forces developers to think about what happens if a response does not arrive within a certain time frame, which is typically beneficial for the resulting source code.

In essence, asynchronous communication makes it transparent that the communication itself can become long-running. Long-running? You got it, this is where a workflow engine can help.

Say you have a business requirement that your service needs to wait for an answer to a certain request before it can actually continue. That response might take some time and is delivered asynchronously. You can handle this situation with the BPMN process model shown in Figure 9-4.

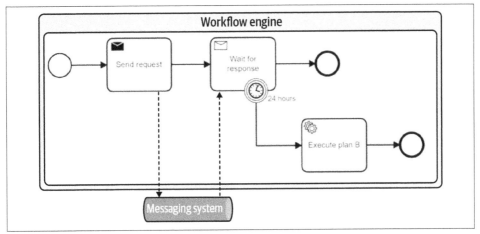

Figure 9-4. BPMN can handle asynchronous communication and take care of timeouts

This example shows that you can easily model timeouts to act on delays. And having a workflow engine in place makes it possible to wait not only for milliseconds, but for minutes or days.

In order to support asynchronous communication, workflow engines offer correlation mechanisms to find the right waiting process instance. Suppose you send out a message to retrieve payment that includes a transaction ID. When the response arrives, it also carries this transaction ID, allowing the workflow engine to identify the process instance waiting for that response.

The following rules have proven themselves in real life for correlation:

- Use artificial IDs like a UUID that is generated just for that communication. When you send a payment request, you generate a new UUID in the client and store it locally in the client (e.g., in its process variables). This ID serves solely for correlation for that single communication, which means that you won't get any interference.

- Don't use IDs from the workflow engine, like process instance IDs. If you need to restart a process instance for operations purposes, it might end up with a different ID, or your workflow engine vendor might change how IDs are generated, in a way that doesn't work at your end. Think of all the applications that used numeric IDs and are now confronted with UUIDs, which are strings.

- Be careful with using business data, like the ID of the order for which the payment is taken. While this is often straightforward and can work well, it has some risks. For example, if for some reason you split the payment into two parts, you'll have two payments for the same order ID at the same time, and you won't be able to correlate the responses distinctly.

BPMN also allows you to combine the send and receive tasks within one service task, as visualized in Figure 9-5.

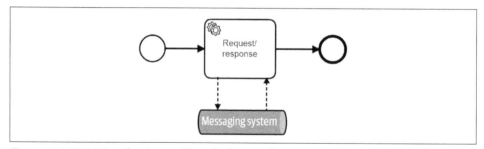

Figure 9-5. BPMN makes it possible to hide asynchronous communication behind a simple service task

This often makes the process model a bit simpler to understand, and hence communication with business stakeholders easier. It can also remove clutter if you use asynchronous communication all over the place.

BPMN and Being Ready to Receive

There is one small but potentially problematic detail in BPMN related to the timing of the incoming messages. The BPMN standard defines message correlation in such a way that a process instance needs to be ready to receive that specific message at the exact time the message arrives. So, strictly speaking, when no token for a specific process instance is waiting in the receive task, incoming messages cannot be correlated and are dumped.

Spoiler alert: some workflow engines allow you to buffer incoming messages with a defined time to live, which gives the process instance enough time to arrive at the receive task.

But let's first explore this issue by looking at a real-life scenario I experienced, which is shown in Figure 9-6. The problem might be a bit surprising at first.

In this case, the process called some external system via SOAP. The SOAP reply just acknowledged that the request was received. The real response was sent via an asynchronous message. For some reason, unwrapping the SOAP reply and committing the process instance at hand took longer than it took for the response to arrive via the messaging system. This led to errors when the response messages were correlated, because the process instances were not yet ready to receive them. It was a matter of milliseconds, but it led to exceptions.

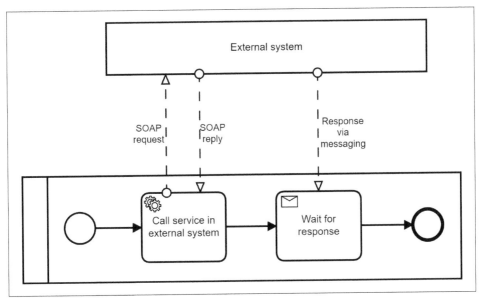

Figure 9-6. A process must be ready to receive the response message when it arrives

The biggest problem was that nobody understood this situation. Looking at the operations tool showed a process instance waiting for the message, yet response messages resulted in exceptions stating that there was no process instance waiting for them.

It took me a while to explain the issue to various stakeholders in that project. I could only convince the developers that this was happening by adding a `Thread.sleep` instruction when a message arrived. This code waited 100 ms before actually correlating the message, which resolved the problem at hand. The final solution was to retry correlating the message, as it only took a few milliseconds for the process to become ready to receive. This way, we leveraged the buffering capabilities of a messaging system.

But this is an unsatisfying solution, for a few reasons. First, it only works when you use communication mechanisms that can buffer, like messages; otherwise, you have to implement some bespoke mechanisms. Second, developers need to understand the situation and acknowledge that errors during message correlation are kind of normal.

So, message buffering in a BPMN workflow engine is a helpful feature. It frees you from worrying about all these dirty details. In this example, the response message would simply have been correlated whenever the process instance arrived in the receive task. Unfortunately, message buffering is a proprietary vendor addition to the BPMN standard, so you need to check if your vendor can provide it. Whenever you have it at your disposal, make use of it!

Aggregating Messages

Process models also allow the expression of more sophisticated patterns around message exchanges, like the *aggregator* (*https://oreil.ly/PxzX3*), as described in *Enterprise Integration Patterns* by Gregor Hohpe and Bobby Woolf (Addison-Wesley):

> Use a stateful filter, an Aggregator, to collect and store individual messages until a complete set of related messages has been received. Then, the Aggregator publishes a single message distilled from the individual messages.

As you guessed, the word "stateful" hints at a workflow engine. You can implement such an aggregator with BPMN as shown in Figure 9-7.

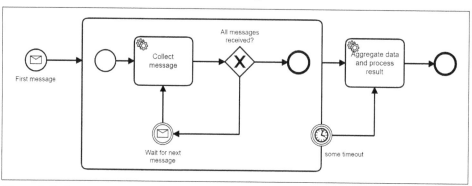

Figure 9-7. An aggregator implemented with BPMN

The workflow engine gives you persistent state as well as easy timeout handling. Of course, this is not limited to a generic aggregator. Oftentimes, you simply need to collect a couple of messages in one specific business scenario, as shown in Figure 9-8.

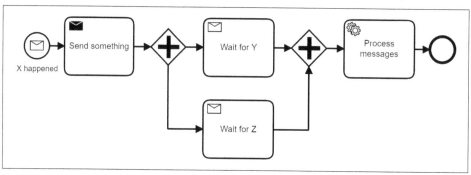

Figure 9-8. Aggregating messages in a process

Remember that you might need message buffering at your disposal to safely execute these models and avoid process instances not being ready to receive at the right moment in time. If your workflow engine doesn't support this, you can find some possible workarounds on the book's website (*https://ProcessAutomationBook.com*).

Poisoned and Dead Messages

Speaking of asynchronous communication and messaging systems, I don't want to leave you without a word of warning. Don't get me wrong, I'm a big fan of asynchronous communication, but I also see a lot of companies and projects struggle with the complexities around it.

My favorite examples are so-called *poisoned messages*. Suppose your service receives new customer orders via messaging. There is a bug in the frontend that puts some broken data into that message, making it "poisoned." Your service will throw exceptions when processing the message.

There is no client you can hand this exception to, so the messaging system has to deal with it. The default is to retry the message, which will not really help, just increase the load. After all the retries are used up, the message is typically put into the dead letter queue (DLQ). But now what?

Even today, most tools don't provide proper user interfaces to monitor the DLQ, inspect the messages, and redeliver them. Customers are forced to build bespoke message hospitals to handle these situations well.

But even if you have the tooling, diagnosing failure reasons is not easy, as a failed message does not provide much context around where that data originally came from. If you receive orders via different channels and route that data through a couple of services, it will take some forensic practices to find the root problem.

This is another great motivation for using executable process models instead of data flowing through various queues, as described in "Data Pipelines and Streaming" on page 96. With a workflow engine, a failed process instance gives you a lot of context about where it started, what path it took, and what data is attached.

Synchronous Facades Hiding Asynchronous Communication

Sometimes you will be forced to provide a synchronous API for certain clients, especially frontends. This becomes a challenge if your architecture embraces asynchronous communication or long-running processes.

The solution to this problem is typically to create a facade that provides a synchronous API, for example via REST. Internally, this facade needs to block and wait for the response that is provided asynchronously:

```
try {
  sendRequestToServiceB(correlationId, ...)
  response = waitForResponseFromServiceB(correlationId, timeout)
  // ...
}
catch (timeoutError) {
  // ?
}
```

There are three ways to receive that response:

- You subscribe to the channel that delivers a response message.
- You provide a callback API.
- You regularly poll to see if the result is available.

All of them have trade-offs, and which to choose depends on your architecture. One thing all of these have in common is that you have to think about timeouts, as you can't wait and block forever. This also implies that you need to think about what to do if there is no response within a certain timeout.

One pattern I regularly see is to return synchronously when everything is all right, and as soon as there is an error fall back to asynchronous processing.

For instance, in the check-in example from "Synchronous Request/Response" on page 174, the check-in service can return a boarding pass synchronously only when everything runs smoothly. This could be easily reflected with HTTP return code 200, meaning "All OK, here is your result." If there is any glitch that prevents the service from creating its result immediately, you instead respond with HTTP 202, which means "Got it, I'll call you back." And then you send the boarding pass via email later on. The source code on this book's website (*https://ProcessAutomationBook.com*) includes a concrete code example.

Of course, switching to asynchronous responses will affect the user experience. Users might not get their boarding passes right away. Is this good or bad? You can dive deeper into that interesting question in "Rethinking Business Processes and the User Experience" on page 262. Spoiler: it's a good thing. Isn't it so much better to receive your boarding pass successfully later than to get an error message right now leaving you alone with the problem?

Transactions and Consistency

Let's switch gears and consider the challenges with transactions in distributed systems. To do this, we'll look again at the example of onboarding new customers.

Remember that we need to insert customers into the CRM and billing systems. In a monolithic application, you simply have different tables in the same database, which allows you to do this in one transaction as illustrated in Figure 9-9. The database offers ACID guarantees: transactions are atomic, consistent, isolated, and durable. If the customer cannot be added into the billing table for whatever reason, such as duplicate or invalid values, the database can simply roll back the transaction. This leads to the customer also being nonexistent in the CRM system. ACID transactions therefore guarantee consistency within the boundary, which monoliths can leverage to offload complexity to the transaction layer.

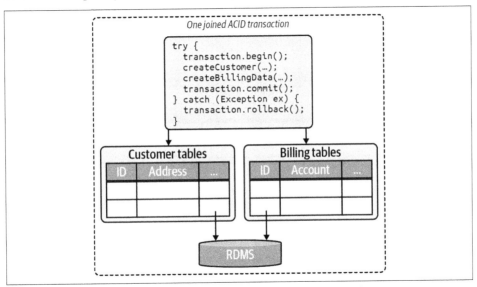

Figure 9-9. ACID transactions ensure consistency within the boundary

If two concurrent threads try to write the same data, the database guarantees isolation, which can be implemented by optimistic or pessimistic locking. This leads to one thread winning and the other getting an exception. The failed transaction is automatically rolled back, as database operations are atomic, meaning all of them are done, or none.

This architecture makes it incredibly easy to implement atomic operations, isolate different threads, and guarantee consistency of data. The business logic can offload a lot of complexity onto the transaction layer of the database.

But in order to do this, the requirements are that all data is in the same database and the application uses a joined database connection. This is only realistic in a monolith, not in a distributed system.

In the onboarding example, CRM and billing are more likely to be two separate services. The onboarding service accesses them via remote communication. Now each service might have its own ACID transaction, but there is no joined one, as illustrated in Figure 9-10.

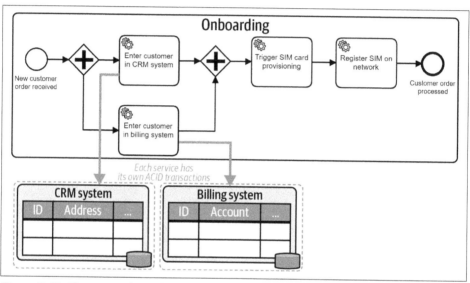

Figure 9-10. If you cross boundaries, you can't do ACID transactions

Therefore, it might happen that a customer exists in the CRM system, even if they have not yet been created in the billing system. This violates the ACID property of isolation, as some outside thread (or human) may be able to see this state already. Furthermore, you have to think about what to do when you hit a problem in billing because you can't roll back the CRM system, meaning the entry will remain there.

Such challenges are typical in modern systems, for a few reasons:

- Components get more and more distributed. And even if there are technologies that offer distributed ACID transactions, like the two-phase commit protocol known as XA, these technologies are either very expensive, very complex, or super brittle. So, normal projects should assume that ACID transactions are not possible when remote communication is involved.

- Different resources, like multiple physical database installations or middleware like messaging, can often not join a common ACID transaction.

- Activities become long-running, because you have to wait for asynchronous responses or humans. And ACID transactions in the database cannot be held open; this would not only lead to deadlocks, but also to transaction timeouts.
- Activities get too complex to be handled in one huge transaction.

In summary, work in modern architectures is increasingly separated into multiple tasks that are *not* combined in a single ACID transaction, as visualized in Figure 9-11. This requires a new way of dealing with consistency on the business level.

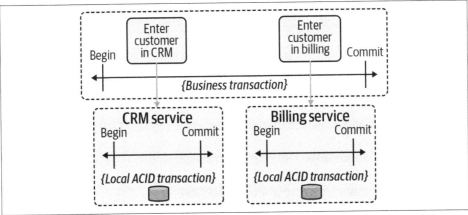

Figure 9-11. Business transactions need to cross boundaries; technical ACID transactions can only happen within a boundary

In order to handle this new normal, you must:

- Weaken your consistency expectations, as not all tasks are isolated from each other during the runtime of a business transaction.
- Make sure that once started, all tasks of a business transaction are either carried out or rolled back.

We'll dig into what this means exactly in the next sections.

Eventual Consistency

Let's recap. Traditional transactions isolate different clients from each other. Nobody can see changes made by somebody else until they are committed (to be precise, most databases allow you to configure that with the so-called *isolation level*). With tasks spread across multiple remote services, you don't have the same level of isolation.

That means that changes made in intermediary steps will be immediately visible to the world. In our example, the customer is already visible in the CRM system, even if they are not in the billing system yet. This violates the invariant that customers always exist in CRM and billing, never only in one system. So this state is considered inconsistent.

It is now important to be aware that these temporary inconsistencies are possible. You also have to understand the failure scenarios they can cause. In this example, you could have created a marketing campaign at a moment when a customer was already in the CRM system, but not yet in billing, so they got included in that list. Then, even if their order gets rejected and they never end up as an active customer, they might still receive an upgrade advertisement.

A good design with the right system boundaries needs to make sure that intermediary steps are not "harmful" in the outside world, or don't make inconsistent information available too early. Or at least, you need to understand the effects of this happening.

Furthermore, you have to think about a strategy to resolve inconsistencies. The term *eventual consistency* suggests that you need to take measures to get back to a consistent state eventually. In the onboarding example, this could mean you need to deactivate the customer in the CRM system if adding them to the billing system fails. This leads to the consistent state that the customer is not visible in any system anymore. We'll look at these strategies in more detail in the next section.

Business Strategies to Handle Inconsistency

There are three basic strategies if a consistency problem occurs: you can ignore it, apologize, or resolve it. Selecting the right strategy is a clear business decision, as none of them is right or wrong, but simply more or less well suited to the situation at hand. You should always think about the cost/value ratio. Let's take a closer look at the three options.

Ignore the inconsistency

While it sounds strange to consider ignoring a consistency issue, it actually can be a valid strategy. It's a question of how much business impact the inconsistency may have.

In the onboarding example, we might decide that a dead entry in the CRM system isn't a problem, so we just keep it there. Of course, the consequences will be that some reports might show incorrect data (including nonexistent customers) and marketing campaigns might keep hitting rejected customers. But still, the business might decide that these effects can be ignored, given that in actual fact this happens quite rarely (e.g., once a month). Sometimes effects pile up over time and require reconciliation jobs to restore consistency later.

Please note that I am not advising you to ignore consistency problems. It is just obvious that ignoring inconsistency is a pretty easy strategy to implement, and in some cases saving the development effort and bearing some inconsistency can be a valid business decision.

Graphical process models might help with this decision, as they can visualize the possible scenarios, and help you see the tasks and their sequences and where failures might occur.

Apologize

The second strategy is to apologize. This is an extension of the strategy to ignore. You don't try to prevent inconsistencies, but you do make sure that you apologize when their effects come to light.

For example, we could decide to ignore failures in the SIM registrations and just wait for customers to complain. When they call in, we apologize, send them a $10 voucher, and trigger the registration manually.

Obviously, this is not a great example, but there are situations where apologies are a good strategy. Again, this is often about the cost/value ratio; it can be much cheaper to run without consistency controls in 98% of the cases and accept the cost of a couple of expensive apologies. It's a bit like airlines overbooking their planes.

Resolve the inconsistency

The third strategy is to tackle the problem head-on and actively resolve the inconsistency. This can be done by different means, such as the reconciliation jobs mentioned earlier. A reconciliation job typically runs as a batch job, with the downsides described in "Batch Processing" on page 94.

The following sections present two other strategies that can resolve inconsistencies on an instance level, without waiting for any batch run: the Saga pattern and the outbox pattern.

Deciding which strategy is most appropriate to resolve consistency issues is a business decision. It typically relates to the volume and the business value of the processes, as well as the business impact of potential inconsistencies. This decision needs involvement from business stakeholders and can't be made by IT alone. Visibility like that provided by BPMN will help you.

The Saga Pattern and Compensation

The Saga pattern describes long-running transactions in distributed systems. The main idea is simple: when you can't roll back tasks, you undo them. The name Saga refers back to a paper written in the 1980s (*https://oreil.ly/Bu0iT*) about long-lived transactions in databases.

BPMN supports this through *compensation events*, which can link tasks with their undo tasks. Figure 9-12 shows this for the onboarding example, given that errors can happen at any time and all affected tasks need to be properly cleaned up. A workflow engine will make sure to execute all the necessary undo actions.

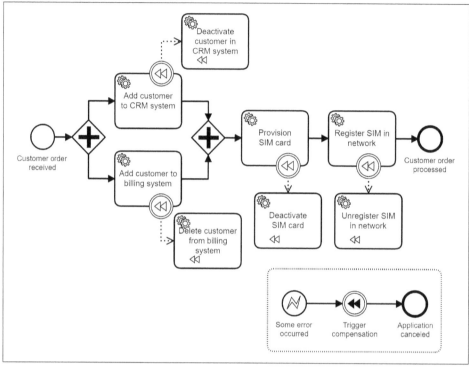

Figure 9-12. A Saga implemented by a BPMN process: compensating tasks have been defined

Such an undo does not necessarily mean a full rollback. A SIM card might already have been shipped to your customer, so you can only deactivate it. The compensation might involve multiple tasks, like also informing the customer.

Compensation logic will make your process model more complicated. This is unavoidable and mirrors real life: without ACID properties, business transactions get more complicated because the rollback is basically moved to the application level.

Of course, you do not necessarily need a workflow engine to implement the Saga pattern. As noted in "Limitations of Other Implementation Options" on page 93, there are always other implementation options. But the workflow engine is of great help, for a few reasons. First, you typically need the long-running capabilities of the engine in remote communication scenarios. And second, discussions of business transactions or any strategy to resolve inconsistencies can gain from the visibility graphical process models provide.

Chaining Resources by Using the Outbox Pattern

Another interesting pattern is the outbox pattern. Suppose you've built a service that executes some business logic, persists the result in a relational database, and sends out an event on an event bus afterward. As explained earlier in this chapter, you can't use an ACID transaction for two tasks that work with different resources (here, the database and the event bus). But it is important that the whole procedure is atomic, meaning that either the business logic is done *and* the event is sent, or *neither* of the two happen.

The outbox pattern, as visualized in Figure 9-13, can solve this problem. In a typical implementation of this pattern, the service writes the event that needs to be published to a separate table in the same relational database where the domain data resides. This table is called the *outbox*. Having a table in the same database allows the service to leverage the ACID transactions of the database, so persisting the results of the business logic and writing the event is atomic. Only after that database transaction succeeds is the event actually published, using some kind of scheduling mechanism. This scheduler will send the event and delete it from the outbox table.

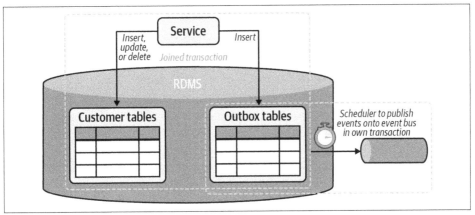

Figure 9-13. The outbox pattern allows elevating consistency to at-least-once

There are two important characteristics to recognize here. First, the outbox guarantees that events are definitely sent, but it might happen at a later point in time (do you recognize the eventual consistency again?). Second, in certain failure scenarios it is possible that events are published twice—for example, if the scheduler reads the outbox table entry, publishes the event on the bus, but crashes before it can commit changes to the outbox table. This transaction semantic is called *at-least-once*, as the design makes sure that the event is definitely sent at least once, but potentially multiple times due to failure conditions.

Implementing the outbox pattern, as shown in Figure 9-13, involves a table, a scheduling mechanism, and very often some additional monitoring capabilities. You may have noticed that this sounds a bit like our discussion of "Wild West Integrations" on page 4.

You can also leverage a workflow engine. In this case you don't need a separate outbox table at all. Instead, you express all the tasks that need to be executed in an atomic fashion in a process model, as shown in Figure 9-14.

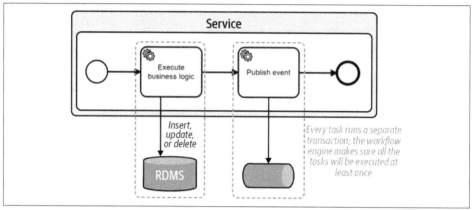

Figure 9-14. You can leverage a workflow engine to eliminate the need for the outbox pattern

The workflow engine will take care of executing the two tasks. First, the business logic will be executed and the results committed. Only if this is successful will the event be published to the event bus in the second task. If something crashes at this point in time, the workflow engine will have persisted the state and will remember that the business logic was already done and the event still needs to be published. In short: the workflow engine will start over at the right task. This leads to the same at-least-once semantics for all tasks as described with the outbox table.

To summarize, you can express all tasks that need to be executed in an atomic fashion as tasks in a process model. Of course, there can also be more than two; the workflow enine will make sure all of these tasks will eventually be executed. There is no need to implement specific infrastructure like an outbox table or schedulers to make the outbox work. At the same time, you can leverage the monitoring and operations capabilities of the workflow tooling.

Eventual Consistency Applies to Every Form of Remote Communication

In the past there were attempts to hide the nuts and bolts of remote communication behind frameworks. For example, it is pretty likely that a REST call looks almost like a local method call in your source code. A developer gets the impression that they get a result right away, which they can directly use in the next line of code. This can make developers forget about the complexity of distributed systems.

Let's examine one quick example to highlight potential problems, starting with a simple REST call. Imagine once more a payment service that can charge credit cards as part of the payment process. To do this, the service needs to call the credit card service via a REST API.

Now assume that this REST call yields a network exception. There is no way to know if the network problem occurred when sending the request to the credit card service or when getting the response back. It is even possible that the credit card service crashed while processing the request. In other words: you have no idea if a credit card was just charged or not.

You need to decide on a strategy to handle this problem. In this case it is pretty likely that you don't want to ignore the problem. Instead, you want to make sure to leave the system in a consistent state. There are multiple possibilities to achieve this. Maybe it makes sense to check if a charge was made in order to determine whether a cleanup is needed. Or you might leverage a cleanup API the credit card service provides. Or you can cancel the charge and ignore any errors saying that this charge doesn't exist. The exact implementation depends on the API of the credit card service, but it is important that this problem is handled. Figure 9-15 shows a possible process model for cleaning up when charging the credit card fails. This example illustrates nicely that you enter the world of eventual consistency with your very first remote call. This requires you to think about consequences and business strategies to resolve inconsistencies, as discussed in this chapter.

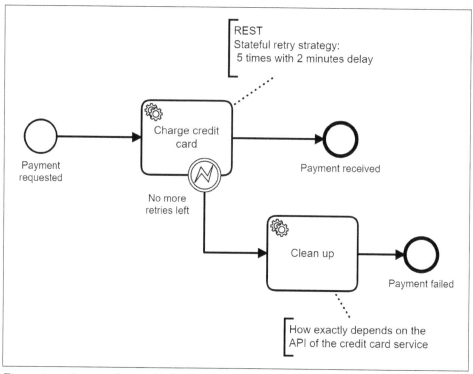

Figure 9-15. Even in the event of network errors you might have triggered business logic, so you might need to restore consistency

The Importance of Idempotency

This chapter talked about at-least-once semantics and retrying. In this context, you also need to learn about *idempotency*. Idempotent operations are defined by Wikipedia (*https://en.wikipedia.org/wiki/Idempotence*) as "operations that can be applied multiple times without changing the result beyond the initial application."

In simpler terms, this means that it is not a problem if an operation call is repeated. And repeating calls is unavoidable in distributed systems. We already looked at deliberate retries for synchronous APIs, and we discussed redelivery of messages. These are important strategies to deal with the unreliable nature of remote communication. In other words: you can't avoid these retries.

Retries always lead to duplicate calls sooner or later. That's why you have to think about idempotency for each and every operation you expose remotely.

Some operations are naturally idempotent. Queries don't cause side effects and thus can easily be retried. Note that idempotency does not imply that the result must be exactly the same. A query might return different results a couple of seconds later because the state of the system might have changed.

Deletions are typically also idempotent, as you simply can't delete the same entity again. But the response might be different: instead of a confirmation the retry might result in an error that the entity is not found.

Other operations are not idempotent by nature, like charging a credit card. In this case a typical strategy is to generate unique IDs in the client that are handed over to the credit card charging service. This service can then detect duplicates if it has its own state to remember calls. Stateless services face a challenge, as you might have to introduce dedicated state for duplicate detection.

It is advisable not to rely on the business payload for detecting duplicates. If there are two credit card charges for the same card with the same amount within milliseconds, it is likely that this is a retry, but you can never be sure. Maybe somebody booked two flight tickets with the exact same price at the exact same time.

 Whenever you design the API for a service, make sure it is designed to support idempotency. If the service doesn't provide this, a client cannot fix it. The result is that you have to guess what calls might be duplicates, which can lead to a lot of problems.

A good workflow engine also offers idempotent operations, so that you can make sure that you only start a new process instance for a given key once. Other operations, like completing a task or correlating a message, are naturally idempotent. If a process instance has moved on in the process, you cannot complete the same task again. And even if you have loops in your model and arrive at the same task again, it gets assigned a different instance ID by the workflow engine. As simple as this may sound, it is important to always keep idempotency in mind and take it into consideration whenever you design any API.

Conclusion

Workflow engines help developers to solve challenges around distributed systems and remote communication.

This chapter described how BPMN can be used to help with typical communication or message exchange patterns. It further showed how automated processes can be leveraged to restore consistency or to implement the Saga or outbox pattern, and it also emphasized the importance of idempotency.

The use cases for workflow engines presented in this chapter were on a smaller scale than typical business process automation projects, but nonetheless demonstrated valid reasons to use process automation technology.

CHAPTER 10

Business–IT Collaboration

In every IT project, different roles need to collaborate. Collaboration is the most crucial aspect of projects. It impacts the development effort, the resulting quality, and the time to value. In short, it is the critical success factor. But as the Wikipedia entry on business–IT alignment (*https://oreil.ly/XFJkK*) notes:

> IT and business professionals are often unable to bridge the gap between themselves because of differences in objectives, culture, and incentives and a mutual ignorance for the other group's body of knowledge. This rift generally results in expensive IT systems that do not provide adequate return on investment.

This chapter dives into the subject of collaboration. It:

- Describes a typical project and the roles involved, to establish a common understanding and vocabulary

- Shows how visual models help to improve collaboration, not only between business and IT but also between IT and IT

- Provides some guidance on creating process models that can be better understood by various stakeholders

A Typical Project

Let's return to the imaginary ShipByButton (SBB) Inc. project presented back in "A Business Scenario" on page 9. Assume that SBB started with that idea four years ago and set up a quick-and-dirty PHP application (note that most parts of this story wouldn't differ much if it were instead an insurance company that's a hundred years old and uses a large mainframe monolith). The PHP application served the company well in the beginning when going to market, but quickly became problematic: it did not scale to a growing number of users, it was really hard to make any changes to the code, and it resisted being broken into smaller pieces that can be maintained by different teams. This meant that the company could not scale its development forces.

So Charlie, the CEO of SBB, announced a big project to rewrite the whole order fulfillment process from scratch. A microservices architecture would be considered to distribute the logic into smaller pieces that work together.

As a first step, the inventory and shipment microservices were defined, and logic from the PHP monolith was refactored out into these services. The communication with the hardware buttons was pretty much untouched, as these devices had been widely distributed to existing customers—so this is still PHP.

Charlie wants you to be the project lead for the order fulfillment service, which is the heart and soul of the company. This sounds exciting and scary at the same time, but you decide to take the risk and jump right into it.

The first thing you do is call Ash, a great business analyst and one of your oldest allies in the company. Together, you start to wander around the premises. First you visit with what feels like a myriad of PHP developers, as you have to do some significant archeology to find out how the current system is processing orders. You checked the wiki documentation first, of course, but found that it was quite outdated. Most developers are excited to help you with the improvement project and walk you through what they know. Unfortunately, they often mix details on the as-is implementation with wishful thinking about the to-be situation. Thankfully, Ash is with you and has experience in getting people back on track. After a long day you not only have a headache, but also a first process model. You print it deliberately in the sketchy mode of your modeling tool; you know this will make it easier to discuss, as people tend to raise fewer objections about something that looks unfinished. The result is shown in Figure 10-1.

The next day, you and Ash go to Reese, who is responsible for revenue and thus has a high interest in order fulfillment. You walk both of them through the process model, which they are very interested in. Reese points out important milestones as well as goals and key performance indicators (KPIs) for the process. All in all, you are well on track and take some time during lunch to thank this book for teaching you about process automation and BPMN.

Strengthened by some good food, you approach the inventory team and ask how you can integrate with their service. Using the process model, you can easily show them where you want to fetch goods from stock, and also explain why you don't need to reserve goods up front. They point you to a wiki page that contains precise information on how to call their service. Awesome!

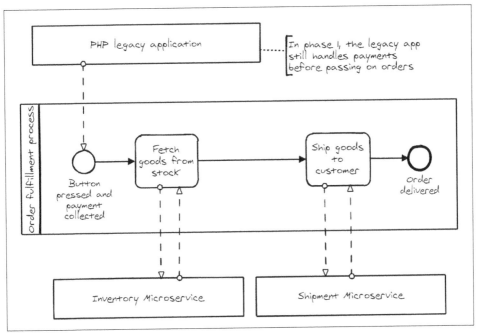

Figure 10-1. Your first sketch of the process

You feel it is time to get started. You remember your colleague Ariel talking about a process automation vendor they were excited about. You call them right away and discuss your project and environment. You learn that this vendor executes BPMN models, which you find essential given that it has served you so well so far. In the end, you are convinced that this is a good way to go. You approach Charlie to ask for a proof of concept, and everyone is on board.

Two weeks later, Dani, a consultant from the vendor, pairs up with Kai, one of your developers. The three of you basically lock yourselves in a room and implement the process model. You quickly set up a development project and add the process model. You write some glue code to call the other microservices. You also write an API that can be invoked from the PHP application speaking to the hardware button. You even write some unit tests for the whole thing. At the end of day two, you are able to process a real order! Enthusiastically, you plan to put this pilot to work and send a copy of every real order to it. This way you can easily verify that it can handle your load.

You briefly check what requirements apply to deploying such an application and happily learn that your company favors a cloud-first approach that allows you to run some containers easily. To do so, you ask Kai to set up a CI/CD pipeline to build Docker images every time a change is made to the process or the code around it.

But you start to worry a bit, because the project concerns the core business process in your company. You ask yourself: what if a process instance gets stuck? What if certain services, like the inventory service, aren't available? What if customers ask about their order status?

You arrange lunch with Georgie, head of operations for the legacy PHP application. You want to learn how it is operated at the moment. Georgie tells you about scraping log files, finding exceptions, looking into databases directly, and guessing about potential fixes. It turns out they have a wiki page that lists common problems and related cures. For anything not on the wiki, they simply open a ticket for a developer to look into it. You're not surprised that Georgie is looking quite tired. You quickly get your tablet and show them your workflow vendor's operations tool. You've prepared some failed process instances, for the purpose of illustration. You explain how operations can be automatically notified, how they understand the process model, and how they can take action. Georgie pays for your lunch.

A few days later, you succeed in getting Reese into a meeting (remember, Reese is responsible for revenue). You show them the pilot case, but looking into the analytics tool fed with real data. Figure 10-2 shows the executable model in the context of an analysis tool.

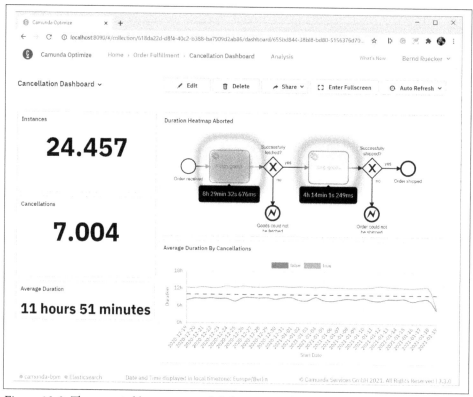

Figure 10-2. The executable process model showing real-life data

Reese is excited and drills into some data on the spot, discovering that the order cancellation rate is disproportionately high when fetching from stock takes more than six hours. Equipped with that data, Reese wants to address this issue with the inventory team and is excited about replacing the legacy system.

Over the next two weeks you manage to get all the missing nuts and bolts developed, the test coverage increased, the notification and monitoring systems connected, and everything deployed on an elastically scalable infrastructure in the cloud that serves the production traffic. Everybody loves you, and the world is unicorns and rainbows.

The Moral of the Story

This story clearly showed how the graphical process model facilitated collaboration between the different stakeholders.

The *project lead* (you) loves that the whole project moves quickly and misunderstandings are reduced. Even if process modeling means more effort in an early phase, e.g., to discuss the model, that effort can be saved during implementation, as requirements are clear. Looking at the whole life cycle, you can also imagine that future changes will be much easier to incorporate without further archeology sessions.

The *business analyst* (Ash) loves to get everybody talking about the same model, which also facilitates a common language. The process model is a great help in gathering, discussing, and documenting requirement, and using BPMN ensures those requirements are clear and coherent.

The *developers* (Dani, Kai) love that it is easy to make the process model executable as part of a normal development project. They can develop in the stack they know, with the best practices they are productive with. The visual model helps them to understand the process intuitively, and probably even helps them navigate through their sources. They see the advantage of the living documentation, recalling problems in the past when nobody knew how something was implemented.

The *operations* or *infrastructure* person (Georgie) loves that they can understand where incidents happen, the visibility they have into problems, and that they can easily resolve them. And even in cases where they can't help, they can easily share a deep link showing the problem including context, which makes incident handling much easier.

And the *executives* (Charlie, Reese) love that the project runs smoothly, the resulting process is really working, and everybody is on board. Of course, they also love the fact that they can now monitor a lot of KPIs that not only allow them to assess the current performance but also to analyze bottlenecks.

I admit that this story is a bit idealistic, but it is not unrealistic. I have seen many projects unfold with such a plot.

Including All the People: BizDevOps

Let's discuss the value of process automation tools in a bit more detail by looking now at the collaboration between business, development, and operations, abbreviated Biz-DevOps, as shown in Figure 10-3.

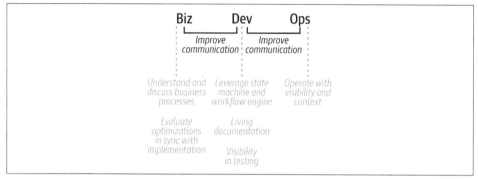

Figure 10-3. Visual process models foster the collaboration of business, development, and operations

Development

Developers can leverage graphical models to communicate with other developers about current projects, or as a visual aid to help them remember what they did a year ago. Executable process models are living documentation; they cannot become outdated when a process is changed, as would happen with any other drawing that's disconnected from the code. Even the most rigid development procedures can't avoid some situations where an urgent fix is rolled out while the documentation is forgotten.

A good example of the value for developers is shown in Figure 10-4. It is a graphical visualization of a test result, showing the exact scenario executed for a single test case.

This is handy when added to a CI/CD pipeline, as it means that developers can immediately identify where a failing process test had problems and which path led to that situation.

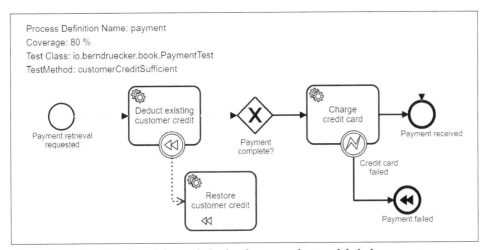

Figure 10-4. Graphical models can help developers understand failed test cases

Business

Visibility is also a key enabler of better communication with business analysts and other business stakeholders, like the project sponsor, the business department, executives, or project leads.

A surprising observation is that projects using process models often report a spike in effort during the first analysis phase. Shouldn't the model help to reduce effort?

Because graphical models can be easily understood by a large group of people, projects often discover a lack of clarity or problems with the process design relatively early in the process. That requires another round of discussion, which takes some additional time. This is not paralysis in analysis, but rather improves the model and saves a lot of trouble in later stages of the project. So, the investment in a better model at the beginning pays off during implementation.

Having said that, you might be reminded of the waterfall approach to software development, where you try to nail down the exact requirements in the very beginning of the project before starting development. This turned out to be pretty unsuccessful in most cases. Of course, that's not what I had in mind when writing the preceding paragraph. Agile development approaches, which develop software in increments and allow learning along the way, proved to be much more successful and should also be applied to process automation projects.

But I want to emphasize that Agile does not mean "analysis free." You should not just start to hack away, as this seldom leads to the right results. The sweet spot is the middle ground where you have a rough understanding of the big picture up front, but analyze the next increment in detail.

Business roles benefit from the model being living documentation. Whenever you need to apply new requirements to a process that is already rolled out, you have a place to go and look at the existing model. If your tooling allows it, you can embed the always-up-to-date model in a wiki like Confluence. Then everybody can easily point out where to make a certain change, and nobody needs to do archeology to understand the status quo.

Another benefit is that workflow engines write a lot of audit data. This can be visualized as overlay in the graphical model, as shown in Figure 10-5. This is a great basis for analyzing and discussing bottlenecks, next iterations, or possible improvements.

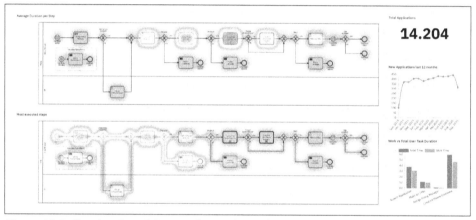

Figure 10-5. Graphical models provide insights to business analysts to allow for process improvements

Operations

Operations—often also called infrastructure—are too often forgotten when talking about business–IT collaboration. These people do a very important job: they make sure that everything runs smoothly in production. Whenever there is a problem, somebody has to recognize and fix it.

Too often, operations folks need to work based on log files and data in databases. This limits their ability to understand the full picture around the process, or to fix problems themselves. Then the only way to solve an incident is to involve developers who know the application by heart.

Using a graphical process visualization helps operations to see incidents in context, which includes the process model, historical information, data attached to a process instance, and detailed information about the error or exception. Figure 10-6 shows an example.

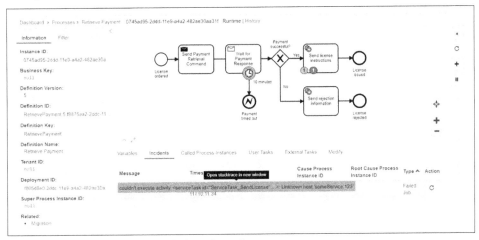

Figure 10-6. Graphical models help technical operators

The workflow tooling allows operators to fix certain scenarios easily. For instance, they can trigger retries once temporal outages of services are over, possibly for thousands of process instances at once, or fix the corrupt data of a process instance using a graphical user interface.

Your company probably embraces DevOps, or might be trying to reduce the operations workload by pushing toward the cloud or serverless scenarios. Easing the load on operations with tooling targeting a wider range of people is even more important in that case, as it allows everybody in your team to detect, analyze, and fix certain problems without being a specialist on certain parts of the source code.

In summary, workflow tools ease developers' work, include business stakeholders in IT projects, and empower operators to do their job well.

The Process Automation Life Cycle

This is a good place to talk about the process automation life cycle, as visualized in Figure 10-7. This figure points out the value of visual process models in the various stages of the life cycle.

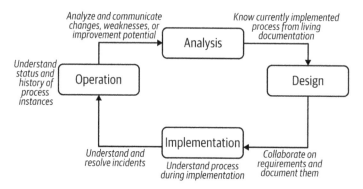

Figure 10-7. The value of visibility in different phases of a project or development iteration

In a typical project, there are four phases: first you analyze what you need to do, then you design a process that will support this goal, then you implement it (including deployment) before you operate it (in production). This will lead to new insights that you analyze before designing and implementing an improvement, which is then operated. And so on. It is a typical PDCA cycle (Plan, Do, Check, Act).

Again, this life cycle does not refer to a waterfall development approach, where you need to go through months of analysis before you implement the whole application. On the contrary, rather than it being a lengthy process that is completed once, with a more Agile software development approach it's expected that every iteration and increment will go through this same life cycle. For example, you might analyze and design for the next sprint in Scrum (a well-known Agile development approach), implement it in a two-week-long sprint, and put it into production right after; you then go straight into the next sprint.

You will see such life cycle pictures everywhere—in fact, most process automation books might even start with one. I personally find it a bit boring, which is why I left it to such a late chapter in the book. Still, you have it now for reference.

The Power of One Joined Model

One important observation that can be made when looking at successful projects is that collaboration between business stakeholders and developers does not mean that one of them forces a model down the others' throats. It really means *collaboration*. Developers should not only think about architecture and technical considerations, but also about the business aspects of a process. And business analysts must understand certain technical aspects, such as why a process model needs to change in order to be executable. This mutual understanding is a big benefit on its own.

Collaboration is not about fighting trench wars to decide who is right, but about gaining a common understanding of the reasons for certain modeling decisions. This allows you to design a model that everybody can agree on.

A critical success factor is that you don't get trapped in the idea of having two different models: a "business model" that captures the business requirements, and a "technical model" that is executable. This idea actually exists in many companies. It is often fueled by slides about process landscapes that allow you to drill into a hierarchy of processes until you finally end up at the executable process—a concept popularized by big consulting companies. It might actually make sense to have a very high-level, strategic model that fits on one page and can give everybody a rough idea of why the process is there and what it does. But it is important to note that this model is like the trailer of a movie: it might highlight some aspects, but it is not a true representation of the actual plot. How a process is really implemented on an operational level might be very different.

On the operational level it's important to have a single, comprehensive model. Of course, this model could have different versions, and may even live in different environments. For example, the business analyst might work on *MightyProcess* in their collaborative BPMN modeler, while the developer works on *mighty_process.bpmn* in their Git repository and the operations person works on *processes/mightyProcess/1* in their operations tool. Physically these are different files in different locations, like source code, which might also be deployed on different servers. Logically, however, it is one model.

Most importantly, this means those files all share the same content. There is no translation, no transformation, no tricks required to get from one to the other. Different people work on different physical "copies" at the same time, but this is like branching or forking source code—which means you also have to think about the moments in time when you sync the models again and merge your changes. This is not always the easiest, but it's doable. In reality it is often sufficient that there is one leading model, let's say in the developers' Git repository. Whenever business analysts make changes, these changes are remodeled in the leading model whenever you want to incorporate them.

Be careful not to get sucked into a never-ending discussion around how exactly this collaboration should work, how different models can be automatically synced, or how a round trip from a business analysis tool to the technical modeler and back works. While this is all important to get right, too much discussion too early in the process of learning process automation can stop projects from moving forward. Normally the approach settles after doing a couple of successful projects.

From a Process Pyramid to a House

I have to make a confession: I am guilty of having distributed a picture indicating a process hierarchy in the past myself! In 2010 I wrote a book about BPMN together with my Camunda cofounder. We published the pyramid shown on the left in Figure 10-8, which advocated for different levels of process models.

We later came to understand that this illustration implied that the business throws a model over the fence for IT to implement, which is exactly what we saw was not successful. So we changed the illustration to a house, as shown on the righthand side of Figure 10-8, where the operational model simply contains human and technical flows in one joined model. This works much better.

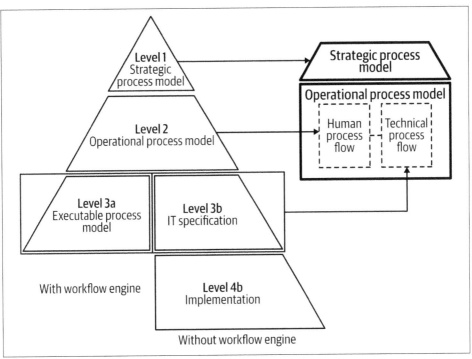

Figure 10-8. Typical illustrations, like the pyramid on the left, suggest separate business and IT models—it's better to use one integrated model like the house on the righthand side (from Real-Life BPMN, 4th Edition)

But what is a human process flow and what is a technical process flow? A human flow is completely handled and controlled by a person, while a technical flow is handled by software—e.g., the workflow engine. Human and technical flows typically interact to represent all aspects of a business process important to various stakeholders. For example, a human may trigger a technical flow in the course of doing their work by clicking a button in their tasklist. Equally, a technical flow may require a human to do something, thus creating a human task for them.

BPMN allows you to model all different flows in one big diagram, called a *collaboration model*. Technically you create separate processes, but place them on one canvas and express the communication relationships. Figure 10-9 shows an example using the customer onboarding process from earlier in this book.

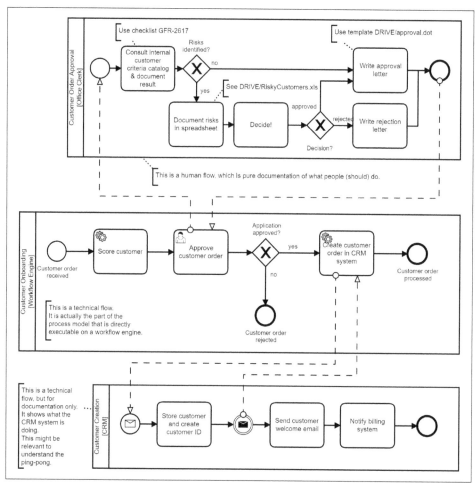

Figure 10-9. A BPMN model containing human and technical process flows

The three different rectangles are called *pools* in BPMN. Each pool is a complete process. You can think of every process as one specific perspective on the overall business process.

The process on the top is a human flow that describes how an office clerk handles approvals. It allows everybody to understand what really happens and how that impacts other processes. For example, it clearly shows that an approval letter is sent manually, and thus must not be part of the automated process (I am not saying this is the most efficient process, but it's often reality). The process model of the human flow can also be used within work instructions; this is why required templates are mentioned.

The process on the bottom shows details of how the CRM system is implemented. While this is a technical flow, it is still solely documentation, as the CRM system does not use a workflow engine. It is still helpful to understand the bigger picture, as often there are a lot of things going on under the hood that you need to know to design your executable process. In this example, you can see that the CRM already sends a customer welcome mail, so you don't want to do that in other places.

The process in the middle is the executable process on the workflow engine, as known from previous examples in this book. It is connected to the other processes by message flows, which could technically mean different things, from user interfaces or emails to API calls or messages. As this is the only process directly executed on a workflow engine, it is the only one that needs to be precise. All other processes are documentation and will solely be interpreted by humans, so they have more freedom and can for example focus only on aspects important to understand the overall ping-pong between components.

Note that such a collaboration model leverages a lot of features of BPMN, and creating one might not be the first thing you do as part of your own BPMN endeavor. On the other hand, this way of showing the interaction between different actors—be they humans, workflow engines, or other software components—is very powerful and often helps everybody involved to really understand the bigger picture.

Unlike the executable technical flow, this collaboration model is seldom kept up-to-date over a system's lifetime. It is more a helpful artifact to use when discovering what the executable process should look like.

Who Does the Modeling?

By now, you should have a good idea of how process models influence your software development approach, how they foster collaboration, and how they can be directly executed.

Against that background, additional questions typically arise: who creates the executable model? Can business folks really model on their own? How do you keep all the physical copies of a model in sync over time? Who owns the model? What do I need to learn in order to master all of this?

In order to find some answers, let's look at the business analyst and the developer and how they typically work with a process model. But let me add a short disclaimer first. I've learned over the last decade that roles vary across enterprises, not only in their responsibilities but in what they're called. Even roles that have the same name can be completely different. And of course, each person fulfilling the role will perform it in their own way. What's more, in smaller projects, one person might fulfill several or even all roles. That's all OK, but I do need to name some roles to move forward in this chapter.

The business analyst thinks about the business requirements and focuses on the what and why, trying to ignore the how (to leave the solution space open, so that developers can decide on the option). Business analysts are typically the ones who create the first drafts of a process model, which of course also shapes the executable process. This is where they should work together with the developers to get it right. The best workshops I have seen were staffed with analysts *and* developers, who together created the first versions of the process model. It is also worth adding some end users, subject matter experts, and operations people for additional perspectives. These workshops foster understanding of the problems faced by the other parties. For example, the business analysts might learn why it is hard to implement a process in the current IT ecosystem, and the developers might learn that legal requirements are what led to such a complicated process. These insights alone have huge value.

Developers are responsible for making the models executable. When trying to do the initial model execution, they often recognize flaws in the model. For example, they could discover that an API needs additional parameters the process is not aware of, or that an API cannot be called as envisioned. Developers need to be empowered to adjust the model if needed. This not only means being able to add attributes to make the model executable, but also to adjust it so that it can cope with real-world challenges.

Of course, all changes need to be communicated back to the business analysts. There must be a reason for every change that can be explained to all stakeholders. This establishes a joint understanding and language between the business analysts and developers over time, which is a huge asset on its own. It also allows a discussion about modeling best practices, which naturally leads to a model that is accepted by different roles. Once business departments understand the reasons behind technical tasks in a model, they tend to accept these.

The adjusted model needs to serve as the basis for later improvements. In Agile projects, you might develop the process solution in increments, meaning you have a conversation about adjustments in every sprint. This is the moment where you might sync the different physical model files referred to earlier. How exactly this is done depends on the tool stack, but generally speaking the simplest approaches work best. For example, your developers could send each executable model to the analysts as soon as it is rolled out. The analysts would then apply all the changes to their current model version to allow for improvements in the next iteration. Some tools provide assistance with this, like support for versioning of models, diffing of models, merges, and even automated round trips. This can of course help, but more importantly you have to find your approach and stick to it. Discipline is more important than tool features.

Keep an eye on the executable models; you need to avoid having business analysts overwrite or remove technical attributes that they might not even see in their tool. That's why the ownership of the executable artifact must be with the developers.

Creating Better Process Models

Many people in different roles need to understand your process models (ideally without much further explanation), and these models are artifacts with a long lifetime. So there are good reasons to invest thought and time into improving your process models, and this section gives you some hints.

However, you should also make sure not to overdo it. Remember what Winston Churchill said: "Perfection is the enemy of progress." In other words: an imperfect model that is in production might be more valuable than a perfect model that never gets executed. Of course, this is subjective, and you might disagree. That's fine, as long as you push something to production—in the words of a colleague, "There is never a perfect solution, so go for the model with the fewest unhappy people."

Extracting (Integration) Logic into Subprocesses

One of the basic questions to ask about any process model is, which aspects belong in the model at hand, and which might be better off in code, in a separate process model that is invoked, or in a completely different service?

We already discussed process modeling language versus programming code in "Model or Code?" on page 59, and we touched on service boundaries in "Respect Boundaries and Avoid Process Monoliths" on page 131. Both are important aspects to consider. This section examines the possibility of extracting parts of the process to create a separate process model within the same service boundary.

Let's revisit the customer onboarding example. Assume that creating a customer listing in the CRM system involves much more than a simple service call, as the CRM system has a clumsy API that demands you create a customer first, and only then can you pass on all the customer data. All of this is asynchronous, meaning you send a message and need to wait for the result. Of course, the legacy system is slow, and the response can take some minutes. As a bonus, sometimes messages get lost on the channel because of a buggy messaging middleware being used.

Figure 10-10 shows a separate process handling these specifics, to avoid polluting the main application process. The technical details to call the CRM system are extracted into a separate model and invoked from the application process. This way, you keep the same level of details for all tasks in the onboarding process, making that model much easier to consume. This is an application of the divide and conquer strategy, which helps you end up with models that people can read more easily.

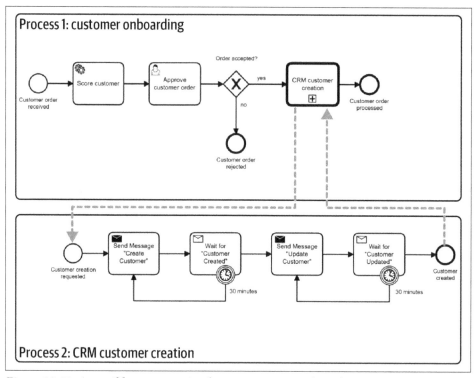

Figure 10-10. A possible process to implement customer onboarding

There is another clear reason to extract logic into a separate model: reusability. For example, imagine that you need to create a customer in the CRM system in multiple places in your process model.

This use case brings up a quite interesting question: do you want to support this kind of reusability on a process model level, or would it be better to create a separate service for customer creation that is globally usable, with a proper API, so that nobody needs to know that it even runs a workflow engine? Yes, that might be the case, as discussed in Chapter 7. Remember that a subprocess in BPMN is only a valid choice if all logic is contained within the same boundary.

Other than that, there are no hard rules available about when to extract logic into separate models. It's like programming—there are no hard rules about refactoring code into separate methods. Still, it influences the readability of the resulting code.

Sometimes, it is a matter of taste. Some people prefer to have bigger models with all details, and then apply modeling conventions to keep them readable. This bears the risk of those process models being too daunting for some viewers. Others like to create a lot of subprocesses to have a clean main process, which on the other side bears the risk that a reader needs to navigate through a lot of models. It also makes it harder to model some circumstances, like going backwards in a process model if a cancellation request comes in.

My recommendation is to avoid using subprocesses if possible, but to introduce them if you clearly have logic at different levels of granularity, as this yields process models that are easier to understand.

Distinguishing Between Results, Exceptions, and Errors

There is another area that is the source of so many discussions in real life that it deserves its own section: dealing with deviations from the happy path. The happy path is kind of the default scenario with a positive outcome, so no exceptions or errors or deviations are experienced. But real life is full of exceptions, so let's talk about them.

BPMN defines the error event as something that allows a process model to react to errors within a task. Figure 10-11 shows an example where the scoring service might raise the error that the customer data is invalid. You can also see that instead of using error events, you can write a problematic result into the process context and model an exclusive gateway later in the process, as is done with customers where no rating is available. This also allows your process to take a different path if that problem occurs. In this case, from a business perspective the underlying problem looks less like an error and more like the result of a task.

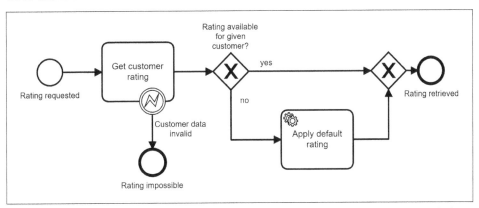

Figure 10-11. Processes can react to errors in services, which is semantically a bit different than getting a negative result and deciding on it

In this example, it might be a valid result from the scoring that a customer cannot be scored, so this should be handled not as an error but as an expected result. It's a thin line, but it's worth giving it some thought as this decision will influence how easy your model will be to understand.

As a rule of thumb, deal with expected results of tasks by means of gateways, but model exceptions (which hinder us in reaching the expected result) via error events.

In real life, you'll also have to deal with technical problems. You can't treat them in quite the same way. Suppose the rating service becomes temporarily unavailable. You might not want to model the retrying, as you would have to add that to each and every service task. This will bloat the visual model and confuse business folks. Instead, you need to configure some technical attributes for retrying rules, or handle incidents in operations. This is hidden in the visual. If you want the retrying to be visible to everyone, you can add text annotations as shown in Figure 10-12.

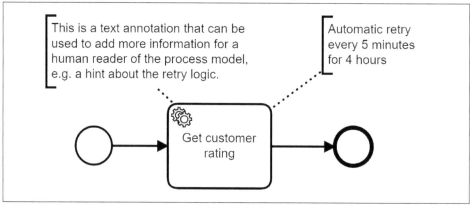

Figure 10-12. Retrying service calls upon failure is typically hidden in attributes; if this is important, text annotations allow you to add information for humans reading the model

The terms *business error* and *technical error* can be confusing, as they emphasize the source of the error too much. This can lead to long discussions about whether a certain problem is technical or not, and if you are allowed to see technical errors in a business process model. Actually, it is much more important to look at how you *react* to certain errors. Even a technical problem can qualify for a business reaction. For example, you could decide that you continue a process in the event that the scoring service is not available, and simply give every customer a good rating instead of blocking all progress. The error is clearly technical, but the reaction is a business decision.

So, I prefer to talk about *business reactions*, which are modeled in your process, and *technical reactions*, which are handled generically in the tooling, like retries or incidents in operations.

Figure 10-13 shows an example where there is a technical reaction (retrying) to the unavailability of the scoring service. But after a certain time, the reaction is escalated to a business level, to avoid breaking any SLA the scoring service has to comply with.

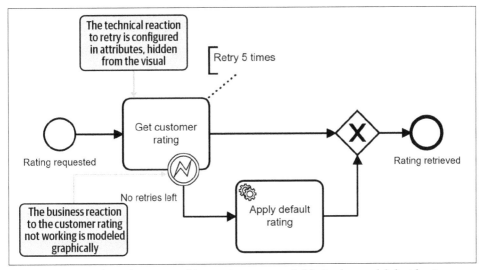

Figure 10-13. Technical reactions like retries are not visible in the model, but business reactions are

Increasing Readability

You want to use visual models to better understand, discuss, and remember processes. Hence, it pays off to invest some effort in making the models easy to read and understand, which boils down to following modeling conventions. Most enterprises define their own conventions over time. You can find example modeling conventions linked on the website for this book (*https://ProcessAutomationBook.com*).

This section gives you two typical examples: labeling elements and modeling to follow the happy path.

Labeling elements

Using labels for all process model elements will make sure that your readers really understand the business semantics of a process. The clarity of a process is often directly linked to how well chosen its labels are.

In Figure 10-14 you can see:

- The start event is labeled with a description in passive voice ("Order placed").
- All tasks are clearly labeled to inform the reader what piece of work needs to be carried out, typically using the pattern verb + object (e.g., "Retrieve payment").

- A labeled gateway makes it clear under which conditions the process continues on what sequence flow, typically by posing a question at the gateway and adding the answer to the sequence flow.
- Labeled end events characterize the end results of the process from a business perspective, typically in the event style ("Order delivered").

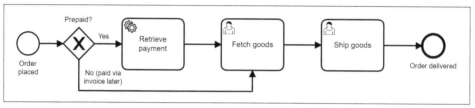

Figure 10-14. A process model sticking to labeling and naming conventions

Model from left to right and emphasize the happy path

Model process diagrams from left to right (or the other way around if that is how you write in your culture), and especially not from top to bottom. This supports the reading direction and also takes the human field of vision into account, which prefers wide screens. Can you imagine a cinema having a screen that is higher than it is wide?

You can further improve the readability of diagrams by carefully positioning symbols from left to right according to the typical point in time at which they happen. While this is not always easy, it makes a big difference.

You may also want to emphasize the "happy path" leading to the delivery of a successful result by placing the tasks, events, and gateways belonging to the happy path on a straight line in the center of your diagram, as shown in Figure 10-15. At least you can try, as this will not always be feasible.

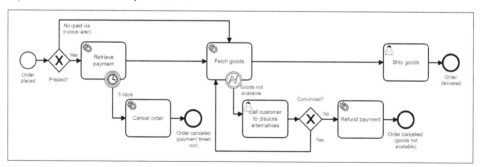

Figure 10-15. A very readable process modeled from left to right, which respects timing and emphasizes the happy path

Conclusion

This chapter highlighted the importance of graphical process models for different stakeholders. This was examined in the context of a typical project, naming project roles and life cycle phases.

You should now have a better understanding of who does the modeling, how different stakeholders can work with a joined model, and what actually makes a good model.

In the next chapter, we'll explore process visibility in practice.

CHAPTER 11

Process Visibility

This chapter:

- Doubles down on the value of process visibility
- Explains how to achieve process visibility, both when using a workflow engine and in heterogeneous environments
- Shows typical metrics and reports that you might want to set up

The Value of Process Visibility

Visibility actually influences process performance on two dimensions:

- (Continuous) process improvement
- Process operation

Process improvement means making the process better. "Better" can mean many things; for example, making it cheaper to operate, reducing cycle times, or allowing for a bigger scale, meaning more instances can be processed in the same amount of time. Sometimes it also means supporting business models that were not possible before. Process visibility is an essential tool for these improvements because it makes it possible to identify bottlenecks in existing processes as well as facilitating discussions of improvement alternatives.

Process operation is about "keeping the lights on." This involves business-oriented operations roles, who are interested in SLAs or instances that are stuck because of business problems. It also involves more technical operations roles who care about incidents with technical causes, for example because required systems are down or input data is corrupt.

In most companies, operations roles cannot be clearly marked as business or technical; it is much more a continuum of being more business or more technical. That's why I decided to just talk about operations in this book.

Process visibility helps all operations roles. One interesting element of this is providing what is called *situation awareness*. There is a lot of research from cognitive psychology in this area that proves that situation awareness is crucial for an operator's decision outcome.

An interesting example of this was studied in the context of air traffic control and the control rooms of nuclear power plants. The authors of the report, "The Impact of Process Visibility on Process Performance" (*https://oreil.ly/gPTjq*), found that "the operator must have knowledge of the current process state at all times, and the ability to use this knowledge effectively in predicting future process states and controlling the process to attain operational goals." This study further reinforced the value of visibility and its influence for process performance by looking at the lean movement: "Visual controls that create immediate transparency about abnormalities are a crucial part of lean production systems, and they are essential for banishing waste to continuously improve processes."

So research confirms the importance of process visibility—but let's conclude this detour and get more practical. Table 11-1 lists typical use cases of various stakeholders where visibility provides a benefit in terms of process improvement or process operation. The use cases are further sorted by the process automation life cycle phases, which were introduced in "The Process Automation Life Cycle" on page 204. This table also indicates how many process instances the person typically needs to look at and (where relevant) how to find that subset. This is an interesting aspect when thinking about the user experience and tool support.

Table 11-1. Use cases that benefit from process visibility

Who?	What?	Phase in life cycle	Benefit	How many instances?
Business analyst	Understand currently implemented process from living documentation	Analysis	Process improvement	All
Business analyst, developer	Collaborate to discuss and document requirements	Design	Process improvement	All
Developer	Understand process during implementation	Implementation	Process improvement	All
Operator	Understand and resolve incidents	Operation	Process operation	One to many (filter for incidents)

Who?	What?	Phase in life cycle	Benefit	How many instances?
Operator, service desk	Understand status of selected process instance	Operation	Process operation	One (find dedicated instance based on business criteria)
Business analyst	Analyze and communicate changes, weaknesses, or improvement potential	Analysis	Process improvement	All or subset filtered by date or business data
Process Owner	Understand process performance	Operation, analysis	Process operation and improvement	All or subset filtered by date or business data

You might want to return to the ShipByButton discussed at the beginning of Chapter 10 to map these use cases to that story.

Getting the Data

Your next question might be, how can I get the right data to achieve the required level of process visibility? Let's look at some options.

Leverage Audit Data from Your Workflow Engine

When using a workflow engine, you get visibility for free. Most products use graphical models and leverage them for design, implementation, and operations.

Nevertheless, you should make sure that the visuals are suitable for all target groups. This book emphasizes BPMN, which does a great job at this. Be cautious with other notations, especially if they claim to be lightweight, as was explained in "Process Modeling Languages" on page 100. Some tools only autogenerate visuals during runtime, which provide very limited help, meaning that you might miss out on a lot of the value.

There are different ways to access the audit data from your workflow engine. The easiest option is to make use of existing monitoring and reporting tools from your vendor, as discussed in "Business Monitoring and Reporting" on page 42. They provide a great starting point and should work out of the box. The power depends on the concrete tool.

Another option is to access the data via the API of the workflow engine. This allows you either to build your own user interface on top of that API or, probably better, to load the data into your own database to analyze it later.

Sometimes you might also read data directly from the database of the workflow engine, bypassing the API. Typical reasons for that design choice are the lack of a proper API or performance issues with using the API for mass data. If you limit yourself to read access to the data, this might be OK. But it should always be a last resort, as a database schema is an implementation detail of the engine and should be treated as such. For example, you don't get the same guarantees in terms of backward compatibility as you would for an API.

If you want to create an ETL job to transfer the data into your own data warehouse (DWH) or business intelligence (BI) solution, this job can also either access the API or fall back to the database.

Some workflow tools also allow history data to be published as an event stream. You can then subscribe to that stream in order to store the data in the format of choice.

So what's the best way to access audit data? As always, it depends. In this case, the "best" option mostly depends on your overall architecture and stack. Your workflow vendor might be able to make recommendations.

Model Events to Measure Key Performance Indicators

With every process execution within a workflow engine you can immediately collect important KPI metrics, for example about the number of process instances per time unit or cycle times.

But often you want to analyze additional performance indicators. For example, you may want to understand how long it takes to deliver an order after payment is received. To support this, you can explicitly add more business milestones to your process model. In BPMN this means adding intermediate events, as shown in Figure 11-1.

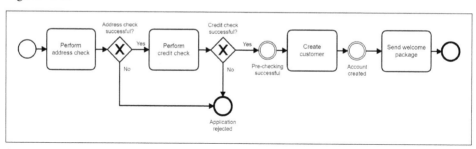

Figure 11-1. You can add measuring points to your process model, often used as milestones

These milestones do not have any execution semantics other than to leave a trace in the audit trail of the workflow engine. A milestone is met as soon as the process has passed the event; its status can therefore be *passed* or *not passed*.

Another approach is to model phases. In BPMN you can use embedded subprocesses, as shown in Figure 11-2.

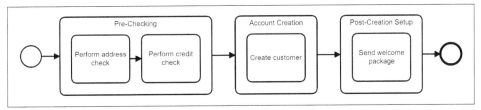

Figure 11-2. You can add phases to your model

In contrast to a milestone, a phase can have a third status: *active*.

You can leverage business milestones and phases for monitoring and reporting, as described throughout this chapter. Most typically, they are used to enable business roles to get an aggregated view or to provide simplified views for end users or customers. Let's briefly investigate the latter a bit more.

Status Inquiries

Imagine you want to answer status inquiries about orders, like "Where is my order?" You probably offer this information in the customer self-service portal. In this case, you can't just use the executable BPMN process, as this typically shows too many internal details that you don't want to disclose, or that may confuse customers.

There are two basic ways to solve this: you can design a custom simplified process model that is specifically intended for the customer (or support agent), or you can leverage milestones or business phases to create a bespoke visualization.

Figure 11-3 shows an example of a custom process model using BPMN. This process model is only used to visualize the status; it is not executed on any engine. This means that the model does not have to be correct, as long as it serves its purpose. In this example, the model simply shows the audit data from certain tasks (including phases) that exist in the real process. Other tasks are removed. As you can see, this model is simply a different visualization—the data can still be accessed from the workflow engine directly, making this easy to implement. A code example is included on the book's website (*https://ProcessAutomationBook.com*).

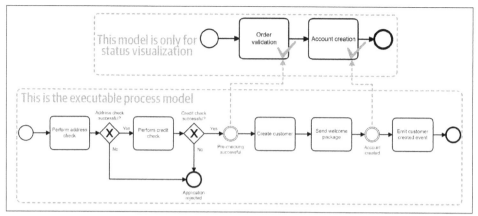

Figure 11-3. A process model only used for status inquiries

However, it's often easier to create a bespoke visualization to show milestones or phases to customers or customer support agents. For example, checklists are very popular for visualizing milestones, as the example in Figure 11-4 shows.

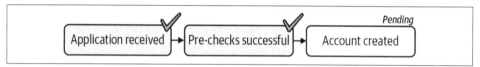

Figure 11-4. Status visibility for customers often has the form of a checklist

A big challenge in this context is finding the right process instances. Customers who call in may not know their process instance IDs. In fact, they might not even know their order number or customer IDs. This means that you need to provide some search capabilities. If this is to be based on workflow engine data alone, you need to make sure to attach the required data to the process instance.

Another observation with status inquiries is that you quickly leave the scope of one process instance. Typically, you want to look at the end-to-end process, and that might start before the workflow engine is involved. As the topic of heterogeneous end-to-end processes is not limited to status inquiries, we'll look at it in a broader scope next.

Understanding Processes That Span Multiple Systems

As you read about in Chapter 7, end-to-end processes are seldom executed in just one context, microservice, or component. Instead, processes cross boundaries. That means end-to-end processes are often not entirely executed on one workflow engine. Take a typical onboarding process—it might start with a paper document (the customer order) being sent, scanned, OCRed, and categorized before a process instance is started in a workflow engine to handle the onboarding flow. In fact, the process might even start earlier, when a prospect downloads the order form.

This means you need to take further action to gain visibility into the end-to-end process. This also applies if your event-driven architecture favors choreography to implement certain parts of the process, as explained in Chapter 8.

This section will briefly introduce approaches used in real life, and their trade-offs. Interestingly enough, many tools in this area are still emerging at the time of writing, so expect some movement in the market.

Observability and Distributed Tracing Tools

A common idea is to leverage existing observability tools from the microservices community. These tools often focus on understanding emergent behavior, as explained in "Emergent Behavior" on page 150, in hindsight.

A common example is distributed tracing, which strives to trace call stacks across different systems and services. This is done by creating unique trace IDs that are added to all remote calls (e.g., in HTTP or messaging headers). If everybody in your universe understands or at least forwards these headers, you can leave breadcrumbs while a request hops through different services. Figure 11-5 shows an example.

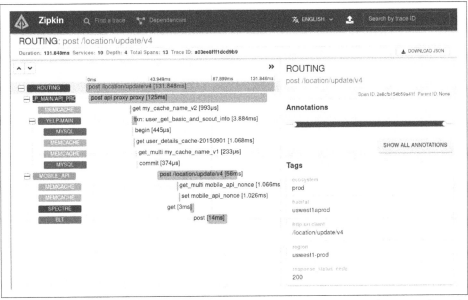

Figure 11-5. Distributed tracing shows distributed stack traces (source: https://zipkin.io)

Distributed traces help you understand how requests flow through the system. This is great for pinpointing failures or investigating the root of performance bottlenecks.

And as there are several mature tools, it is relatively easy to get started, even if you have to instrument your applications or containers to support the traces.

But two factors make it hard to apply distributed tracing tools to the problem of understanding end-to-end business processes:

- Traces are hard for non-engineers to understand. My personal experiments where I showed traces to non-tech people all failed miserably. It was far better to invest some time in redrawing the same information with boxes and arrows. And even if all the information about method calls and messages is useful to understand communication behaviors, it is too fine-grained to understand the essence of cross-service business processes.

- To manage the overwhelming mass of fine-grained data, distributed tracing uses sampling. This means only a small portion of all requests are collected. Typically, more than 90% of the requests are never recorded, so you never have a complete view of what's happening.

Custom Centralized Monitoring

Instead of collecting technical traces, you're better off collecting meaningful business or domain events. This allows you to get the right granularity of information. You can then build your own centralized monitoring tool on top of these events, which is basically a service that listens to all events and stores them in a separate data store. The important aspect is to use technology that can handle the required load and perform the desired queries. This is visualized in Figure 11-6.

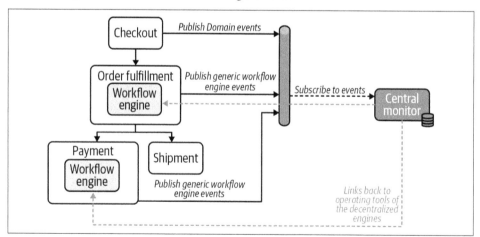

Figure 11-6. Custom centralized monitoring allows you to monitor end-to-end processes in heterogeneous architectures

Events can originate from multiple sources; they can include existing events from your event-driven architecture, custom events emitted for monitoring purposes, or events extracted from legacy systems. Furthermore, good workflow engines support sending relevant events automatically (e.g., that a process instance started, that a milestone was reached, that a process instance failed, or that an instance just ended).

In the easiest case, the centralized monitoring solution shows a list of events, process instances, and current incidents for every end-to-end process instance. This view might provide links to the right operational support tool of the respective workflow engine, which allows you to dive into all the details or to resolve incidents. Figure 11-7 shows an example.

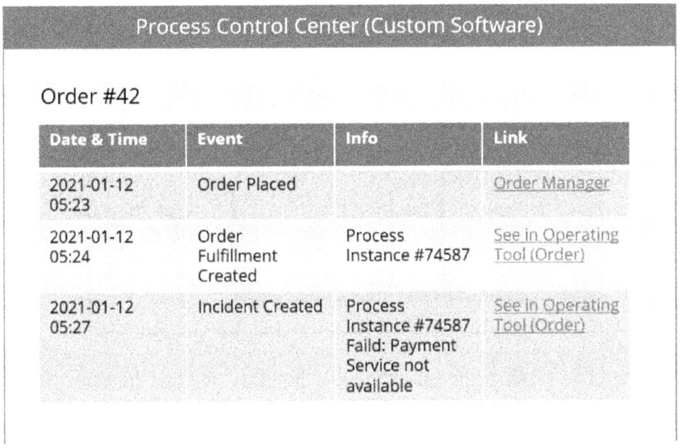

Process Control Center (Custom Software)

Order #42

Date & Time	Event	Info	Link
2021-01-12 05:23	Order Placed		Order Manager
2021-01-12 05:24	Order Fulfillment Created	Process Instance #74587	See in Operating Tool (Order)
2021-01-12 05:27	Incident Created	Process Instance #74587 Faild: Payment Service not available	See in Operating Tool (Order)

Figure 11-7. Central tooling can provide all the relevant information for an end-to-end process, including links to the decentralized operating tools

You can also leverage graphical process models to visualize this information. Lightweight and open source JavaScript frameworks like those from the bpmn.io project (*http://bpmn.io*) make it easy to create HTML pages, as shown in Figure 11-8.

Of course, you can also build multiple models highlighting different aspects of the same end-to-end process. This is especially handy for business analysts who want to focus on a certain hypothesis or process phase.

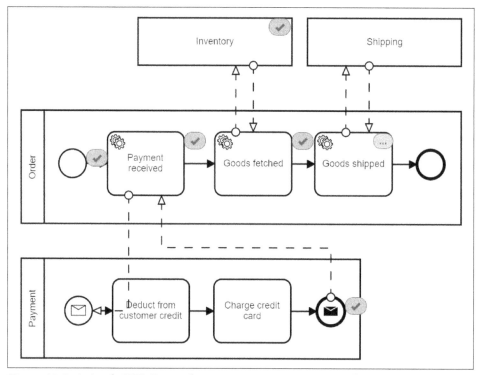

Figure 11-8. A simple HTML page leveraging a BPMN viewer to show status on a graphical process model

Custom monitoring solutions are a powerful mechanism, but need additional effort to build. And a big barrier to introduction in large enterprises can be lack of clarity on the ownership of such a component: who will build, operate, and maintain it?

Data Warehouses, Data Lakes, and Business Intelligence Tools

Of course, you can also leverage existing data warehouses or data lakes. In fact, maybe your existing business intelligence, analytics, or reporting tools can even handle some requirements for end-to-end process monitoring out of the box. This might be a good starting point, as it means you can avoid the hassle of introducing a central tool. This approach is visualized in Figure 11-9.

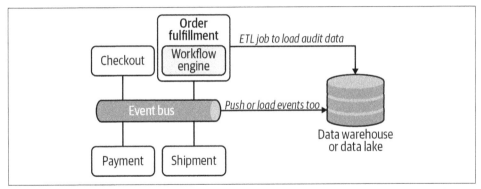

Figure 11-9. Data warehouses can be leveraged to provide insights and therefore collect data from workflow engines

But this approach comes at the price of losing process context and typically also the visualization as process models.

Loading audit data from workflow engines into these tools is often a challenge, as it is hard to preprocess and store the relevant data in a way that leads to actionable data in the DWH.

It might be a good compromise to leverage the DWH as the data store, but still develop a custom user interface on top of it. This has more flexibility when it comes to providing process context, e.g., by showing process diagrams.

Process Mining

A completely different breed of tool is process mining tools. They solve the problem of understanding how a process is actually automated using a mixture of different tools like ERP or CRM systems. Typically, this involves loading and analyzing a bunch of log files from these systems to discover correlations and process flows.

Process mining tools can discover a process model and visualize it graphically. They also allow you to dig into detailed data, especially around bottlenecks or optimization opportunities. A sample is shown in Figure 11-10.

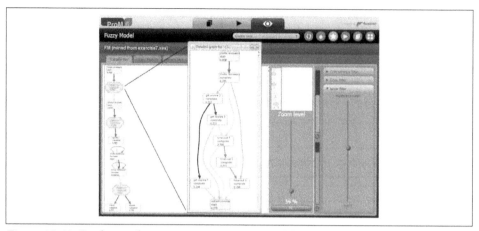

Figure 11-10. Exploring data in a process mining tool (source: https://www.prom tools.org/doku.php)

Process mining adds interesting capabilities for achieving visibility into your business processes. Unfortunately, the focus of most of the tools is on discovering process flows within legacy architectures.

That means these tools are good at log file analysis but not really good at ingesting live event streams. They enable analysis of the discovered process models, but do not serve monitoring or reporting use cases. And they typically leverage direct follower graphs instead of BPMN, making it hard to show these graphics to all stakeholders involved.

Furthermore, in most scenarios, process mining tools are used in extensive analysis projects intended to discover, understand, and analyze a big legacy chaos. In these projects, it can take weeks to discover what events can be leveraged and where to find them.

So, while process mining is valuable, it has a different focus than allowing real-time process monitoring and reporting.

Process Event Monitoring

An emerging category for solving this problem is process event monitoring. The idea is that you can define a process model for monitoring and then map events to certain tasks, as visualized in Figure 11-11.

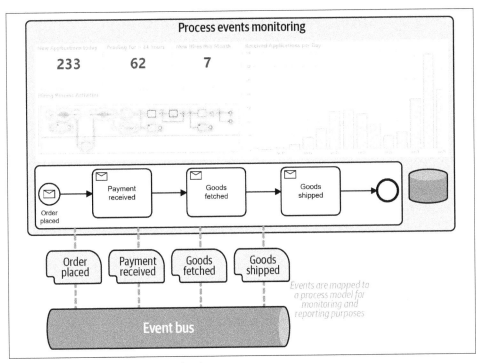

Figure 11-11. Process event monitoring

Events carry a unique trace ID (as described with distributed tracing) and can be ingested from various sources. This solution is comparable to custom monitoring, with the main difference that a lot of functionality comes prebuilt from the vendor.

Current Market Dynamics

By the time you're reading this these categories might have blurred: typical process mining tools might have gotten better at process event monitoring and vice versa; observability tools might add business perspectives; and lightweight tooling might be used as a basis for custom monitoring solutions, reducing implementation effort.

In summary, there are already a few options available today, and in the future I expect this to get a lot easier. I'm excited myself to see exactly how this happens.

Setting Up Process Reporting and Monitoring

To be successful with your process automation project, you have to set up the right reports and metrics. Let's explore this in a bit more detail.

Typical Metrics and Reports

The most important metrics are relatively straightforward. Some are based on process *duration*. These include:

- Cycle time, which refers to the duration of the entire process (either a process running in one workflow engine, or the end-to-end process). This is a key indicator when judging process performance. It is further interesting to analyze trends and outliers, for example in order to understand the reason behind and impact of extremely slow process instances.
- Duration of specific parts or phases of the process. This can be useful if you want to limit your analysis to a smaller part of the process.
- Duration of a single tasks. For example, you might want to verify SLAs or analyze improvement potential for individual steps.

Other typical metrics are based on *count*. For example:

- Number of started and ended instances
- Number of instances visiting a specific path
- Number of instances reaching a specific end state (end event in BPMN)

Ideally, you want to access these metrics in (near) real time, at a large scale, and of course they must be accurate. Furthermore, you might need some alerting in case metrics pass a certain threshold—for example, if delivery time for orders spikes and you need to investigate why. Ideally, all stakeholders involved should be able to access relevant information in a self-service form, possibly even creating their own process-focused visualizations and reports.

This is quite a wish list. But it is actually feasible, if you have monitoring and reporting tools that know about the process context. These tools can spit out all of these numbers and do analysis around them out of the box. However, if you miss the process context, for example because you base your reporting on your own DWH, this analysis might get cumbersome, if not impossible. Typically, real-life projects have to tweak their DWH loading jobs (ETL) to precalculate metrics, like the cycle time for processes, in order to have them available in the DWH. This impedes the business agility you want to achieve with process visibility.

This is why setting up dedicated process monitoring and reporting tools makes a lot of sense. Ideally, you can even provide real-time dashboards with process context. Figure 11-12 shows a real-life example from a customer.

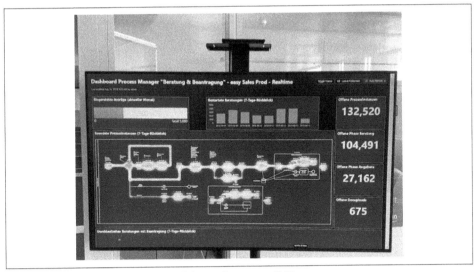

Figure 11-12. Example dashboard for real-time visibility

Allowing for a Deeper Understanding

These generic metrics, aggregated at a relatively high level, are not always enough to facilitate process improvement. You also need to provide more fine-grained data to allow for deeper analysis.

For instance, you might want to be able to distinguish differences depending on the process context, meaning that you need to examine the data attached to process instances. Or you might want the ability to track changes over time; for example, to analyze trends. It can be useful to incorporate the process state when doing reports, as it makes a difference if processes are still running, if they completed, or if they were canceled. Furthermore, you also want to be able to look into the path a process took, as certain special cases will need investigation.

Imagine an insurance onboarding process, where people can apply for a new car insurance contract. An example is shown in Figure 11-13. In this process, some contracts need manual approval. This means that the overall cycle time also varies greatly, as customers are served very fast in the fully automated case, but relatively slowly in the manual case.

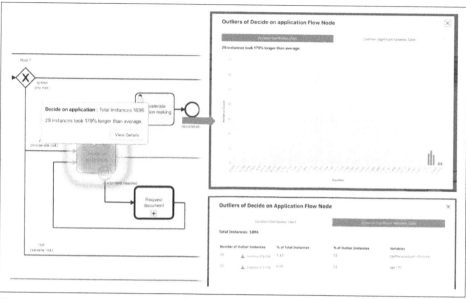

Figure 11-13. With process context knowledge you can make sense out of the data, like analyzing outliers

Now suppose that you investigate the data and learn quickly that even the duration for the human task instances also varies widely. You're curious as to why this is the case, especially as you want to discover how to speed things up. So, you analyze the outliers with regard to the duration of that task. You get some insights as soon as you look into the data attached to the process instances, because all of the slow processes involve older drivers applying for fast sports cars. This gives you a good basis to talk to the team lead of the clerks, to clarify why these cases seem to be more complicated than others. The process context helps you to find the important indicators to improve process performance and thus customer satisfaction.

Conclusion

You get some degree of process visibility for free when using workflow engines to automate processes.

However, many processes, especially end-to-end processes, are heterogeneous. This chapter described how to gain visibility in this case, either by using off-the-shelf products geared toward process event monitoring or process mining, or by implementing a custom monitoring solution. Typical DWH and BI tools don't cut it, as the process context is missing, which makes generating even simple reports hard and flexible, deep analysis impossible. Finally, this chapter gave you some starting points regarding what metrics and reports you want to set up.

PART III

Get Going!

This last part of the book will focus your attention on introducing process automation successfully in your company.

Chapter 12

Here, you'll learn what a successful adoption journey can look like, highlighting a pragmatic, Agile, and iterative process to introduce process automation. This chapter describes the difference between top-down directives and bottom-up success stories; it will help you understand not only how to set up your first project for success, but also how to scale adoption later.

Chapter 13

The concluding chapter of the book presents some closing thoughts.

CHAPTER 12

The Journey to Introduce Process Automation

This chapter will answer questions like: how can you introduce process automation into your organization? How can you make your first project successful? And how do you establish a company-wide practice to scale adoption?

To achieve this, it:

- Sketches two typical adoption journeys and derives a pattern from them
- Describes the first steps in this journey, which are the crucial ones (particularly in the first one to three process automation projects)
- Dives into scaling adoption across the entire organization, and all the challenges that come with that

You might wonder why you're reading about these topics in a technical book. The reason is twofold. First, as a developer or software architect, you need be aware of certain challenges to be able to address them. Even if politics are beyond your direct control, you will be affected by them, and you need to take actions that will help avoid major problems with your projects.

Second, if you are an enterprise architect, it is vital to learn best practices on how to introduce process automation into your enterprise. Your job is not only to understand capabilities and architecture, but also to find the right balance between giving important guidance, defining necessary guardrails, and letting projects breathe. Instead of defining "the right architecture" for your company, you will much more likely end up as an internal consultant and facilitator. This chapter will equip you with the basics to achieve that.

Understanding the Adoption Journey

But first things first, let's understand the typical journey to adopt process automation. I find it most helpful to learn from examples, so we'll look at two stories here. One is a made-up failure story that contains many elements from real life. It will help you understand failures you definitely want to avoid. The second is a real-life story from a customer I have observed over many years. This story will emphasize the elements that led to their success.

Failures You Want to Avoid

Imagine you are an IT executive at the fictional company DontDoItAtHome Inc. DontDoItAtHome provides a marketplace for handcrafted goods that customers don't want to build themselves at home.

After a vendor event, your CIO returns to the office enthusiastically talking about the potential of process automation and the great impact workflow automation platforms can have on the productivity of your developers. They explain how process orientation is a strategic topic and suggest that you should set up a central workflow engine to enable broad adoption throughout your enterprise.

You ask them how they want to start that initiative—and what project should first adopt the new methodology. They tell you that process automation is too strategic to start with a trivial project. No—they plan to set up a whole program for it! They even promise all of the funding—isn't that great? Although you do wonder where that money will come from; they told you just last month that there was no budget left for an important feature your customers are begging for.

Your CIO assembles a team to evaluate a workflow tool, specifically asking that they don't forget the vendor that hosted the great event they attended. After choosing a product, this team will build a company-specific platform around the core product to support your specific IT infrastructure. The plan is that once this platform is in place, projects can race through automating important business processes.

In order to prepare input for this race, another team is pulled together. They collect all the relevant business processes and sketch them on a process landscape. As proposed by a big consultancy company, they follow a layered approach for the process architecture. They describe relevant business processes down to a very detailed level, which should serve as input for the automation projects that will soon implement the executable processes on the new platform.

Six months into this endeavor, your CEO starts to get nervous and wants to see results. Neither the workflow platform nor the process architecture team has delivered any immediate business value. Your CIO is being pressured to show real achievements that translate into a proper business case for such a huge investment.

The CIO wants to make a statement and decides to automate the most crucial process first, which is the order fulfillment process. This will get a lot of visibility in the business, and they are convinced that they'll be able to show how great and important the workflow platform is for the company.

A new project team is formed to implement order fulfillment. They have no experience with workflow engines, and certainly not with the new internal platform. And learning about that internal platform is difficult because it is poorly documented. They need to consult the platform team regularly.

Upon learning more about the underlying workflow product by doing some research on the internet, the project team discovers that the in-house platform blocks them from using more than half of its features. On top of that, it uses a version of the tool that is a year old and has severe shortcomings, all of which the vendor has fixed in the latest version.

And the platform team has no time to work on any of their requests: several additional process automation projects have been kicked off, and the platform team's capacity is fully consumed by simply explaining the platform to everybody involved.

As a result, the order fulfillment team has to work with half the features of an already outdated engine, plus bespoke features that are either useless, undocumented, or unstable (or all three at the same time).

On top of that, they get a process model from the process landscape project as a requirement. The expectation is that they just need to implement it. How hard can that be? As it turns out, it is impossibly hard. That process model is basically not usable. It's missing a lot of details needed for implementation and also contains a lot of wishful thinking about what a to-be process could look like. The project team discovers that the process model needs severe changes that will also influence how a lot of employees throughout the organization will work in the future.

At the same time, business departments are tired of discussing the process model, as they've already held too many meetings six months ago to model the process as part of the process landscape setup. Unfortunately, these efforts did not yield tangible results or improvements for the business.

Of course, nobody in the company wants to hear this reality, especially given the fact that the same workflow tool works nicely for other companies, and that a ton of money was just invested in this program. As a result, the organization might not even learn from their failures, so it will be doomed soon after.

You can derive a lot of insights from this example:

- Don't start with big strategic endeavors too early in your journey. Start with a project, not a program.
- Avoid a top-down adoption motion; create an environment that allows bottom-up growth instead. A great balance is to have an environment where grass-roots initiatives can start, and then support the most promising ones to drive adoption. Scaling adoption should always come as a second step.
- Resist the temptation to create your own platform.
- Pick the right processes to be automated first. The most important core process in its entirety might be a bit too big, too risky, and too complicated to attempt as a first step.
- Don't start too many projects at once.
- Concentrate on delivering business value. Your process solution needs to solve a real business pain.
- Don't start with process architecture or process landscape initiatives. You cannot expect to derive ready-to-be-used process models for your process automation projects up front. You'll be better able to sketch process architectures later, when you know how process automation really works.
- Let your own learnings influence your target picture, which includes embracing a culture where failures are openly discussed to learn from them. Vendors' or consulting companies' best practices (or books) can serve as a good starting point, but can't replace finding your own way.
- Make sure to let project teams breathe and make their own decisions.

A Success Story

Let's contrast DontDoItAtHome with a real-life success story. This story is about an insurance company with around 7,000 employees, which I won't name here. I also can't deliver the same amount of detail as in the fictional story, but will concentrate on a summary instead.

In 2014, the insurance company formed a team to automate the handling of specific car insurance claims. There was a real pain point here, as the existing claim handling was mainly manually driven and spanned a couple of organizational units. This made it easy to build a business case for the project and get buy-in from top management. This was further backed (not driven) by the strategic initiative to intensify "process orientation," which was a hot topic for insurance companies back then.

As part of this project they:

- Evaluated a workflow tool
- Analyzed and modeled the one executable process
- Implemented the whole process solution
- Integrated it with their existing user interface
- Integrated it with their existing SOA infrastructure
- Exported relevant data into their data warehouse
- Put it into production and operated it

The big secret to the success of that initial project was that the focus was on solving a business pain. Introducing workflow automation technology was an important step in that project for strategic reasons, but they managed to keep a good level of pragmatism. For example, when they discussed process reporting in their DWH, the project manager cut off discussions that went into too much detail. Instead, they pushed for implementing the minimum viable feature set required for this project in a timely manner.

I also remember one nice anecdote around that project. During the evaluation phase, some big vendors pitched their workflow tooling, but so did my company, as the only open source vendor. We were small at that time, and could not yet show long lists of insurance references. Still, we were invited to a first sales meeting. I only heard later that the project team was deeply impressed by the pre-sales consultant (me) choosing not to focus on slide shows and white papers, but insisting instead on showing a demo, explaining source code, and kicking off a proof of concept as soon as possible. It was the exact opposite of the big vendors' pitches, and this resonated with them so well that they also convinced their CEO. The rest is history.

After the initial project, the team was reorganized into its own department. They were given the responsibility of helping other teams with the design and development of process solutions. In the first two or three years, they did a lot of the implementation work for these teams, but over time evolved into an internal consulting task force that "just" helped other teams to get started.

In an organic way, they became the go-to place for any questions or discussions around workflow tooling. As such, they not only made sure experiences and insights were kept, but also facilitated knowledge sharing across the entire organization. Today, they also run an internal BPM blog, organize their own training classes, and manage an annual internal community event where different teams can share best practices.

While they did develop some tools on top of the workflow engine, they never forced anybody in the company to use them. And while they started operating a central BPM platform back in 2015, they moved away from this model soon after and now allow solution teams to run their own engines. They still provide reusable components around the engine, e.g., to hook into Active Directory or to talk to their internal ESB, but these are provided as additional libraries.

They are now in the process of starting an internal service to provide managed workflow engines, to ease provisioning and operations for their project teams.

By the end of 2019, this company had almost one hundred different process solutions running in production. Not only is the BPM team super satisfied, but so too are upper management.

The key takeaways from this story are:

- Go step-by-step until you are ready to scale.
- Get buy-in from the decision makers, which requires your process solution to solve some real business pain.
- Make sure to give experienced people the opportunity to help in follow-on projects.
- Capture best practices and ensure knowledge sharing.
- Provide reusable components if they increase productivity, but as libraries that teams want to adopt.
- Establish an internal consulting approach, perhaps organized as a center of excellence. At least identify and nurture one well-known champion in the enterprise that can drive the topic.
- Define learning paths for new people or teams.

Having looked at these two very different examples, let's dig deeper into what defines successful adoption journeys.

The Pattern of Successful Adoption Journeys

From hundreds of real-life stories like the two sketched here, my colleagues and I have derived a simple pattern that is most successful when introducing workflow tooling into an organization. It is shown in Figure 12-1.

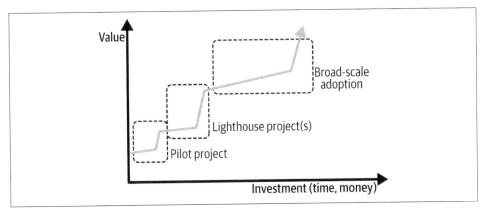

Figure 12-1. Typical adoption journey

While evaluating your stack you need to setup a proof of concept project. The goal of this project is to define and validate the architecture and stack, the exact code is most often thrown away.

Right after this POC, start with a pilot project. It is essential to go live with the pilot to really learn about all aspects of the process solution throughout the full software development life cycle. You should choose a scenario where you can show at least some of the benefits of process automation (e.g., increased efficiency, effectiveness, compliance), as many people, including decision makers, will be interested in quantifiable results.

Favor Agile development approaches to develop process solutions iteratively and incrementally. This allows you to learn fast and let these learnings correct your course. This is a very positive and motivating spiral that I have seen working often. It's especially important for projects using new tools or architectures.

While this is the case in some organizations, the pilot project might not be centrally planned as "the process automation starting point." Very often these projects simply start as projects intending to solve a business pain, and adopt process automation technology along the way. This is totally fine and might even make it easier for the project to avoid too much politics in the beginning.

After running a successful pilot, start a lighthouse project. This is either a deliberate step in your journey to introduce process automation, or it naturally follows a successful grassroots pilot initiative where you recognized the potential of process automation.

A lighthouse project has a broader, more realistic scope and can be leveraged to show off architecture, tooling, and the value of process automation to other people and teams within your organization. It acts as a lighthouse to guide other peers in the company toward the value of process automation. Make sure that you select a relevant use case.

Ideally, the team that did the pilot also works on the lighthouse, as this allows all of their learnings to be taken into account. This is important as the lighthouse might serve as a template for later projects. This is why you should also plan some time to review the lighthouse project after it has been completed and gone live. Keep in mind that it is far better to invest in that overhaul than to try to make things perfect in the first run.

Make sure that the lighthouse gets visibility within the company. Follow a "show and tell" approach, giving internal presentations, sharing the source code (including documentation), and inviting people to discussions. Typically you should prefer live demos over slideware and concrete company projects over generic vendor showcases.

Only then should you take the next step, which is to scale process automation across your enterprise. You should enter this phase slowly. Make sure not to go too broad before you have gathered enough relevant experience from a handful of projects. Ideally, this scaling works in a "pull" manner, meaning that project teams hear of the advantages of process automation and decide they want to apply it in their own projects.

The whole journey is visualized in more detail in Figure 12-2, which is taken from a best practice called the customer success path (*https://oreil.ly/CF44F*).

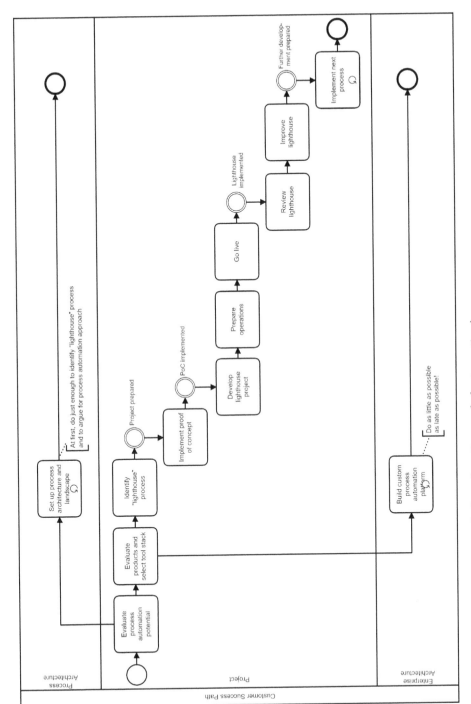

Figure 12-2. Customer success path (based on Camunda best practices)

Different Journeys for Different Scenarios

Of course, some specifics about the adoption journey will vary depending on your status quo at your organization and your main driver for introducing process automation. Let's quickly discuss some typical situations.

Replacing existing workflow products

In my consulting engagements, I work with a lot of companies that already have some workflow product in place and want to replace it. This might be a tool that's been discontinued by its vendor, an open source framework that has proved too low-level for the company's needs, or simply a tool that did not deliver on its promise. As part of digital transformation or IT modernization programs, companies might also deliberately decide to replace "old-school BPMS" or homegrown workflow engines that will not be maintained any longer.

This is a special situation, as the organization is already aware of what process automation means and what a workflow engine is. Teams already have experience with process modeling and know what it means to execute such a model. Even if they need to adjust in terms of architecture and stack, a lot of the basics concepts are familiar, which can make the whole journey much easier.

However, you need to keep an eye on preconceptions. Remember "Not Your Parents' Process Automation Tools" on page 14? Other people might have a different view of process automation than you have after reading this book. You might need to have some strong discussions.

An additional challenge might be that you need to justify why you want to introduce a new tool. I have seen many companies that required sophisticated studies to justify replacing an old tool, even if everybody hated it and nobody was productive with it. This can be an important consideration, as it might shift the focus of a pilot or lighthouse project. You might not need to make a case for process automation, but you might need to justify the migration to a new tool.

Finally, you might need to investigate the root of the problems with the old tool. Sometimes the issue is not so much the tool itself, but mistakes in how it was used; e.g., applying it to the wrong problems or setting up weird architectural patterns. In this case, you need to avoid the same mess occurring with the new tool, so people might need to unlearn some of their practices or be made aware of and admit mistakes made in the past.

Introducing process automation in SOA environments

If you work for a company that has adopted SOA, the strategy for introducing process automation will depend on the internal viewpoint on this architecture. There are plenty of companies that are basically happy with SOA and want to keep going with it. That's fine; you don't have to switch to a microservices approach to apply process automation! But you should be careful about introducing a process automation approach that is too centralized, even if that can also work out if it fits into your organization and culture.

Introducing process automation in event-driven architectures

Maybe you work for a company that embraced event-driven microservices, and you're now facing an unmanageable amount of services with a lot of emerging behavior, as described in Chapter 8. In this case your journey might be very different.

For example, you could first try to gain some visibility without the need to change too much. You could create a process model that expresses your expectation of what happens. You will make that model executable, but special in the sense that it is only tracking events, and not doing anything actively itself. It does not steer anything—it simply records.

This will allow you to leverage the complete toolchain around your workflow engine, including monitoring, so you can see what's currently going on, monitor SLAs and detect stuck instances, or do extensive analysis on historical audit data.

And this model can be the first step in a journey toward more orchestration. A simple example is that you start to monitor timeouts for your end-to-end process. Whenever a timeout is hit, some action is taken automatically. In the example in Figure 12-3, you would inform the customer of a delay after 14 days—but still keep waiting. After 21 days, you give up and cancel the order.

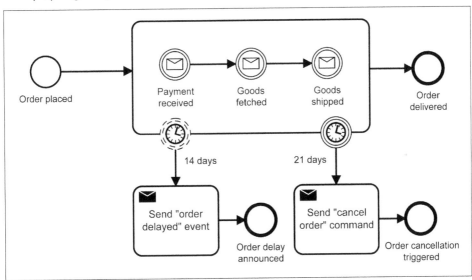

Figure 12-3. A BPMN model that tracks events can also get active in certain scenarios

This is a good basis to evolve the process to take over end-to-end responsibility for order fulfillment. You can do this step-by-step. For example, you might start with orchestrating payment deliberately from this process, removing a part of the ongoing event chain.

I know of many real-life examples where such a tracking process was the beginning of a modernization project. More often than replacing a choreography, these processes pick up events from various legacy systems, where connections under the hood are slowly removed and replaced by orchestration.

Strategic initiatives driving process automation

Another situation is if your company has started a strategic program that drives the adoption of process automation. At the time of writing, these are typically digital transformation programs.

These programs own budget. This gives you a great opportunity to introduce process automation and solve some real business problems—but it is super important to follow the advice to start small and with a concrete project fulfilling a business need. Too often, I see strategic programs end up in the situation sketched with DontDoItAtHome.

In that context, I even see many successful process automation projects deliberately flying under the radar of these programs, to avoid them getting in the way. Flying under the radar can make sense.

As a summary, every situation is a bit different. Try to become aware of the status quo, the history, and of course the goal of your process automation endeavor and adjust accordingly.

Starting Your Journey

Whatever your journey will look like, at some point in time you always have to start it. And the first steps are the most important, so let's examine these in more depth.

Of course, when starting any process automation endeavor you have to select a tool stack first, described in "Evaluating Workflow Engines" on page 123. The recommendation is to start creating POCs as soon as possible. Modern tools allow you to automate your first process within hours, so you can do POCs with more than one vendor. You might want to partner with a consulting firm you trust that has some experience with different vendors, as they can help you get started right away. The hands-on experience of doing POCs will greatly help you shape your direction.

Bottom-up Versus Top-down Adoption

Before diving into the characteristics of the POCs themselves, let's consider the two typical motions that are in play in bigger enterprises when it comes to the adoption of methods and tools: bottom up and top down.

Adoption can start at the bottom and work its way up. This often happens with open source components. Developers might learn about a tool somewhere and start to play around with it. Once they understand the possibilities, they become enthusiastic about it; they might apply the tool right away to solve a problem at hand, or even push it into production.

At this point, a proper evaluation of the tool has not been done; basically the company jumped into a POC right away. If it is successful, this project gets noticed and serves as a lighthouse, and other projects start adopting the tooling.

If the project scope or visibility grows bigger, at some point in time a business, legal, or compliance department might kick in and ask for guarantees. Or someone might request support, or the company might find that it really needs features that are only available in a paid version of the tool.

In this case, the company basically starts the procurement process at a stage where the tool is already settled and an evaluation does not make much sense. This isn't necessarily a bad thing, as the tool has proven its value. Personally, I'm a big fan of this motion as I have often seen it be very successful.

This is in contrast to a top-down adoption motion, where the tooling is basically decided on at the top and handed over to development projects. In an extreme form, an enterprise decides on a company-wide process automation tool stack that every project has to use. This is the adoption motion that was typically in play with SOA projects. Looking at the history of SOA, you can see that developers still played a decisive role, though—in this case usually by either just not using these tools or failing to use them successfully.

So even if this top-down motion often plays to my own company's advantage (if Camunda is chosen as the platform), I recommend being very careful with it. You can define company-wide recommendations, but you should still leave the projects enough room to decide on their own. This will increase the chances of tools being embraced, rather than rejected.

Proofs of Concepts

Now let's explore what makes a good POC, and how you can prepare and run it properly. With a POC, you typically create a prototype application within no more than three to five days. The result is intended to be thrown away, which is very important to keep in mind. Its sole purpose is to try to show that your project will fly, including all aspects relevant for your specific situation. Questions to consider might be:

- Is it possible to use the workflow tooling in your own architecture and stack?
- Does the development approach fit into your organization?
- Can you model the specific business domain problem?
- What kinds of know-how are needed for the different roles?
- How much effort will be needed for these kinds of projects?
- What is the impact of process automation for operations?

Often it makes sense to implement a POC together with the workflow vendor or a specialized consultant, in order to get quick results and focused feedback with respect to your specific challenges. However, you should always at least co-develop in order to really understand what is going on. A team size of two to four people has proven to be quite optimal.

Before planning a POC, you need to consciously clarify the specific goals you want to achieve. This will have a great influence on the POC, so make up your mind about what really matters. Often it's better to make a clear choice about whether, for example, it is more important to be able to show off a nice user interface at the end of the week or to have clarified all the technical questions and to understand the workflow engine of choice in depth, maybe using nothing more than unit tests.

Typical goals for a POC include:

- To verify that the approach or the tool works under specific circumstances
- To show a case that convinces internal stakeholders that the approach makes sense
- To work through a complete example and get specific questions sorted out
- To learn more about the tool and understand how it works

When planning your team, consider that you need knowledge about the business domain, the targeted technical solution, and the modeling language (e.g., BPMN), as well as analytical and moderation skills. Define a moderator to avoid too many detours and keep your POC on track. Let people learn on the job by developing the POC together with an experienced consultant.

In some companies, people want to build a minimum viable product (MVP) instead of a POC. An MVP is basically a first simple version that already delivers some value. The big difference is that it is not thrown away. While I see great value in putting such an MVP into production and learning throughout the entire life cycle, I would still only do it after creating an initial POC. The POC can also be seen as a quick prototype to validate the architecture. It is almost always better to throw it away and start from scratch after, as this allows the POC to focus on learning instead of production-quality code. And with a POC taking just a few days, the time investment is not too big either.

Make sure to present the results of the POC internally. Select a speaker who is comfortable with presenting, prepare a set of focused slides illustrating your progress and the lessons learned, and test your solution and presentation at least once. It is surprising how often teams do some awesome work over the course of a week and then expect that a spontaneous demo will speak for itself. It typically does not—invest some extra time to think about a storyline so that people can follow and understand why and how you applied process automation.

Presenting the Business Case

A proper presentation should also talk about the business case. A great example I saw recently was a meeting where a customer was discussing the start of their process automation adoption journey. They described their first use case, a process that replaced a couple of emails and one spreadsheet with a BPMN process that had five tasks. So far, that sounds kind of boring. But then they presented a slide where they calculated their ROI. This was the exact opposite of boring!

The company had invested roughly $100,000 in this project, which took three months to go live. By saving manual labor, they were able to assign several people to new roles. The savings in salaries alone amounted to roughly $1 million every year! Of course, nobody in the company questioned this project's success, and it helped them greatly in fostering adoption of process automation practices.

Another great example I saw was at a large bank that replaced a legacy application for tax operations operated by an external service provider with a workflow engine-based in-house solution. This saved them service and licensing costs of roughly €1 million in the first year and about €3 million in each year that followed. Additionally, they were able to bring the ownership of and capability for a key regulatory system in-house. The new system has received glowing feedback from its users, with comments that it is a "night and day difference" to its predecessor enables them to serve customers much more effectively and efficiently.

If you have such numbers, make sure to present them. Important decision makers internally need to be aware of the business case.

But often, I see scenarios where the value is more qualitative and harder to calculate. For instance, one customer with a microservices architecture told me that they would have been in serious trouble if they had not introduced process automation, because pure choreography would have resulted in chaos.

This is hard to put in numbers, as it is more about avoiding risk or technical debt. Fortunately, upper management understood that reasoning and backed the introduction of process automation.

Sometimes it helps to search for success or failure stories in the same industry. Your process automation vendor of choice may be able to help with this. As a summary, Table 12-1 shows typical value propositions with examples for inspiration.

Table 12-1. Value propositions of workflow automation

Value proposition	Type	Measurability	Example
Reducing development effort around state handling	Quantitative	Hard to measure	Implementing and maintaining bespoke state handling was estimated to account for roughly 10 person years over the lifetime of the software, which corresponds to around $1,000,000. A workflow engine is used now out of the box. License, training, and ramp-up costs summed up to roughly $100,000. As a bonus, your best developers can focus on important things.
Automating manual tasks	Quantitative	Easy to measure	A new onboarding workflow is going live that does a first validation automatically. This saves four hours of work in sales on every business day. Additionally, the tracking of the onboarding workflow is automated, and customers can see their current status in a self-service portal online. This sums up to saved effort equivalent to one person. You save roughly $100,000 and improve quality for everybody involved.
Building the right thing	Qualitative	Hard to measure	Process visibility allows a variety of people to understand the process design in early phases. So, while implementing a process to provision new mobile phone contracts, a developer from another team is able to spot a fundamental flaw in the process model: a particular service cannot be used "that way," as they know from previous projects where they learned this the hard way. The problem is discussed and the model updated right away, taking about a person day of effort. That problem could have stayed hidden until the rollout, when it would have cost many days of effort to discuss the required change, plan it, implement it, retest everything, and so on and so forth.
Avoiding stuck process instances	Qualitative	Hard to measure	Whenever there is some failure in processing, an order does not simply get stuck and wait for the customer to ask for their goods. Instead, operations gets notified of any incidents and can easily look into the problems and fix the instances before the customers even notice the delay.
Understanding the current status	Qualitative	Hard to measure	Getting set up with cable internet can be a time-consuming process. Gaining visibility into the exact current status is important to keep customers and support agents happy. The alternative is frustrating, when customers call the company and they can't give a good answer about the status of an order.

Value proposition	Type	Measurability	Example
Saving effort by using prebuilt functionality	Quantitative	Easy to measure	Workflow tools come with ready-to-use components like GUIs for operations and for human task management. The latter can actually be a huge gain, as they involves task life cycle support, extensive APIs, and prebuilt user interfaces. You can save the cost of a team of full-time developers, quickly summing up to $500,000 or more every year.
Scaling processes	Qualitative	Hard to measure	Your latest commercial went viral, and people are storming your service. You couldn't keep the lights on without process automation, as you would simply be overwhelmed by manual work. A workflow engine makes sure you stay in control when incidents occur on a bigger scale.

Note that process automation technology is an enabler for certain architecture paradigms that would not be possible without it. When organizations want to apply these paradigms for strategic reasons—say, moving toward a microservices architecture in order to handle organizational scale and allow for business agility—this can be sufficient motivation to introduce a tool, even if there is not a concrete business case in the first project.

Don't Build Your Own Platform

Having talked so much about the business case, let's briefly discuss the exact opposite of providing immediate business value: building a company-wide process automation platform on top of a vendor's tool. Some companies even assemble a whole SOA or integration stack with components from different vendors.

I see this happen so often that it is worth its own section. The reason to build such a platform is typically twofold: companies don't want to be dependent on the vendor, and they need some integration into company specifics that all projects can leverage.

But building such a platform is a risky endeavor, for multiple reasons. It is quite hard to set up a process automation platform, and attempting it will distract you from delivering business value. It makes it hard to include learnings gleaned from later projects, as you settle on certain architecture primitives very early in your journey. Also, it is complicated and time-consuming to keep this platform up-to-date or to fix bugs—or simply to make all the features of the underlying products available, or to include new features introduced in new versions. And finally, users can't do internet searches for help with problems in the bespoke platform, which they can do for well-known open source products.

So far, every one of these initiatives that I have seen has struggled. You should not think about creating a bespoke platform before you have a couple of projects live, as only then can you really understand the common characteristics and what is likely to be valuable and applicable in all projects.

Of course, you might still do some work in the initial projects to make operations or enterprise architects happy. For example, you might integrate with your authentication and authorization infrastructure, or make sure the workflow tooling adds its logs into your central logging facility. This kind of code may be valuable for upcoming projects, and you might want to reuse it.

Dos and Don'ts Around Reuse

Reuse can make a lot of sense, as it means you can save effort and costs. If all of your process solutions need to communicate with your messaging infrastructure or your mainframe, you don't want to reinvent that wheel in every project.

But instead of building a bespoke platform, another pattern usually turns out to be more successful. Think of reusable components or libraries as internal open source projects. You offer them to your company and provide some resources and help. If a library is helpful, most people will happily apply it. But nobody has to. These libraries can develop and evolve in the very first projects. If later projects need some additional feature, then they are not locked out from extending the library themselves—as they can always provide pull requests—or fork the project.

This kind of reuse scales really well and helps your developers. At the same time, it does not block anybody from being productive.

 Always focus on providing helpful guidelines instead of putting constraints in place.

Many process automation initiatives also take up the idea of extracting process fragments that can be reused in different business processes. I am skeptical about this. If the scope is limited to one project team, it's fine, but these fragments should not be shared across teams. In the latter case you are better off extracting this logic into its own service with properly defined capabilities and APIs that can be used in different contexts, as discussed in Chapter 7.

From Project to Program: Scaling Adoption

After the first five or six successful projects, including the pilot and lighthouse, it starts to make sense to think about a more structured approach to scaling adoption within your organization. Make sure not to start scaling earlier, as you will miss important learnings and risk making the same mistakes in parallel projects, possibly even leading to friction between these projects.

This section discusses some challenges and proven practices around scale.

Perception Management: What Is Process Automation?

Customers use workflow engines for very different use cases. In my company's customer base, a common theme is to build solutions that are essentially Java applications, but also contain an executable process. Internally these applications are seen as "Camunda projects," even if the process part of the application is very small.

While this is not a problem, it comes with a risk. If customers build huge bespoke applications, it can take a lot of time before they are actually put it into production. This kind of project tends to get very expensive, or might even be canceled due to too many problems in the implementation. These factors are not at all related to the workflow engine, but because the projects are "Camunda projects," this ends up damaging the reputation of process automation.

So, be careful about what you connect to the topic of "process automation."

Establishing a Center of Excellence

If you have one team doing the pilot and probably also the lighthouse project, they will not only become very familiar with the technology and architecture, but also learn a lot of valuable lessons. Make sure these learnings can be leveraged in the projects that follow.

One option is for these people to simply continue building process solutions as a team. This is definitely efficient, but does not scale. You could also split up the team and send the individual people to work on different projects. This is an approach I have seen work very well, but it means you need to have some flexibility in team assignments. A third possibility is the one sketched in the success story presented earlier: transform the project team into a center of excellence (COE), as visualized in Figure 12-4.

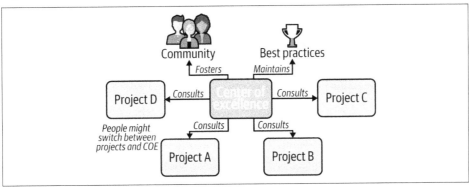

Figure 12-4. A center of excellence can help you scale the adoption of process automation

This can be set up as dedicated tool-specific COE, but more often it is a general process automation COE charged with evaluating process automation technology and helping decide what is the right tool for the job at hand. Typically, these COEs also manage technologies around robotic process automation (RPA) or skill-based routing for human tasks.

The COE creates and maintains internal best practices, often leaning on vendor documentation and best practices as a basis. You should also document decisions, constraints, or additions that apply to your company. For example, you might want projects to always use a specific distribution of a tool. You can describe how the tool is hooked into your central Active Directory. You can also link a couple of internal projects that provide integration into messaging, SOAP web services, or FTP.

One big bank told me how it had developed a "self-service portal" within the COE over the course of two years. This portal contains getting started guides, Java project templates, and some reusable components as maintained libraries. This setup allows most projects to get going on their own, including projects staffed by big offshore IT integrators. The COE team developed the first six workflow solutions themselves, but seven additional projects have already been completed via self-service, which proves the efficacy of their approach.

The COE can also foster a community, simply by being available to talk to. They might provide a forum or a Slack channel, or run regular face-to-face or web meetings. The right approach depends heavily on your company's culture.

It is also worth investing in internal marketing, as it is important that other projects know about the COE. You might even want to talk publicly about your use case, if possible.

Managing Architecture Decisions

I am not a fan of rigid standardization. Project teams need some freedom to choose the right tools. In many situations it is even best if the team can, for example, decide if it needs a workflow engine at all. Your COE and lighthouse projects might have generated enough internal marketing for people to know the benefits of using one, so they should be able to decide for themselves.

But of course, it is risky to let every team choose whatever they fancy in that moment, as those decisions may be swayed by trends, hype, personal preferences, or simply people having a go with something they've "wanted to try for ages." It is important for everybody to understand that certain technology decisions are a commitment for years, and sometimes even decades. So these decisions and the resulting maintenance will affect more than just the current team.

What works well is to combine the freedom of choice with the responsibility to operate and support the software solution in production, which is known as "you build it, you run it." This important primitive makes teams aware that they will be held accountable for their decisions. When this is truly the case, teams tend to make more sensible decisions and are more likely to choose what Dan McKinley calls "boring technology" (*https://mcfunley.com/choose-boring-technology*).

Another common approach is to establish an architecture board that defines some guardrails. Ideally, this board does not dictate arbitrary standards but maintains a list of approved tools and frameworks. Whenever a team wants to use something that is not (yet) on the list, they have to discuss it with that board. Teams need to present the framework and the reasons why they need exactly this tool. This can even lead to a fruitful sparring around the tool choice. Teams might learn about alternatives that are better suited, or they might get questions around maintenance they have not thought of. But of course, they can also convince the board and get a green light. These boards should not block progress, so either they must decide very fast or allow teams to go ahead without permission but understanding that if they do something outrageous, they might be asked to rethink their approach.

I have also seen more rigid gatekeeping, especially around bridge technologies that can easily be abused. For example, one big customer requires every team that wants to use RPA to pitch its use case first. The goal is that these teams are fully aware that they're increasing technical debt. They need to present a strategy to pay the debt back (e.g., to migrate to proper APIs later).

Decentralized Workflow Tooling

This book suggests that you should prefer an approach where every team runs its own workflow engine, especially in a microservices context. The main advantage is to allow for scale by isolating teams. This also means that you deliberately accept the potential of a wild mix of workflow platform installations.

This raises questions. How can you get an overview of what is actually running? How can you make sure the installations have all the important patches? Are all engines doing well? How do you collect metrics from various engines to check if you are within your license limits? Typically, these questions are asked by the center of excellence, your workflow champion, or an enterprise architect with responsibility for process automation.

How these questions are answered depends on the tool at hand, but often it is as simple as automatically harvesting the relevant data from different engines within the company using APIs the tool provides. You might even go further and allow updating or patching engines with the click of a button.

Of course, all of this gets even easier if you use managed services in the cloud, as they already have control planes built-in that provide these capabilities. This might also apply to private cloud installations.

Roles and Skill Development

In order to scale you need to actively develop the right skills internally, some on the job, some in training. The exact needs depend on the tool in use. As a rule of thumb, the more developer-friendly a tool is, the less proprietary training you need.

Let's quickly sketch typical learning paths for different personas in a project. For developers, I differentiate between different types.

Rockstar developers
> These are the early adopters who can sometimes perform miracles. They are highly motivated and passionate. You simply give them the workflow engine and a getting started guide, and get out of their way. They will most probably Google their way through. These folks are probably best suited to the early projects and perhaps the COE. They come with the challenge that they always want the latest and greatest technology and sometimes tend to overengineer. They are not always good at coaching others. And please pay attention, as such people are easily distracted.

Professional developers
> These developers are trained software engineers. They are productive in their environment of choice with a very individual selection of tools. In order to be productive with a workflow engine, they need to learn the basics of the process modeling language (e.g., BPMN) as well as get a solid foundation in core workflow engine concepts and APIs. Having a training session with your tool vendor is recommended, maybe flanked by some ongoing consulting hours so they can ask questions in case of any problems. These people often make good coaches as part of your COE.

Within the process automation space, you often hear about *low-code developers* (as discussed in "The limitations of low code" on page 16). Low-code developers are not trained software engineers, but often have a business background. They likely slipped into development using Microsoft Office tools, macros, or RPA. They often dedicate their working time to developing solutions in these environments. For some companies, the key to scaling their process automation efforts is enabling these developers to model executable workflows. Low-code developers need a very constrained environment and a highly customized training course in the exact environment they will be working in.

You might also have heard of *citizen developers*. These folks are not software engineers, but typically end users with some IT affinity. They want to solve an active pain with a technology they can master. These solutions are outside the scope of this book.

Business analysts basically need to learn the process modeling language (BPMN). While they might use different techniques to discover and discuss workflow models (e.g., creativity techniques), they should be able to create a process model as input for development, as well as understand models built by developers.

Operations (or infrastructure) people need to understand what it takes to deploy and run the tooling as well as how to troubleshoot failure situations. Most vendors have a dedicated training for this target group.

Enterprise architects need to understand the role of process automation in the bigger picture and the overall architecture. If possible, architects should also have some training in the tool of choice to understand its specifics.

Some customers also report that they have additional *process methodology experts* that are really good at checking if a particular process design is the most reasonable one. They try to get to the bottom of all design decisions, with the goal of simplifying process models. These people are typically organized within the COE.

Of course, roles and responsibilities can vary, and every person fulfilling a role will "live" it in their own way.

Note that a good training course can only be effective if you start using the knowledge for a real-life project right after. Try to have the training as close as possible to your project start.

Also, you should always try to organize some additional coaching on the job. This can be delivered by the vendor, a partner, or your own COE. A remote consulting offering often works well.

Conclusion

As this chapter showed, a successful adoption journey is typically a step-by-step approach that starts with a pilot, followed by a lighthouse project that really showcases the benefits. Lessons learned are used to guide the next projects. Think about scale after the first five or six projects have successfully gone live.

Experience suggests that offering guidance, for example, in the form of a center of excellence or reusable libraries, tends to be more successful than imposing rigid rules, as does a bottom-up path to tool adoption. You should also think about learning paths for your key roles, to give your process automation journey the best chance of success.

CHAPTER 13

Parting Words

You've reached the end of the book—I hope you enjoyed the experience, and that it has improved your understanding of process automation. For me, as a process automation enthusiast, there are still many things left unsaid. This final chapter provides a very quick look at a few topics that I felt needed to be mentioned. It:

- Summarizes how architecture trends influence process automation, and where this is covered in this book

- Looks at how modern architectures influence user experience, customer journeys, and business processes

- Gives you some advice on what to do next

Current Architecture Trends Influence Process Automation

Currently there is a big trend toward using more fine-grained components that run in a distributed fashion. This is a key necessity to master the growing complexity and scale of modern systems.

It also has a few interesting implications, which were touched on in various places in the book:

- Business logic is distributed, and many components need to interact to fulfill customer demands and to implement end-to-end business processes. This was introduced in Chapter 7.

- Systems get more reactive and event-driven and thus need to balance choreography and orchestration, as described in Chapter 8.

- Remote communication introduces new challenges, especially around consistency, as described in Chapter 9.

- In order to enable developing, operating, and maintaining a large number of components, companies need to improve their practices around continuous delivery. Workflow engines need to be flexible enough to support this, as discussed in Chapter 6. Testing procedures for executable processes are an important piece of that puzzle, as described in "Testing Processes" on page 62.

- Components move to the cloud quickly, basically because it eases operations and deployment. A shift to a microservices architecture often goes hand in hand with a shift to running things in a public (or private) cloud. This means that workflow automation technology needs to be available in the cloud, as was touched on in Chapter 6.

- Developers have more freedom than ever to choose technology stacks for single components. This makes architectures more polyglot, and as mentioned in "Combining Process Models and Programming Code" on page 54, good workflow engines should support writing glue code in different languages.

- There is more automation happening in general. This means that workflow engines need to support the required scale, as well as near real-time applications, as touched on in "Performance and Scalability" on page 121.

The need for workflow engines will certainly increase over the next years, and the tooling needs to be lightweight and flexible. If and how workflow technology achieves nonfunctional requirements will differ between vendors and products, but it is possible and I personally have seen workflow engines being applied in modern architectures and at a huge scale.

Rethinking Business Processes and the User Experience

As architectures undergo the changes described here, I regularly observe that business departments don't understand the opportunities that arise as a consequence. On the contrary, long-running capabilities are often shoehorned into synchronous facades to avoid altering familiar customer experiences.

Let's take an example. Assume you want to book a train ticket. This is often a synchronous user experience. You select the route, select a seat for your reservation, choose the ticket type and fare, and finally provide your personal details together with a payment method. After you have entered all the data and hit the checkout button, you can watch some animated GIF while waiting for your booking to go through.

Providing this synchronous user experience is actually hard to implement in modern architectures, as you saw in Chapter 9.

But that's not the point I want to make here. The problem is the strong desire to have this synchronous user experience in the first place. When discussing this, I am often confronted with a strong opinion from business departments that such a communication needs to be synchronous. In the train ticket example, there are two typical reasons for this:

- "If there is a problem during the booking process, then we need to talk to the customer. This is only possible with a synchronous experience."
- "We need to create a ticket as a PDF for the customer to print out. This needs to be displayed right after the booking has succeeded."

I totally challenge both.

Concerning the first point, when there is a problem in the booking process, you can pause that process in some intermediary step and inform the customer. They might still be waiting on the website, but the site does not need to be blocked by a loading wheel. Maybe customers can be shown a nice status overview page instead, that is constantly updated in the background. The customer knows they can walk away and come back later, still seeing their progress, perhaps using a unique deep link. They might get an email or a notification in the app whenever something goes wrong and needs their attention.

There is an interesting observation to make here. You have to think about the problem anyway, even if you provide a synchronous behavior. If, for example, you reserve a seat for a customer and the service crashes right afterward, you ideally offer a way for the customer to regain their reservation, or at least you need to make sure the reservation times out.

Whenever requirements sit in between asynchronous architectures and synchronous customer experiences, you can see their weird effects even as a customer. Has your browser ever crashed while you were in the middle of booking a flight? Mine has. Do you think I was able to get the same seat I'd selected during that first session, which was never completed? Of course not.

Why not tackle these eventual consistency issues head-on and give the customer the opportunity to finalize their booking within a certain time frame?

As for the second argument about printing out tickets, I'm sorry, but this is 2021. Who prints out tickets anymore? Smartphones, apps, and the ubiquity of computers have changed the customer experience. Customers want tickets in their apps. And even if they prefer to print them, customers will happily take them via email. This makes the customer experience much more resilient. If for some reasons PDFs cannot be generated at the moment of booking, everything works fine and the customer simply gets their ticket a couple of minutes later.

With a synchronous user experience, however, the whole booking would fail. What do you think customers will like better?

As a bonus, you don't have to translate between synchronous and asynchronous worlds all the time, which makes it easier to implement your system. The only thing you have to do is get your business folks to rethink the customer experience from the ground up. Yes, this is a hard undertaking, but a growing number of successful industry examples might help you on the way. Surprisingly often, I can make progress by simply asking what Amazon would do. In the words of Eliyahu Goldratt:

> You've deployed an amazing technology, but because you haven't changed the way you work, you haven't actually diminished a limitation.

Where to Go from Here

Congratulations, you made it! Thank you for reading this book. I hope I've been able to pass on some of my enthusiasm to you.

My goal in writing the book was to equip you with the most important knowledge around process automation, to help you get started on your journey. Using new concepts and technologies is never possible without making your own mistakes, but I hope what you've read here will reduce their number and effect.

With that being said, the best advice I can give you is to practice. Use process automation technology now. Literally, now. Stop reading and automate a process. Setup a process solution and apply what you just read—ideally in a real-life use case, but a fun or hobby project will also do. The examples and links on the book's website (*https://ProcessAutomationBook.com*) might help you get started.

I wish you all the best with your endeavors and hope to hear about your experiences one day, via email (*feedback@ProcessAutomationBook.com*), on the Camunda forums, on the O'Reilly learning platform, or at some conference somewhere in the world.

Index

A

ACID transactions, 183-185, 189
actor model, limitations of, 98
adoption journey
    about, 238
    failures to avoid, 238-240
    pattern of successful, 242-244
    scaling adoption, 254-259
    starting your journey, 248-254
    success story of an, 240-242
aggregating messages, 180
aggregator pattern, 180
API calls, 139, 141-144
applications
    external tasklist, 86
    relationship between processes, workflow
        engines and, 37
    tasklist, 42, 87
architecture (see solution architecture)
artificial IDs, 177
asynchronous communication, 181
asynchronous request/response, 176-178
audit data, 25, 221
auto-deployment, 32
auto-generate/generation, of graphical repre-
    sentation, 104
automation, 2
    (see also process automation)
    motivations for, 3
    of control flow, 2
    of tasks, 2
autonomy
    about, 127
    bounded contexts, 129

cohesion, 127
coupling, 127
decentralized workflow tooling, 144
domain-driven design, 129
services, 129
AWS Step Functions, 73
Azure Durable Functions, 73

B

batch processing, 94-96
behaviors, 138, 150
bespoke platform, 254
BizDevOps
    about, 200
    business, 201
    development, 200
    operations, 202
    process automation life cycle, 204
blockchain, process automation with, 108-111
boring technology, 256
bottom-up adoption, 249
boundaries
    about, 127
    bounded contexts, 129
    business processes and, 130-139
    call activities and, 140
    cohesion, 127
    coupling, 127
    crossing, 10, 60
    crossing as an API call, 141-144
    decentralized workflow tooling, 144
    defending, 138
    domain-driven design, 129

synchronous communication and, 168
communication
  asynchronous, 181
  between microservices, 71
  patterns for service invocation, 173-182
  processes across boundaries, 139-144
  remote, 191
  using workflow engines as channels for, 119
compensation events, 188
compliance conformance, as a motivation for
  automation, 3
consistency, 183-190
Constantine's law, 127
continuous delivery, solution architecture and,
  122
control flow, 2, 48
count metrics, 232
coupling, 127
creating
  customized tasklist applications, 87
  process models, 211-216
  process solutions, 45-65
  user interfaces, 122
  workflow platforms, 253
crossing boundaries, 10, 60, 141-144
custom centralized monitoring, 226-228
cycle time, 232

D

data
  audit, 25, 221
  getting, 221-223
data lakes, 228
data pipelines, 96-98, 123
data streaming limitations, 96-98
data warehouses, 228
database triggers, Wild West integration and, 6
DDD (domain-driven design), 129
dead letter queue (DLQ), 181
dead messages, 181
decentralized workflow engines, 117
decentralized workflow tooling, 144, 257
decision engines, 77
decision logic, 77
Decision Model and Notation (DMN), 78-79
decision tables, 78
decisions
  Decision Model and Notation (DMN),
    78-79

in process models, 80
orchestration, 76-81
validating, 166
decoupling, choreography and, 170
defending boundaries, 138
delegating tasks, 83
deletions, 193
dependency, direction of, 161
deployment, 122, 125
deployment coupling, as a coupling category,
  128
designing responsibilities, 165
detecting duplicates, 193
Deutsch, Peter, 174
developer experience, 107, 122
developers
  about, 199
  citizen, 17, 258
  low-code, 258
  professional, 258
  rockstar, 258
  self-image of, 107
development
  in BizDevOps, 200
  of roles, 258
  of skills, 258
  speed of, 107
DevOps, 203
diff, diffing, 100, 107, 210
distributed computing, 174
distributed monoliths, risk of, 154-155
distributed tracing tools, 124, 225
DLQ (dead letter queue), 181
DMN (Decision Model and Notation), 78-79
DMS (document management system), 139
document management system (DMS), 139
domain coupling, as a coupling category, 128
Domain Storytelling, 136
domain-driven design (DDD), 129
duplicates, detecting, 193
durable state (persistence), as a core capability
  of workflow engines, 23
duration, of processes, 232

E

EAI (enterprise application integration) tools,
  14
elements, labeling, 215
emergent behavior, 150

implementation, 48, 93-100
implementation coupling, as a coupling category, 128
in-house workflow platforms, 120
inconsistencies, handling business strategies using, 186
increasing readability, 215
information richness, as a motivation for automation, 3
infrastructure, 199
infrastructure people, 199, 202, 259
integration
    as RFP criteria, 125
    communication patterns for service invocation, 173-182
    eventual consistency and remote communication, 191
    importance of idempotency, 192
    logic into subprocesses, 211-213
    processes for, 11
    solving challenges with workflow engines, 173-193
    tools for, 124
    transactions and consistency, 183-190
    via database, Wild West integration and, 6
IoT (Internet of Things), 91
isolation
    about, 127
    bounded contexts, 129
    cohesion, 127
    coupling, 127
    decentralized workflow tooling, 144
    domain-driven design, 129
    services, 129
isolation level, 185

J

JUnit tests, 62

K

Kafka, 157
KPIs (key performance indicators), 60, 222

L

labeling elements, 215
latency, processing, 95
leveraging audit data from workflow engines, 221

license, as RFP criteria, 126
life cycles, 38-43, 204
logic, extracting into subprocesses, 211-213
long-running behavior, 138
long-running processes, 10
low code, 16
low-code approach/developers, 258
low-code platforms, 123

M

market dynamics, current, 231
McKinley, Dan, 256
message events, 52-53
messages
    about, 157
    aggregating, 180
    dead, 181
    poisoned, 181
metrics, 232
microservice team, 148, 150, 152
microservices, 70
microservices architecture, 56, 127, 152, 173, 196, 252, 262
migrating process instances, 64
minimum viable product (MVP), 251
modeling, 209-211
models, 38
    (see also process models)
    actor, 98
    code versus, 59-62
    collaboration, 207
    executable, 210
    executable process, 7-9, 210
    graphical process, 38, 108
modular monoliths, 74-76
monitoring
    architecture decisions, 256
    custom centralized, 226-228
    flow of execution, 49
    process event, 230
    processes, 232-234
    workflow engines, 117
Monolith to Microservices (O'Reilly), 127
monoliths, modular, 74-76
MVP (minimum viable product), 251
myths, about orchestration and choreography, 168-170

N

naive point-to-point integrations, Wild West integration and, 6
Newman, Sam, 127, 162
non-developers, 17
non-programmers, 78
non-technical people, 16

O

Object Management Group, 47
observability, 225
OCR (optical character recognition) tools, 56
onboarding process, 68
operations people, 199, 202, 259
operations tooling, 41
optical character recognition (OCR) tools, 56
orchestration
    about, 67
    avoiding event chains using commands, 158-161
    balancing with choreography, 147-171
    centralized, 170
    commands, 155-157, 158-165, 168
    decisions, 76-81
    designing responsibilities, 165
    direction of dependency, 161
    evaluating change scenarios to validate decisions, 166
    event-driven systems, 147-155
    events, 157, 162-165
    humans, 81-88
    messages, 157
    myths about, 168-170
    physical devices and things, 91
    RPA (robotic process automation) bots, 88-91
    software for, 68-76
    terminology, 158
Outbox pattern, chaining resources using, 189-190
ownership, of process models, 119

P

Parallels, running versions in, 63
perception management, 255
performance, solution architecture and, 121
persistence (durable state), as a core capability of workflow engines, 23

physical devices, 91
POCs (proofs of concept), 126, 249-251
poisoned messages, 181
pools, in BPMN, 208
prebuilt connectors, 58
presenting business cases, 251
process automation
    about, 1-4, 255
    adoption journey, 238-248
    architecture trends and, 261
    business drivers, 13-19
    business processes, 11
    business scenario, 9
    business-IT collaboration, 12
    examples of, 4-7
    executable process models, 7-9
    history of, 14-18
    in event-driven architectures, 247
    in SOA, 246
    integration processes, 11
    journey to introduce, 237-259
    life cycle, 204
    long-running processes, 10
    scaling adoption, 254-259
    starting your journey, 248-254
    strategic initiatives in, 248
    tools for, 14-19
    value of, 13-19
    value propositions of, 252
    with blockchain, 108-111
    workflow engines, 7-9
    workflows, 11
process definitions, 7, 122
process event monitoring, 230
process improvement, 219
process instances, 7, 64
process methodology experts, 259
process mining tools, 124, 229
process modeling languages, 100-111
    about, 100
    as RFP criteria, 125
    benefits of graphical process visualizations, 102-104
    textual process modeling approaches, 104-111
    Workflow Patterns, 101
process models
    combining with programming code, 54-62
    creating, 211-216

About the Author

Bernd Ruecker is a software developer at heart who has been innovating in the field of process automation for two decades. Solutions based on his work have been deployed in a range of organizations, from "normal" companies to highly scalable and Agile environments of industry leaders such as T-Mobile, Lufthansa, ING, and Atlassian. He has been contributing to various open source workflow engines for more than 15 years and is the cofounder and chief technologist of Camunda—an open source software company reinventing process automation to automate any process, anywhere. Along with his cofounder, he also wrote *Real-Life BPMN* (CreateSpace Independent Publishing Platform), a popular book about process modeling and automation that is now in its sixth edition and available in English, German, and Spanish.

Bernd loves to write code, especially to prove concepts. He regularly speaks at international conferences and writes for various magazines. He focuses on new process automation paradigms that fit into modern architectures around distributed systems, microservices, domain-driven design, event-driven architecture, and reactive systems.

Colophon

The animal on the cover of *Practical Process Automation* is the barred rabbitfish (*Siganus doliatus*). These fish inhabit the reefs of the Western Pacific, from the Philippines south to northwestern Australia.

Barred rabbitfish are sky blue with white bellies and two dark bands over the eyes and gill slits. They have luminous yellow striping as well as darker yellow patches over their mouths and on their dorsal fin and tail. They can grow up to 10 inches long, and can live up to 12 years. Another common name for them is "spinefoot," from the envenomed spines in their rear fins; they also have protective spines in their dorsal fin. They use their short, sharp teeth to feed on algae.

Juveniles swim in schools to find food and as protection against predators. They exhibit the classic schooling behavior, with many individuals swimming together in a coordinated way as to speed and direction, as though they were a single entity. Maturing fish form pairs for breeding.

The cover illustration is by Karen Montgomery, based on a black and white engraving from Cuvier. The cover fonts are Gilroy Semibold and Guardian Sans. The text font is Adobe Minion Pro; the heading font is Adobe Myriad Condensed; and the code font is Dalton Maag's Ubuntu Mono.

Ingram Content Group UK Ltd.
Milton Keynes UK
UKHW031813120423
420063UK00003B/6